Biblical Words
and Their Meaning:

Biblical Words and Their Meaning:

AN INTRODUCTION TO LEXICAL SEMANTICS

Moisés Silva

ZONDERVAN
PUBLISHING HOUSE
OF THE ZONDERVAN CORPORATION
GRAND RAPIDS, MICHIGAN 49506

BIBLICAL WORDS AND THEIR MEANING: AN INTRODUCTION TO LEXICAL SEMANTICS
Copyright © 1983 by The Zondervan Corporation
Grand Rapids, Michigan

Library of Congress Cataloging in Publication Data

Silva, Moisés.
    Biblical words and their meaning.

    Bibliography: p.
    Includes index.
    1. Bible—Language, style. I. Title.
BS537.S54   1983   220.4   82-17561
ISBN 0-310-45671-1

Edited by Ben Chapman
Designed by Louise Bauer

Printed in the United States of America

TO PAT

Contents

Part Two: Descriptive Semantics

Preface

Authors of an earlier century who filled title pages with never-ending qualifications knew what they were doing. How can one adequately describe the contents of a book in one or two phrases? The present work, for example, makes the pretension of covering the broad field of word meanings in the Bible, a task that cannot be executed in one volume without oversimplifying the material. But on the other hand, unsuspecting readers who have not given much prior thought to linguistics may notice the subtitle and decide to tackle the book, only to wonder what my brand of semantics has done to the simple word "introduction."

It is possible for students innocent of modern linguistics to understand this book—provided they like a challenge. In the interests of such students I have supplied summaries for each chapter, a glossary, and a brief, annotated bibliography. Furthermore, a special effort has been made not to introduce new concepts without some explanation. Of necessity, however, these definitions are rather compressed, for it did not seem appropriate to make this book an elementary text in general linguistics. Those readers are thus most likely to enjoy and profit from this work who, recognizing the importance of the subject, have already acquired some understanding of standard linguistic concepts.

This introduction is intended for theological students who are familiar with the basic issues and methods of biblical scholarship and who know the elements of Greek and Hebrew, although a knowledge of the latter is not essential (Hebrew words are always transliterated;

moreover, sections that presuppose acquaintance with Semitics may be skipped without losing the flow of the argument). A second-year seminary student should have no difficulty following and appreciating the material discussed here. I even cherish the hope that advanced students of linguistics, though unfamiliar with biblical scholarship, may profit from seeing their discipline applied to the ancient documents that constitute the Bible.

The chapters that follow aim at establishing the theoretical foundations that are logically prior to the development of procedure and thus should be regarded as a contribution to general hermeneutics (theory), not, at least not primarily, to exegetical method (practice). To be sure, examples and various kinds of illustrations are used repeatedly; moreover, certain parts of the book (portions of chaps. 1, 2, 6, and the conclusions) include material that has a direct practical bearing. Still, the dominant concern embraces principles and scientific assumptions. Any how-to manual that shortcuts these issues thereby invalidates itself. As a concession to the flesh, however, I should point out that chapters 3–5 need not be mastered before a reader can profit from the rest of the work.

What profit is there, however, in reading a book on this topic? One of the standard qualifications for becoming a linguist is the ability to express, as persuasively and unaffectedly as possible, complete astonishment that not every human being shares a passion for the scientific study of language. Biblical linguists are no exception. Acquaintance with up-to-date systematic work on the nature of language seems an indispensable foundation for proper exegesis. It could hardly occur to a serious student to make historical judgments without reference to the latest and most reliable archeological publications. How does one then explain the fact that even reputable scholars have attempted to shed light on the biblical languages while working in isolation from the results of contemporary linguistics? One could just as easily try to describe Jewish sects in the first century without a knowledge of the Dead Sea Scrolls.

Lexical semantics is that branch of modern linguistics that focuses on the meaning of individual words. The field of semantics is of course subject to a much broader interpretation, for several other disciplines —philosophy, literary studies, anthropology, sociology, psychology, and even mathematics—have demonstrated their direct relevance to the study of human communication. Any of these disciplines may be regarded as a valid starting point for the analysis of biblical semantics;

the present work, therefore, although it draws on data from them at a few points, can make no claim to provide a full semantic description of the biblical languages. It does, however, assume the central importance of linguistics for the proper understanding of meaning.

But even after we have narrowed our concerns to the area of *linguistics*, and within this discipline to the area of linguistic *semantics*, a further qualification is necessary: *lexical* semantics. Linguistic meaning can be studied at the level of individual words, or at the sentence level, or at the level of discourse. These levels are so closely interrelated that to isolate one of them, as we are doing in this book, is somewhat artificial and ultimately unsatisfactory—yet pedagogically it is both justifiable and necessary. The strong emphasis that chapter 6 places on the intrinsic significance of context should aid the reader in dispelling false conceptions regarding these issues. Perhaps someone can be persuaded to write a sequel on "Biblical Sentences and Their Meaning."

Although some portions of this work (particularly in chaps. 3 and 6) may have a claim to originality, granted a modest definition of the word, my main intention has been to synthesize critically the results of scholars in the field of linguistic semantics. If the text is considered an introduction to the *subject* of semantics, the notes can be regarded as an introduction to *current scholarship* on that subject. The numerous bibliographic items there—they barely scratch the surface—are not paraded for show but are rather intended as an enticement for eager students to dip more fully into this promising area of research. The notes also provide an opportunity to qualify and expand some controversial positions taken in the text. It follows that, although the text as a whole can be understood without reference to the notes, the latter are in fact integral to the composition of the book and ignoring them could have the effect of distorting some portions of the material.

The present work had its origins in, and still bears the marks of, a Th.M. thesis at Westminster Theological Seminary, to whose faculty I am greatly indebted for instilling in me a desire to meet the highest standards of scholarship within the context of a commitment to the full authority of the Scriptures. I received most of my training in Semitics at Dropsie University; of particular value were a two-year sequence in comparative Semitics by Federico Corriente and a rigorous study of Canaanite inscriptions with M. H. Goshen-Gottstein. My doctoral work at the University of Manchester concentrated on historical semantics and semantic borrowing; I remember with deep appreciation the sober advice of my supervisor F. F. Bruce, the detailed and incisive criticisms of T. Muraoka, and the encouragement and intellectual stimulation of James Barr. During my stay in England I also had the delightful privilege of consulting with T. E. Hope (Leeds) and the late Stephen Ullmann (Oxford).

While much of the basic research for this book was thus completed by 1972, time was needed for mature reflection. During the following nine years I held a position in New Testament at Westmont College that provided an ideal opportunity for professional growth generally and for the testing and further development of ideas. The teaching of interdisciplinary language courses and the stimulus of academic contact with colleagues in other departments proved an invaluable complement to my regular assignments in the Department of Religious Studies. I owe a special debt to Robert H. Gundry, Professor of New Testament, and to John W. Sider, Professor of English, for their active interest in my work; to Betty Bouslough, who typed most of the manuscript, for the dedication and excellence that characterize all her work; and to the administration and board of the college, who granted me a sabbatical for the spring of 1979, without which the writing of this book might have been indefinitely delayed.

I am grateful to many individuals who read and criticized this material at various stages of its production. I must also thank my devoted parents for their unflagging and sacrificial support through many years of education. To my wife, who has endured more than one could reasonably ask, this book is lovingly dedicated.

Abbreviations

AASF	Annales Academiae Scientarum Fennicae
ALGHJ	Arbeiten zur Literatur und Geschichte des hellenistischen Judentums
AmSp	*American Speech*
AnBib	Analecta biblica
ApSem	Approaches to Semiotics
ArRom	*Archivum romanicum*
ASTI	*Annual of the Swedish Theological Institute*
Bauer	Bauer, *A Greek-English Lexicon of the NT*, 2nd ed.
BDB	Brown-Driver-Briggs, *Hebrew and English Lexicon of the OT*
BHS	*Biblia hebraica stuttgartensia*
Bib	*Biblica*
BIOSCS	*Bulletin of the International Organization for Septuagint and Cognate Studies*
BJRL	*Bulletin of the John Rylands Library*
BRE	Biblioteca románica española
BSac	*Bibliotheca sacra*
BT	*The Bible Translator*
BZAW	Beihefte zur ZAW
CahLex	*Cahiers de lexicologie*
CBQ	*Catholic Biblical Quarterly*
CCent	*Christian Century*
CT	*Christianity Today*
CTL	*Current Trends in Linguistics*
DBSup	*Dictionnaire de la Bible, Supplément*

DePrLit	De proprietatibus litteratum
EncJud	*Encyclopaedia Judaica* (1971)
EtLingAp	*Etudes de linguistique appliquée*
ExpT	*Expository Times*
FL	*Foundations of Language*
FTL	Forum theologiae linguisticae
GerTT	*Gereformeerd theologisch tijdschrift*
IB	*Interpreter's Bible*
ICC	International Critical Commentary
IDB	*Interpreter's Dictionary of the Bible*
IJAL	*International Journal of American Linguistics*
Int	*Interpretation*
IRM	*International Review of Missions*
JanL	Janua linguarum
JAOS	*Journal of the American Oriental Society*
JBL	*Journal of Biblical Literature*
JETS	*Journal of the Evangelical Theological Society*
JSS	*Journal of Semitic Studies*
JTS	*Journal of Theological Studies*
KB₃	Koehler-Baumgartner, *Hebräisches und aramäisches Lexikon zum AT*, 3rd ed.
KG	Kultur der Gegenwart
Lg	*Language*
Ling	*Linguistics*
LSJ	Liddell-Scott-Jones, *Greek-English Lexicon*
LSM	Language Science Monograph
LXX	Septuagint
MLR	*Modern Language Review*
MM	Moulton-Milligan, *Vocabulary of the NT*
MSU	Mitteilungen des Septuaginta-Unternehmens
NICNT	New International Commentary on the NT
NIDNTT	*New International Dictionary of NT Theology*
NovT	*Novum Testamentum*
NTS	*New Testament Studies*
OTS	Oudtestamentische studiën
PPS	Publications of the Philological Society
PRFE	Publicaciones de la *Revista de filología española*
QSem	Quaderni di semitistica
RB	*Revue biblique*
REL	*Revista española de lingüística*

RL	*Revue de linguistique*
RLR	*Revue de linguistique romane*
RSR	*Recherches de science religieuse*
SBL	Society of Biblical Literature
SE	*Studia evangelica*
SEL	Studies in English Literature
SJLA	Studies in Judaism in Late Antiquity
SJT	*Scottish Journal of Theology*
SNTSMS	Society for NT Studies Monograph Series
StSem	Studi semitici
Sup	Supplement
TBL	Tübinger Beiträge zur Linguistik
TDNT	*Theological Dictionary of the NT*
TDOT	*Theological Dictionary of the OT*
Thayer	Thayer, *Greek-English Lexicon of the NT*
Theol	*Theology*
TLL	*Travaux de linguistique et de littérature*
TLZ	*Theologische Literaturzeitung*
TTod	*Theology Today*
TWNT	*Theologisches Wörterbuch zum NT*
TZ	*Theologische Zeitschrift*
USQR	*Union Seminary Quarterly Review*
VT	*Vetus Testamentum*
WTJ	*Westminster Theological Journal*
ZAW	*Zeitschrift für die alttestamentliche Wissenschaft*
ZNW	*Zeitschrift für die neutestamentliche Wissenschaft*

TYPOGRAPHICAL CONVENTIONS

Hebrew letters are transliterated according to a simple system in which spirantization (in the consonants *bgdkpt*) and certain vowel distinctions (such as length) are not marked.

An asterisk (*) is used to mark unattested forms and ungrammatical expressions. Square brackets indicate a phonetic transcription: [a], [b], etc; obliques indicate a phonemic transcription: /a/, /b/, etc.; italics indicate sounds as orthographically represented (that is, letters): *a*, *b*, etc.

Double quotation marks are used for words and sentences when citing a context, but italics are used when dealing with them as linguistic entities. Meanings are enclosed in single quotation marks.

Full bibliographical information is given only at the first mention of a work. These first occurrences can be located readily through the index of authors and titles.

Introduction

In 1935 it seemed that the work of British and American Semitists —most of whom were primarily interested in Old Testament interpretation—was founded "upon the shifting sands of superficial resemblance and sporadic analogies," not "upon the firm rock of scientific method."[1] In his lively presidential address to the American Oriental Society, Roland G. Kent claimed that research in comparative Semitic grammar had ignored the scientific methods worked out by the Indo-Europeanists of the nineteenth century. He took sharp issue, for example, with C. F. Burney's assumption that n and l should be considered equivalent in dealing with Semitic roots; Kent remarked that we could just as easily "assume from some scattered Indo-European words that the *nude* is ipso facto, etymologically, the *lewd*." And again, after reviewing a certain linguistic argument by C. J. Ball, Kent tells us that it is all "nonsense."[2]

The next few decades saw much progress in the specific area of Semitic linguistics.[3] However, they also saw the growth of a new movement, "Biblical Theology," which created the need for another linguistic rebuke. Concerned with the original revelation of the Bible,

[1]Roland G. Kent, "Linguistic Science and the Orientalist," *JAOS* 55 (1935): 115–37, 137.

[2]Ibid., pp. 130, 133.

[3]For a capable assessment see Edward Ullendorff, "Comparative Semitics," in *Linguistica semitica: presente e futuro*, ed. Giorgio Levi Della Vida (StSem 4; Rome. Centro di Studi Semitici, 1961), pp. 13–32, and his article by the same title in *CTL* 6:261–73.

theologians insisted that we must lay off our Western thought and lay bare the genuine Israelite and Christian faith. But many of them, convinced that this original situation manifested itself in the very structure of language, began to read off theology from Hebrew and Greek morphology, syntax, and etymology. Finally in 1961 James Barr spoke his piece.

> Unafraid of great names, voluminous works, rigorous research—though they be called Pedersen, Boman, Gerleman, though they be inscribed TWNT. Like David, who training with lions and bears later faced the Philistine, so Barr begins with specific authors before facing TWNT.[4]

BARR, LINGUISTICS, AND EXEGESIS

Barr's book, *The Semantics of Biblical Language*, was a trumpet blast against the monstrous regiment of shoddy linguistics. Controversial throughout, undiplomatic at times, it has been recognized as a major contribution to biblical studies. What are its theses?

Theologians have been particularly concerned with pointing out the differences between Greek and Hebrew thought. The former, we are told, is static, contemplative, abstract, intellectualized, divisive; the latter is dynamic, active, concrete, imaginative, stressing the totality of man and his religion. Whatever we may think of this contrast, Barr claims that the *linguistic arguments* used to support it are "unsystematic and haphazard." Evidence of the kind adduced by these theologians is valid only when the biblical languages are rigorously examined and when the method is integrated with general linguistic science. Modern theology fails on both scores.[5]

Underlying much of the work criticized by Barr is the conviction that language and mentality can be easily correlated. For example, the fact that Hebrew *baśar* corresponds to *two* Greek words ($\sigma\acute{\alpha}\rho\xi$ and $\sigma\tilde{\omega}\mu\alpha$) has been interpreted as a reflection of the Israelite's concern with the totality of man in contrast with those Greek presuppositions

---

[4]Luis Alonso-Schökel, "Teología bíblica y lingüística," *Bib* 43 (1962): 217–23.

[5]James Barr, *The Semantics of Biblical Language* (Oxford: Oxford University Press, 1961), pp. 21ff. These criticisms took on added significance when, one year later, Barr focused on a specific subject, *Biblical Words for Time* (SBT 1st ser. 33; London: SCM, 1962, 2nd ed. 1969). From a different perspective Chaim Rabin expressed similar concerns in "Is a Biblical Semantics Possible?" (in Hebrew), *Beth Mikra* 7-2 (1962): 17–27.

that posited a distinction between flesh and body.[6] Barr pointed out that it is outmoded and unscientific to assume such neat correspondences between linguistic and thought structures.[7]

Of special importance for our purposes is Barr's evaluation of the *Theological Dictionary of the New Testament*. His discussion, largely negative in character, points out the confusion inherent in the very nature of a theological dictionary: a dictionary is supposed to offer word substitutions, whereas *TDNT* contains essays on the history of ideas. Or to put it differently, if the purpose of the book is to investigate the theological thought of the New Testament, why do it in a book organized under words?[8]

The importance of Barr's book is indicated by the reaction it has elicited.[9] If nothing else, Barr has brought out the best in his reviewers' figures of speech. We have already seen him compared with David of old. H. T. Kerr thinks of him as a spanner tossed into the theological machinery and as a maverick "within the midst of the Biblical herd."[10] C. F. D. Moule tells us that Barr flashed "a red light at the reckless driver who tries to take a short cut across a mine-field. We must be grateful that some of the explosives have been detonated for us."[11]

What is striking, however, is the consistently favorable attitudes expressed in these reviews; only one of them is wholly negative in character.[12] Most of them commend Barr enthusiastically and lavish scholarly admiration on him. To quote Moule again, the irritating quality of the book "does not affect its truth or timeliness. It is an investigation carried out on the highest level of scholarly exactness and in a temper of honest inquiry; and biblical theologians will ignore it at

---

[6]*Semantics*, p. 35 (he takes the example from J. A. T. Robinson, *The Body: Study in Pauline Theology* [SBT 1st ser. 5; London: SCM, 1952], p. 12).

[7]Ibid., p. 33.

[8]Ibid., pp. 215, 233.

[9]The *Elenchus bibliographicus biblicus* through 1967 lists nearly forty reviews of *Semantics*. For a superb critical summary of the controversy see Richard J. Erickson, *Biblical Semantics, Semantic Structure, and Biblical Lexicology: A Study of Methods, with Special Reference to the Pauline Lexical Field of "Cognition"* (Ph.D. diss., Fuller Theological Seminary, 1980), pp. 12–65.

[10]*TTod* 18 (1961–62): 346.

[11]*Theol* 65 (1962): 27.

[12]The negative review is by Thorlief Boman (who had been severely criticized by Barr) in *SJT* 15 (1962): 319–24. Notice also G. Friedrich, "Semasiologie und Lexikologie," *TLZ* 94 (1969): 801–15, and *Auf das Wort kommt es an* (Göttingen: Vandenhoeck & Ruprecht, 1978), pp. 507–50.

their peril."[13] Even those reviewers who are strongly critical of Barr make clear their appreciation for his work.[14]

The book has been criticized on various grounds: some question Barr's philosophical stand, some resent his use of a particular school of semantics as though it alone were scientific, some reject his statements concerning biblical translation.[15] These and other criticisms cannot be ignored, but they do not affect the significance of Barr's contributions to biblical exegesis. The question remains then whether biblical scholars have incorporated these contributions into their exegetical work.[16]

The answer must be a qualified yes. According to Barr himself, the "change of theological climate" in the 1960s led to a reduced dependence on word studies,[17] while scholars who wish to preserve the method as important for biblical theology have usually tried to take note of Barr's criticisms.[18] Furthermore, a few exegetes[19] have vigorously pursued the areas in modern linguistics that appear most promising as aids to biblical interpretation. Particularly encouraging is the inclusion of a fine article on "Semantics" in the Supplementary Volume to *The Interpreter's Dictionary of the Bible*.[20]

[13]*Theol* 65 (1962): 26. Moule's praise is not at all untypical: notice G. Fohrer (?), ZAT 73 (1961): 337–38; R. B. Y. Scott, *TTod* 18 (1961–62): 515–17; S. H. Hooke, *JTS* 13 (1962): 128–30; J. Alberto Soggin, *TZ* 18 (1962): 211–13; B. Mickelsen, *CTod* 6 (1961–62): 150; J. L. Swellengrebel, *IRM* 51 (1962): 206–10. A linguistic anthropologist, B. Siertsema, supported Barr in "Language and World View (Semantics for Theologians)," *BT* 20 (1969): 3–21. See also E. Ullendorff's recent tribute in *JSS* 26 (1981): 356–57.

[14]E. g., G. E. Wright, *USQR* 17 (1961–62): 350; J. D. Smart, *CCent* 79 (1962): 139. Less critical is B. S. Childs, *JBL* 80 (1961): 374. Notice also Nic. H. Ridderbos, "Is het Hebreeuws één van de bronnen van de openbaring?" *GerTT* 64 (1964): 209–29.

[15]For Barr's answers, see his "Common Sense and Biblical Language," *Bib* 49 (1968): 377–87, and the 2nd ed. of *Biblical Words for Time*, pp. 188–207.

[16]I bypass the effect of Barr's work on contemporary theology; cf. Brevard S. Childs, *Biblical Theology in Crisis* (Philadelphia: Westminster Press, 1970), especially p. 72; Erich Dinkler, "Die ökumenische Bewegung und die Hermeneutik," *TLZ* 94 (1969): 481–90; Paul Ronald Wells, *James Barr and the Bible: Critique of a New Liberalism* (Phillipsburg, N.J.: Presbyterian and Reformed, 1980).

[17]*Biblical Words for Time*, pp. 170–71.

[18]E.g., David Hill, *Greek Words and Hebrew Meanings: Studies in the Semantics of Soteriological Terms* (SNTSMS 5; Cambridge: Cambridge University Press, 1967).

[19]We shall discuss some important contributors in chap. 6.

[20]Nashville: Abingdon, 1976 (the article is by Charles R. Taber). Also worthy of note is Anthony C. Thiselton, "Semantics and New Testament Interpretation," in *New Testament Interpretation: Essays on Principles and Methods*, ed. I. Howard

However, two qualifications must be entered. In the first place, from time to time one comes across works that seem completely untouched by the contemporary discussion. A recent lexicographical work by Nigel Turner is perhaps the most obvious example.[21] A conservative textbook speaks of the "biographical suitability" of Hebrew and quotes with approval the judgment that "the Hebrew thought in pictures, and consequently his nouns are concrete and vivid. There is no such thing as neuter gender, for the Semite everything is alive."[22] Less extreme, but still disturbing, comments are anything but rare in the literature.

Second, the majority of biblical scholars, although aware of the problems and wishing to handle the material responsibly, can hardly be expected to master the results of modern linguistics. We may note that even David Hill, who wants to take direct account of Barr's criticisms, refers to linguistic authorities almost exclusively in the introduction to his book: his actual exegetical work shows little integration of linguistics.[23] Again, the *New International Dictionary of New Testament Theology*, which seems to provide a corrective to *TDNT*, proves disappointing in this regard.[24]

In short, then, we may agree that the past two decades have seen

Marshall (Exeter: Paternoster Press, 1977), pp. 75–104. More recent is the fine work by J. P. Louw, *Semantics of New Testament Greek* (Semeia Studies; Philadelphia: Fortress, 1982).

[21]*Christian Words* (Edinburgh: T. & T. Clark, 1980); see my review in *Trinity Journal* 3NS (1982) 103–9.

[22]Norman L. Geisler and William E. Nix, *A General Introduction to the Bible* (Chicago: Moody Press, 1968), p. 219; the quotation itself predates Barr's work. Note also Otto A. Piper, "New Testament Lexicography: An Unfinished Task," in *Festschrift to Honor F. Wilbur Gingrich*, ed. E. H. Barth and R. E. Cocroft (Leiden: Brill, 1972), pp. 177–204, especially p. 184.

[23]Only on pp. 97ff. of *Greek Words* does Hill attempt this kind of integration. One misses a linguistic analysis of the semantic changes with which he deals and an appreciation of the various questions on bilingualism which the book raises; Barr himself (see "Common Sense," p. 387) found considerable divergence between Hill's alleged principles and his word studies. We may also note the recent and valuable work by G. B. Caird, *The Language and Imagery of the Bible* (Philadelphia: Westminster Press, 1980), which makes some interesting use of linguistic semantics, but at a superficial level. The failure of current scholarship to assimilate Barr's criticisms is documented by Arthur Gibson, *Biblical Semantic Logic: A Preliminary Analysis* (New York: St. Martin's Press, 1981).

[24]E.g., the grouping of semantically related terms in this recent work does not really evince sensitivity to linguistic theory; it appears to be only a matter of convenience. Cf. my review in *WTJ* 43 (1980–81): 395–99.

considerable progress in the proper use of language for biblical interpretation, but we must not fall under any delusion that linguistics and exegesis have been genuinely integrated in modern scholarship. And beyond that, modern linguistics—and semantics in particular—continues to develop at a very fast pace. The present work then seeks to synthesize the results of contemporary lexical semantics insofar as they touch more or less directly on the concerns of biblical scholars. But first we need to define more precisely the focus of our interest by contrasting it with so-called "theological lexicography."

THEOLOGICAL LEXICOGRAPHY

> Modern biblical theology in its fear and dislike of the "proposition" as the basis of religious truth has often simply adopted in its place the smaller linguistic unit of the word, and has then been forced to overload the word with meaning in order to relate it to the "inner world of thought."[25]

With these words Barr calls attention to a rather anomalous situation in biblical studies. It has become customary in articles and books dealing with biblical topics to begin the discussion with an examination of "the terminology." Occasionally, the author may even think that a study of the relevant terms completes his research of the topic.

Such an approach is inadequate. When a discussion depends primarily or solely on the vocabulary, one may conclude either that the writer is not familiar with the contents of Scripture or that Scripture itself says little or nothing on the subject. This latter situation, Barr claims, is what obtains in modern discussions of the biblical view of time. The fallacious lexical arguments used by several theologians are due primarily to

> the very serious shortage within the Bible of the kind of *actual statement* about "time" or "eternity" which could form a sufficient basis for a Christian philosophical-theological view of time. It is the lack of actual statements about what time is like, more than anything else, that has forced exegetes into trying to get a view of time out of the *words* themselves.[26]

[25] *Semantics*, p. 246.
[26] *Biblical Words for Time*, p. 138.

Now we have seen that Barr attributes this concern with lexicography to the theologians' aversion to propositions; their fear of proof texts has led them, with questionable progress, to the use of proof words.[27] This judgment may be partly, but only partly, accurate. As great an interest in word studies is quite common among conservative students who hold zealously to the orthodox view of propositional revelation.[28] A good example is Knight's examination of the "faithful sayings," a conservative work of the highest quality, but nevertheless weakened by the author's unbalanced emphasis on words; as a result, "in his scrupulous examination of the lexicography of the sayings, Mr. Knight has all too often missed the wood for the trees."[29] There can be no question then that biblical scholars and ministers influenced by them have been much too worried about words; the approach was not deemed necessary by the great theologians of the church, nor is it the normal method in other areas of philology (classical studies, modern literature). How did this situation come about?

As is well known, it was Hermann Cremer who gave the original impulse to the discipline of "theological lexicography."[30] Assuming

[27] *Semantics*, p. 271.

[28] One may speculate that, ironically, the verbal view of inspiration has led conservatives to a similar error. It seems to me a distortion of the doctrine, however, to argue or imply that the *content* of revelation resides in the scriptural words themselves rather than in the sentences. Philip E. Hughes points out that although these words are vitally important, they are that "only in combination. Words isolated from their context have lost their significance and are not sacrosanct. What is essential is *the truth which the words unitedly reveal*" (my emphasis); see "The Reformers' View of Inspiration" in *The Word of God and Fundamentalism* (London: Church Book Room, 1961), p. 99. We may incidentally note the preposterous claim (sometimes attributed to B. F. Westcott) that "NT doctrine is largely based on its prepositions"; see W. Graham Scroggie's foreword to W. E. Vine, *An Expository Dictionary of New Testament Words*, originally, *A Comprehensive Dictionary of the Original Greek Words with Their Precise Meanings for English Readers*, 4 vols. (London: Oliphants, 1939–41).

[29] Review of George W. Knight III, *The Faithful Sayings in the Pastoral Letters* (Grand Rapids: Baker, 1979, originally published 1968), by Anthony Hanson, *JTS* 20 (1969): 719.

[30] His *Biblisch-theologisches Wörterbuch der neutestamentlichen Gräcität* first appeared in 1867 and went through nine editions (latest English ed. 1895); the tenth edition (1911–15, not translated into English) was put out by Julius Kögel. After Kögel's death in 1928, G. Kittel revamped the work and *TWNT* began to appear in 1932; the project, under the direction of G. Friedrich beginning with vol. 5, was completed forty-five years after its inception. Cf. Friedrich's essay in *TDNT* 10:613–61. For a general survey of Greek lexicography see Javier L. Facal, "Historia

that the Greek terms chosen to express Christian doctrine had "received a new impress and a fresh power"—indeed, that the Holy Spirit Himself had transformed linguistic elements and molded distinctive expressions—Cremer set about "to reform and scientifically to reconstruct N.T. lexicography."[31] The method to be followed was that of pointing out both the affinities and the differences between the biblical usage and the extrabiblical range of meaning.

He realized, of course, that he must restrict his investigation to terms having a biblico-theological import; in other words, he would only deal with "that department of the linguistic store which is necessarily affected by the influence which we have described, i.e. . . . the expressions of spiritual life, moral and religious."[32] It is therefore strange to find in his work numerous terms that are used in identical fashion by classical authors.[33] More surprisingly, Gerhard Kittel later argued that the number of theological terms in the New Testament "is much greater than that handled by Cremer and [his successor, Julius] Kögel"! He therefore proposed a massive enterprise that would not only deal in much greater detail with all theological terms, but would also include proper names, "some of the theologically more important prepositions," and numerals.[34]

It should be stressed, however, that Kittel's formulations marked a shift in method. Cremer, whatever his weaknesses, was concerned with scientific lexicography in its usual sense; Kittel, on the other hand, wished to go beyond the work of "external" lexicons and deal fully with "internal lexicography." As it turns out, internal lexicography is not lexicography at all, but rather the study of *concepts* on the

de la lexicografía griega moderna," in *Introducción a la lexicografía griega*, ed. E. Gangutia (Manuales y Anejos de "Emérita," 33; Madrid: C.S.I.C., 1977), pp. 107–42.

[31]Cremer, *Biblico-Theological Lexicon of New Testament Greek*, 3rd English ed. (Edinburgh: T. & T. Clark, 1883), pp. iv and vii; cf. Robert C. Duncan, *The Contribution of Hermann Cremer (1834–1903) to Theological Hermeneutics* (unpublished Ph.D. thesis, University of Edinburgh, 1957), p. 23.

[32]Cremer, p. iv.

[33]Such terms as ἀκολουθεῖν, ἑκών, and προστιθέναι, may indeed occur in theologically significant passages, but so do definite articles and inflectional morphemes. Duncan (p. 26) tells us that Cremer dealt with approximately one fifth of the New Testament vocabulary.

[34]Preface to *TDNT* 1: vii. Some of the dangers involved in expanding the material were soon pointed out by Erich Fascher in a perceptive review, *TLZ* 63 (1933): 4–8.

basis of the terms used to express them. This understanding of lexicography was first formulated by Kögel,[35] and it may be argued, at the risk of oversimplification, that it was made necessary once papyrological discoveries had weakened Cremer's own formulations.[36] I would further suggest, however, that the Kögel-Kittel theory was not compatible with Cremer's *original* conception of the nature of his work.[37] At any rate, one would have naturally expected Kittel to elaborate on the nature of "internal lexicography" during his Cambridge lectures in 1937. Instead, he shifted his emphasis back and claimed that the *TDNT* is "genuine lexicography and genuine philology" because it "arises out of genuine history."[38]

Now the lexical approach to theology seems simple enough: when we come across a significant word in the New Testament, we see how it differs from Attic Greek, find its Hebrew equivalent (especially through the help of the Septuagint), study its usage in the New Testament, and then apply our findings to the original passage. Throughout this excursion the student faces several pitfalls. In the first place, paying so much attention to a word and (usually) its derivatives often leads to an exaggerated estimate of etymological studies. In the first chapter we shall deal with this question in detail. For now we need only keep in mind the fascination that preachers (with "a little learning" of Greek) can develop for etymological sermons.

Second, there is the danger of "illegitimate totality transfer," a somewhat awkward phrase intended to stress the simple fact that any one instance of a word will not bear all the meanings possible for that word.[39] It would be admittedly invalid to overload Acts 7:38 with all

[35]See the preface to the tenth edition.

[36]Cf. Barr, *Semantics*, pp. 238–44. Of course, Kögel's ideas did not seem an innovation because Cremer had already in the preface to the third edition spoken of his work as both linguistic and conceptual; he went on to add, however, that it would be unscientific to write a biblical theology in lexical form.

[37]Friedrich himself admits that there was a difference between Cremer and Kittel (see the last paragraph in the preface to *TDNT*, vol. 5). More recently ("Semasiologie," col. 804) he has claimed that Kittel was really adopting L. Weisgerber's method: "In der Tat hat Kittel nichts anderes unternommen, als die beschreibende, vergleichende und historische Untersuchung des neutestamentlichen *Begriffsschätzes*, seiner Eigenart und seines Werdens durchzuführen" (my emphasis).

[38]Gerhard Kittel, *Lexicographia sacra* ("Theology" Occasional Papers, 7; London: SPCK, 1938), pp. 8, 30.

[39]Barr, *Semantics*, p. 218. The points under discussion amount to a summary of criticisms found at various places in Barr's book; cf. also *Biblical Words for Time*, pp. 159ff.

the senses in which ἐκκλησία is used by the apostles; some of these senses (e.g., reference to the so-called universal church) would actually be contradictory in this verse. However, it is easy, especially in the course of a sermon, to comment on the broad meanings of a word at the risk of obscuring its specific function in a given text.

Third, one is rather likely to ignore what may look like small differences between the ways the word is used; that is, one may import into a particular passage a meaning discovered elsewhere, without noticing that the word in the latter passage is modified by a particular phrase or by some syntactical feature (preposition, article, inflection). For example:

> The use of ὁ λόγος with the article in the very special case of John 1 is really a special meaning which cannot be mingled indiscriminately with other cases simply because they also contain the word λόγος. In other words a simple syntactic relation like the adding of the definite article and the absence of other qualification can establish a different semantic field just as well as the transition to another word can.[40]

Fourth, we should point out that concentrated study on one word seldom leads to the very important examination of semantically related terms. This point will be explored fully in part 2.

A final and fundamental danger is that of confusing the word for the reality. The Spanish word *llave* is used in some Latin American countries for three different objects: key, wrench, and faucet; no one would conclude, however, that Latin Americans use only one instrument for opening doors, working on pipe, and drawing water.[41] Yet it is not at all uncommon to arrive at theological conclusions on similar grounds, as when *TDNT* bases the New Testament relationship between exhorting and comforting on the fact that the same word (either παραμυθεῖσθαι or παρακαλεῖν) can express both ideas.[42]

To use a different sort of example: if the word we are interested in is ἁμαρτία, it must be clear in our minds whether we want to know all

---

[40]*Semantics*, p. 222.

[41]The example, which however is not restricted to Mexican Spanish, is used in a different connection by R. E. Lonacre, review of Benjamin Lee Whorf's *Four Articles on Metalinguistics* in *Lg* 32 (1956): 302.

[42]*Semantics*, pp. 323–24. The analogy with *llave* may seem equivocal, yet it is valid for showing that linguistic data *cannot be assumed* to reflect reality— demonstration is necessary for each individual example.

that the Bible teaches concerning the doctrine of sin (the "concept"), or the range of meaning covered by the specific word ἀμαρτία. But these two things are constantly confused. Indeed, the confusion may be inherent in the nature of *TDNT*, which seeks to deal with conceptual history *(Begriffsgeschichte)*[43] in the form of a dictionary of words. Kittel seems to have thought very little about the serious problems raised by such a method.[44] Sawyer, who reports some progress in the later volumes of *TDNT*, comments that "the 'word-bound' approach to what are really concept-studies still persists"; in a "dictionary" one naturally expects a discussion of words, yet the section dealing with "tension in the ξένος concept" says nothing about ξένος.[45]

This point takes us back to the beginning of the present discussion (p. 22). If we are studying *words*, then the most important tool is Bauer's *Lexicon*, but if we are interested in *ideas* (the real concern of Cremer and Kittel), it is not reasonable to base our study primarily on words. Surely if we wanted to study Kant's epistemology, it would not occur to us to examine Kant's use of the word *wissen*, for we would encounter many passages where a theory of knowledge was the last thing in the philosopher's mind. But further, examining Kant's use of *wissen*, and then concluding our investigation, would leave us with a distorted picture. In fact, it is not hard to imagine the possibility that a relevant chapter from one of his *Critiques* may not contain the word at all; missing that chapter, however, might be disastrous for our conclusions.

To take a biblical example: a very important passage on the subject of *hypocrisy* is Isaiah 1:10–15, but the student suckled at the concordance would never find it; instead, he would come to an unrefined understanding of the topic. This is apparently what happens at times in *TDNT*, where the "extremely valuable discussion of education . . . is marred by being restricted, thanks to the format of the dictionary, to passages where παιδεία, παιδεύω, etc., occur"; or in

---

[43]Preface to *TWNT*, vol. 1.

[44]So Barr, *Semantics*, pp. 206ff. A similar criticism, though with less justice, had been made of Kittel's forerunner in 1911: "If Cremer had written a connected theology of the New Testament, a number of scientific scruples against his position would have been removed or mitigated, for then it would no longer have been a matter of words, of lexicographical questions, but of the presentation of concepts in the sphere of New Testament religion . . ." (H. Jordan, quoted by Duncan, *Cremer*, pp. 119–20).

[45]John F. A. Sawyer, review of vol. 5 in *SJT* 23 (1970): 241. This problem is still present in *NIDNTT*, e.g., in the discussion of κλῆρος (2:290).

the article on ὄνος, where "the curious omission of any reference to the role of the ass at Solomon's coronation is presumably due to the accident that the term there (3 Reg. 1.38 LXX) is ἡμιόνος, not ὄνος."[46]

Now the thrust of the last few pages may be summarized by quoting Barr's most significant but really quite simple and disarmingly reasonable thesis.

> Theological thought of the type found in the NT has its characteristic linguistic expression not in the word individually but in the word-combination or sentence. . . . [Since] important elements in the NT vocabulary were not technical . . . the attempt to relate the individual word directly to the theological thought leads to the distortion of the semantic contribution made by words in contexts; the value of the context comes to be seen as something contributed by the word, and then it is read into the word as its contribution where the context is in fact different. Thus the word becomes overloaded with interpretative suggestion. . . .[47]

The point is that we learn much more about the doctrine of sin by John's *statement*, "Sin is the transgression of the law," than by a word-study of ἁμαρτία; similarly, tracing the history of the word ἅγιος is relatively unimportant for the doctrine of sanctification once we have examined Romans 6–8 and related passages.

THE SCOPE OF BIBLICAL LEXICOLOGY

In the previous section we have seen the inadequacy of overemphasizing, or rather *misusing*, lexical study in the task of interpretation. We may indeed argue that it is impossible to do too much lexicography—the present work itself is intended to encourage the

[46]Sawyer, review, p. 241.

[47]*Semantics*, pp. 233–34. On p. 272 he encourages the use of stylistic research as much more rewarding than lexicography. This whole discussion, however, should not be interpreted as a denial of the "autonomy" of words (Friedrich's misunderstanding in "Semasiologie und Lexikologie," col. 813, where he quotes Ernst Leisi's misleading statement that sentences are not as significant as words); cf. Stephen Ullmann, *The Principles of Semantics*, second ed. (New York: Philosophical Library, 1957), pp. 64–65. For a valuable and well-known philosophical discussion, see Gilbert Ryle, "The Theory of Meaning" (1957), reprinted in Charles E. Caton, ed., *Philosophy and Ordinary language* (Urbana: University of Illinois Press, 1963), especially p. 138.

study of words! Difficulties arise when lexical research is forced into a mold that it cannot fit, as when it becomes the exclusive basis for exegesis. We have also challenged, however, the very conception of "theological lexicography" (perhaps "lexical theology" is a more accurate and revealing description). How do our interests, then, differ from the concerns of *TDNT* and similar works? To answer this question, we need to recall the distinction between the word, or linguistic symbol, on the one hand, and the extralinguistic referent (the concept or theological idea) on the other. As might be expected, our concern is with the former of these.

To be sure, the question of how word and concept should be related is beset with complex (and primarily philosophical) problems.[48] These problems pose some well-known dilemmas for the lexicographer. On the one hand, "meaning" in the broadest sense does include the extralinguistic thing denoted by a word along with cultural interpretations and individual attitudes, so that if a lexicographer is not familiar with all these aspects, "his identification of meaning will be vague or wide of the mark."[49] On the other hand, lexicographers are supposed to define words, not things.[50] How to reconcile these two principles is perhaps an insoluble problem of lexicography.[51] But we

---

[48]I have no contribution to make in this area, neither do I care, for purposes of the present discussion, to commit myself to a specific philosophical solution. I merely wish to plead that, however we may decide to *relate* the linguistic to the extralinguistic, these two must be *distinguished*. This was of course Barr's real concern (*Semantics*, p. 217; "Common Sense," p. 385), so that both Hill (*Greek Words*, pp. 11–12) and Friedrich ("Semasiologie," cols. 803–4) becloud the issue.

[49]Hans Kurath, ed., *Middle English Dictionary*, "Plan and Bibliography" (Ann Arbor: University of Michigan, 1954), p. 3. We should note that some linguists have a much narrower conception of meaning; cf. Lázló Antal, "Meaning and Its Change," *Ling* 6 (1964): 14–28, especially p. 19. Even Antal acknowledges, however, that "in a description of meaning, the denotata cannot be overlooked, because they are the sole indication by means of which we can draw conclusions as to the meanings themselves" (p. 24).

[50]Alf Sommerfelt, "Sémantique et lexicographie: remarques sur la tâche du lexicographe," *Norsk tidsskrift for sprogvidenskap* 17 (1954): 485–89, especially p. 486.

[51]For example, Bauer cannot define δεπόσιτα without describing the Roman custom to which it refers, but sometimes he oversteps the limits of lexicography, as in his "definition" of σάρξ in Paul's writings, or in his extended note on ὄνομα. Interestingly, the *Patristic Greek Lexicon*, ed. G. W. H. Lampe (Oxford: Clarendon, 1961), without solving the problem, admits to being only partly linguistic and warns its readers that the articles deliberately describe patristic theology (p. viii; unfortunately, this means that we still lack a scientific description of the patristic vocabulary). Note

unnecessarily aggravate the situation by collecting numerous theological and historical essays, arranging them alphabetically according to the corresponding Greek words, and calling the final product a *Wörterbuch*.[52] Again, David Hill tells us, rightly, that we should do more than linguistics, that we should "penetrate beyond the words and matters of usage" and move into "the inner world of thought";[53] but if that is his real object, why does he call his work "our lexicographical studies"?[54]

Our discussion so far may appear hair-splitting. After all, we agree that *full* semantic description requires the study of theology and of the history of ideas; we even agree that the actual *contents* of *TDNT* often prove valid and useful. Does it really matter then what term is used to describe that type of research? It does, not only because we need scientifically rigorous terminology, but also because we need "real" lexicography.[55] Purely linguistic studies, though not an end in themselves, are of utmost importance if we expect our broader semantic discussions and specific exegetical decisions to rest on a solid footing. This point has been made, from a different perspective, by T. E. Hope. Although his argument has reference to loan words, it is so obviously relevant to the study of theological terms that I quote in full:

> In the past a cultural or historical approach to the interpretation of borrowed vocabulary has held the field. It has inspired a long series of scholarly works and its value has been amply demonstrated. But it has also proved open to abuse. The tendency has been in the past to write history [and theology] in terms of loan-words [and theological terms],

also that Baumgartner (in KB₃, p. xvi) describes Koehler's method as *Wörter und Sachen*.

[52]This unfair caricature is meant only to stress the dangers in the format and in the (indirect?) claims of *TDNT*: I certainly do not wish to denigrate the content of the articles, most of which are, as no one would care to deny, quite indispensable.

[53]Hill, *Greek Words*, p. 12.

[54]Ibid., p. 300. That there is some confusion as to what he is really doing may be seen from his discussion of the *idea* of righteousness in Israel; the discussion itself is of course appropriate, but it certainly should not be characterized as a description of "the development of the meaning and content of the צדק-*words*," nor as a "study of Old Testament *usage*" (pp. 92, 96, my emphasis). Notice, however, that his first two studies are excellent examples of *linguistic* investigation.

[55]Is it just a coincidence that since *TDNT* began to be produced, we have not had linguistic descriptions comparable to those of Kennedy and Nägeli (discussed below in chap. 2)?

rather than to interpret loan-words with reference to history. There is no intrinsic fault in this; the fault lies in the exaggeration of a valid principle rather than the principle itself. It would be idle to deny that loan-words for the most part do bear witness to historical events . . . ; but to construct a monograph by fitting a number of words into a prepared historical pattern, to use borrowings as a text upon which to write a chronicle of political and cultural events (which are in any case well known beforehand) and no more, is to produce work which is *essentially extra-linguistic,* and which the historians, I fear, would not approve of either. Words are elements of language. *As linguistic entities they must be handled according to linguistic principles.* Loan-words must be interpreted not only in terms of social, political, economic and literary influences, or as evidence of these influences, but appraised straightforwardly, directly, *in their own right.*[56]

We wish in this book, therefore, to establish principles and develop methods for the study of all types of words (not only theological terms) as elements of language in their own right. Our goal is *not* to deduce the theology of New Testament writers straight out of the words they use, nor even to map out semantic fields that in themselves may reflect theological structures.[57] We have the relatively modest goal of determining the most accurate English equivalents to biblical words, of being able to decide, with as much certainty as possible, what a specific Greek or Hebrew word in a specific context actually means.

To some students, this task may seem only a bit less boring than, say, textual criticism. But just as the establishment of the correct text—no matter how tedious the process involved or how unsensational the results—is a fundamental step in biblical interpretation, so lexicology takes priority in the exegetical process. We may pursue the analogy and suggest that, although not every exegete need become a

[56]*Lexical Borrowing in the Romance Languages: A Critical Study of Italianisms in French and Gallicisms in Italian From 1100 to 1900,* 2 vols. (Oxford: B. Blackwell, 1971), p. x (my emphasis).

[57]This qualification distinguishes our concern—which does involve the study of lexical fields, but only for linguistic purposes—from the method of scholars such as John F. A. Sawyer, who seem interested in developing an approach somewhat intermediate between the purely lexicographic and that of *TDNT.* Some portions of their work, however, are directly relevant to ours and will therefore be discussed in chap. 6.

professional textual critic, every exegete must have sufficient involvement in that work to evaluate and assimilate the results of the "experts." Similarly, all biblical interpreters need exposure to and experience in lexicographic method if they would use the linguistic data in a responsible way.

In a survey of biblical scholars and students conducted in the late 1960s, some respondents commented on the need for "a better understanding of the nature, use, and limitations of a lexicon" on the part of dictionary users.[58] The point, which could hardly be disputed, is still valid today. This requisite understanding, however, can only be developed on the basis of a solid grasp of the theoretical foundations of lexicology. It is to these principial questions that the present book is devoted.

[58]John Edward Gates, *An Analysis of the Lexicographic Resources Used by American Biblical Scholars Today* (SBLDS 8; Missoula, Montana: Society of Biblical Literature, 1972), p. 134.

PART 1

HISTORICAL SEMANTICS

SUMMARY OF CHAPTER 1

SYNCHRONY AND DIACHRONY

The study of the history of words must be guided by Saussure's fundamental distinction between synchronic (or static) and diachronic (or evolutionary) linguistics and by his emphasis that the former should take priority over the latter.

ETYMOLOGICAL SCIENCE

The study of etymology focuses on word origins, but we must distinguish several approaches: identifying the component parts of a word, the earliest attested meanings, the prehistorical forms and meanings, or the forms and meanings in the parent language. Etymological research is of special value for the translation of ancient documents written in poorly attested languages, such as Ugaritic. Since Greek is richly attested, the study of etymology is not as important for the New Testament as it is for the Old Testament. The abundance of *hapax legomena* in the Old Testament requires the use of other Semitic languages for determining the meaning of many Hebrew words, but care must be taken not to abuse this method.

ETYMOLOGY AND EXEGESIS

Although the use of etymology is hardly ever needed for determining the meaning of Greek words in the New Testament, both ministers and scholars often appeal to etymology as the key to interpretation. However, the priority of the synchronic approach demands that we pay regard to etymology only if it can be shown that the biblical writers intended the word to be taken in its etymological sense. We may demonstrate such an intention through the notion of transparency, but further qualifications are necessary.

1 Etymology

One hundred years ago linguistics was, almost by definition, historical in method; indeed, the discipline took its place among the sciences only when the "neogrammarians" of the 1870s demonstrated the regularity of phonetic *changes*. Although scholarly interest in historical and comparative research has never waned, modern linguistics is to be sharply contrasted from earlier stages by its essentially *descriptive* character. No doubt many factors contributed to this new outlook, but the work of a Swiss scholar, Ferdinand de Saussure, is generally regarded as the foundational influence.

SYNCHRONY AND DIACHRONY

In the all-important first part of his *Course in General Linguistics*, Saussure dealt with the arbitrary manner in which language associates a word with its mental content (a combination called "the linguistic sign"). After discussing other related questions, however, he proceeded to formulate a distinction that would have telling repercussions on the study of language.

Some sciences—Saussure begins—deal with systems in which things of different orders must be equated; economic science, for example, seeks to equate labor and wages, and this means that it is concerned with *values*. Linguistics too is concerned with values, since it deals with signs: linguistics must correlate the *signifier* (the word, the sound image) and the *signified* (the concept for which the word is used, the mental content).

Now it is especially the sciences concerned with values that must distinguish their subject matter on the basis of *time*. "In these fields the scholars cannot organize their research rigorously without . . . making a distinction between the system of values per se and the same values as they relate to time." The distinction becomes absolutely essential in the study of language, for "nowhere else do we find such precise values at stake and such a great number and diversity of terms, all so rigidly interdependent."[1] There are then really two sciences of language *diachronic* or evolutionary linguistics, and *Synchronic* or static linguistics.

The speaker, it must be noted, is aware only of the present state of language, so

> the linguist who wishes to understand a state must discard all knowledge of everything that produced it and ignore diachrony. He can enter the mind of speakers only by completely suppressing the past. The intervention of history can only falsify his judgment.[2]

Saussure illustrates his point by reference to the French words *décrepir* ('to remove mortar') and *décrépit* ('decrepit'). In the present state of the language, the speakers sense a relation between the two words and even speak of the *façade décrépite* ('decrepit façade') instead of the *façade decrepi* ('a façade from which mortar is falling') of a house. In fact, however, the first word is a verb formation from the root *crep*, whereas the second is a direct loan from Latin *(decrepitus)*. "It is obvious that the diachronic facts are not related to the static facts which they produced. They belong to a different class."[3] In other words, these terms are related synchronically but not diachronically.

Saussure goes one step further. Not only should these two approaches be distinguished as independent and self-contained; we must also recognize that one is more important than the other.

> Here it is evident that the synchronic viewpoint predominates, for it is the true and only reality to the community of speakers. . . . The same is true of the linguist: if he takes the diachronic perspective, he no longer observes language but rather a series of events that modify it.[4]

[1]Ferdinand de Saussure, *Course in General Linguistics* (New York: McGraw-Hill, 1966, originally published in 1915), pp. 79–81.

[2]Ibid., p. 81.

[3]Ibid., p. 83.

[4]Ibid., p. 90.

To summarize his conclusions, he defined the concern of synchronic linguistics as "the logical and psychological relations that bind together coexisting terms and form a system in the collective mind of speakers"; diachronic linguistics, on the other hand, studies those relations, unperceived by the collective mind, that "bind together successive terms."[5]

Saussure's contribution was not assimilated immediately. A decade later (1924) as distinguished a scholar as Jespersen was still speaking of *historical* grammar as "the pride of the linguistic science of the last hundred years or so."[6] But eventually Saussure's axiom won the day; at present

> most scholars tend to see in it the most fruitful contribution of the whole Saussurean theory. It has rescued descriptive linguistics from the purely practical and ancillary status to which it had been relegated by the rise of the historical method in the last century.[7]

Ullmann is impressed with the practical results that Saussure's distinction has helped to achieve,[8] and offers the following illustration to confirm the importance of synchronic study: French *pas* may be a negative particle or the noun for 'step,' and English 'ear' may refer to the organ for hearing or to the spike of a cereal plant (*ear of corn*). Philologists, knowing that both French words derive from *passus*, but that the English words have different etymologies, have considered the former a case of *polysemy* (multiple meaning) and the latter a case of *homonymy* (two different roots that have come to sound alike). As a matter of fact, the French speaker does not perceive that these two *pas* are related, so they should be regarded as homonyms; conversely, the English example should be considered polysemous, since English speakers usually perceive *ear of corn* as a metaphor. Psychologically, these phenomena are "all-important," and attention to Saussure's warnings would have prevented "the obstinate recurrence of these fundamentally distorted views even in products of serious scholarship."[9]

[5]Ibid., pp. 99–100.

[6]Otto Jespersen, *The Philosophy of Grammar* (New York: Norton, 1965, originally published, 1924), p. 30.

[7]Ullmann, *Principles*, p. 143.

[8]Ibid., p. 139.

[9]Ibid., p. 140 (see also pp. 128ff.). We shall return to these questions in chaps. 4, 6.

This whole discussion is of the greatest relevance for biblical studies. We must accept the obvious fact that the speakers of a language simply know next to nothing about its development; and this certainly was the case with the writers and immediate readers of Scripture two millennia ago. More than likely, even a knowledge of that development is not bound to affect the speaker's daily conversation: the English professor who knows that *nice* comes from Latin *nescius*, 'ignorant,' does not for that reason refrain from using the term in a complimentary way. It follows that our real interest is the significance of Greek or Hebrew *in the consciousness of the biblical writers*; to put it baldly, "historical considerations are irrelevant to the investigation" of the state of the Koine at the time of Christ.[10]

This last statement needs some modification—our own inclusion of a section on historical semantics bears out the importance of the diachronic approach; and, as we shall see, the two approaches are not mutually exclusive. As a guiding principle, however, the priority of the synchronic viewpoint is a reliable result of modern linguistics that we dare not ignore. It is therefore advisable to divide the body of this study into two distinct parts: the present one, where diachronic considerations will be discussed, and part two, the most important and substantial section, which will deal with synchronic principles.

ETYMOLOGICAL SCIENCE

In order to obviate possible confusion, we shall maintain a distinction between *etymology* and *semantic change*. By the former we mean that area of linguistic study that seeks to determine the *origins* of

---

[10]Cf. John Lyons, *Introduction to Theoretical Linguistics* (Cambridge: Cambridge University Press, 1968), p. 46. Contrast the claim that, since the Koine is a popular language showing development, "he who would know the Koine must know earlier Greek as well. Otherwise, he lacks the base line from which the definition of the Koine moves" (E. C. Colwell in *IDB* 2:481). The measure of truth contained in that statement is better formulated by Lyons: "It may be that the way in which rules are integrated in the system of description will reflect particular historical processes in the development of the language. If so this is an important fact about the structure of language. But it does not affect the general principle of the priority of the synchronic, since the native speakers of a particular language are able to learn and apply the 'rules' of their language without drawing upon any historical knowledge" (*Introduction*, pp. 48–49; see also p. 407). In his later book, *Semantics*, 2 vols. (Cambridge: Cambridge University Press, 1977), Lyons reviews the objections that can be raised against an uncritical acceptance of Saussure's distinction and adds: "Within certain limits [which correspond to those that concern us in this book] . . . the distinction . . . is not only defensible, but methodologically essential" (1:243–44).

particular words; by the latter we mean the analysis of semantic *developments*, beginning with a word's first attested meaning. This distinction, however, cannot be pressed, particularly since the former is so often dependent on the latter.[11]

Having thus narrowed the scope of etymological study, some further distinctions are necessary, for the word *origins* itself can be interpreted in a variety of ways. In the first place, the investigator may simply be interested in identifying the *component parts* of a word. We can therefore say that the etymology of English *speaker* consists of the verb *speak* and the suffix *-er*; of Hebrew *miqneh* ('property,' especially 'cattle'), the preformative *mem* and the verb *qanah* ('acquire, buy'). So-called synthetic languages like German and Greek are especially susceptible to this kind of analysis; the Greek vocabulary, for example, is made up of thousands of derivations consisting of preposition + verb, such as ὑπό ('under') + μένειν ('remain') > ὑπομένειν ('endure'). It is important to understand that such an identification of origin does not *necessarily* take us to primitive times; in fact, a Greek writer may easily coin such a compound at the moment of writing. On the other hand the method may indeed uncover prehistorical meanings.

Second, etymological study may involve determining specifically the *earliest attested meaning* (from which, one may speculate, all other meanings were subsequently derived). In practice, this simply involves examining a particular word in our earliest sources and ascertaining its meaning there.

---

[11]Indeed, the word *etymology* is normally used today with reference to the history of words (though always with special interest in the earlier stages); see below, chap. 2. James Barr suggests the following description: "Etymology is the traditional term for several kinds of study, working upon words as the basic units and interested in the explication of them in relation to similar elements which are historically earlier, which are taken within the scope of the study as 'original,' which appear to be more basic as units of meaning, or which appear to have a prior place in some generative process"; see "Etymology and the Old Testament," in *Language and Meaning: Studies in Hebrew Language and Exegesis*, ed. A. J. van der Woude (OTS 19; Leiden: E. J. Brill, 1974), pp. 1–28, especially p. 20. In this article Barr proposes a classification somewhat different from the one suggested in the present chapter. For a significant paper on the autonomy and aims of etymological research, see Yacov Malkiel, *Essays on Linguistic Themes* (Berkeley: University of California, 1968), pp. 175–98. The etymology of the word *etymology* itself (from ἔτυμον, 'true, real') is noteworthy, since the term goes back to Hellenistic times (of course the practice of etymology is even older than the word used to describe it); for some Greeks—not all—to discover the origins of a word was to discover the very nature of things, and in this approach they are followed by several notable moderns (see the next note).

Third, the researcher may be interested in the *prehistorical stages*: what meaning (or form, or both) did a particular word have prior to its earliest attestation? Since such a meaning cannot be verified, the etymologist becomes engaged in the process of reconstruction (the relative certainty of which will vary tremendously from word to word). Various methods can be used for this task, such as the previously mentioned analysis of a word's component parts; for example, it is often argued that the word ἀλήθεια ('truth') originally meant 'concealment,' since it is apparently composed of the privative *alpha* and a derivative of λανθάνω.[12] Another method is to look for cognate terms in related languages; for example, if Greek εἶρος ('wool') is a cognate of Hittite *warḫunu*[13] ('to make rough, leafy, inaccessible'), this information helps us establish the prehistory of the Greek word.

Finally, etymological study may lead to the more ambitious reconstruction of the form and meaning of a word *in the parent language* by a careful examination of the cognate languages. For example, in biblical Hebrew we find the word *barur* ('sharp,' Isa. 49:2; Hifil 'sharpen,' Jer. 51:11—both with reference to arrows); some Akkadian cognates refer to 'luminosity, radiance, mistiness'; the Ethiopic *barara* means 'to pierce.' A careful investigation of that (and additional) information leads Pelio Fronzaroli to posit a Semitic root **brr*, 'to penetrate,' a meaning that he believes accounts for all the data.[14]

---

[12]It should be made clear that, even if we could establish conclusively that this is in effect what the word used to mean in prehistoric times, that fact would not necessarily tell us what the ancient Greeks understood truth to be, for the semantic development may have been fortuitous; much less does such a fact tell us what truth *is!* This kind of fallacious argumentation is an irritating quality of M. Heidegger and his followers. For example: "Revelation suggests some kind of unveiling, whereby what has hitherto been concealed from us is now opened up. This, however, would be true of all knowing. The Greeks thought of truth itself as ἀλήθεια, 'unhiddenness.' We have attained truth when that which was concealed is made unhidden, brought out into the light" (John Macquarrie, *Principles of Christian Theology*, 2nd ed. [New York: Charles Scribner's Sons, 1977], pp. 85–86). Even if the author's main point is valid, the reference to Greek lends, illegitimately, a kind of scientific authority to his statement.

[13]According to the laryngeal theory of Francisco Rodríguez Adrados; cf. *Introducción*, ed. Gangutia, p. 202.

[14]"Problems of a Semitic Etymological Dictionary," in *Studies on Semitic Lexicography*, ed. Pelio Fronzaroli (QSem 2; Firenze: Istituto di Linguistica e di Lingue Orientali, 1973), pp. 1–24, especially the preliminary specimen on pp. 18ff., where he summarizes: "The meaning 'to penetrate' is shown as original by its preservation in the marginal areas. Contexts in which the two literary words for 'ray' and

These four levels of etymological investigation do not exhaust the approaches used. A researcher, for example, may wish to determine a specific meaning—but not necessarily the earliest one—from which a later meaning was directly derived. Or again, etymological studies very often focus on *borrowings* from other languages.[15] But enough has been said to show the need for great care and precision when speaking about the etymology of a word.

Now what are the uses of etymology? To begin with, etymological research is the backbone of comparative linguistics; it is only by the proper identification of cognates that linguistic reconstruction is possible. In other words, etymology is a legitimate field of study in its own right. Second, etymological identifications can serve, if used cautiously, to illumine certain kinds of historical and cultural questions; in fact, the reconstruction of original Indo-European words has played an important role in prehistoric anthropology. Third, and more relevant to our purposes, etymology is often important for the translation of ancient documents.

Let us elaborate this third point. When Ugaritic was discovered in the early part of this century, scholars depended heavily on its relationship to the other Semitic tongues in order to decipher and translate the tablets. If a particular word happened to occur very frequently, its numerous contexts helped to determine the meaning easily; however, due to the paucity of Ugaritic materials, many *hapax legomena* remain. Scholars therefore search the other Semitic languages for possible cognates. For example, the Ugaritic word *ṭwy* occurs in one obscure passage; some scholars relate it to the Hebrew root *šwh* ('to

---

'radiance' appear in Akkadian, do not bear evidence of referring to the quality of light; they refer to the strength of penetration of the rays of Šamaš (or other gods), that reach the most secret places. . . ."

[15]Borrowings, which can take place between related as well as unrelated languages, must be sharply distinguished from *cognate* terms: the former result from external contacts, the latter from a genetic relationship. E.g., the Hebrew *hekal* ('palace, temple') comes from Akkadian *ekallu*; even though these two languages are related, however, we are not dealing here with a proto-Semitic word preserved by them, but with a non-Semitic, Sumerian word, *e-gal*, borrowed by Akkadian and then in turn by Hebrew. Very frequently, a violation of patterns in phonological changes alerts us to the presence of noncognate terms. A classic example is English *day*, Latin *dies* (these languages belong to the same "family," Indo-European); though similar both in form and in meaning, these two words are not related, since Latin /d-/ corresponds to English /t-/.

rule') and others to the Arabic *ṭwy* ('to stay') in their attempt to make sense of the passage.[16]

The relative value of this use of etymology varies inversely with the quantity of material available for the language. For example, so much Greek literature was written and preserved, that the number of words occurring only once or twice are proportionately very few, and they can normally be explained by reference to cognates within Greek itself. One example in the New Testament is the important word ἐπιούσιος in the Lord's Prayer (Matt. 6:11; Luke 11:3), which may be derived from ἐπί + εἰμί or from ἐπί + εἶμι (several different interpretations are then possible).

But if the use of etymology plays a very minor role in Greek New Testament lexicography, the situation is quite different for the determination of meaning in the Hebrew Old Testament, which contains no fewer than 1300 *hapax legomena*[17] and about 500 words that occur only twice out of a total vocabulary of about 8000 words. Most of these, to be sure, cause no serious problems, either because they are clearly derived from well-attested words or because they occur frequently in postbiblical Hebrew literature.[18] Even after we eliminate these, however, we are left with several hundred rare words, occurring particularly in poetic passages, many of which are relatively obscure (i.e., the contexts are not clear enough to establish the meanings of these words).

---

[16]This example is taken from Johannes C. de Moor, "Ugaritic Lexicography," in *Studies*, ed. Fronzaroli, pp. 61–102, especially pp. 89ff.

[17]Cf. *EncJud* 7:1318. On the basis of more inclusive principles, Chaim Rabin has suggested 2,440 *hapax legomena*; see Edward Ullendorff, *Is Biblical Hebrew a Language? Studies in Semitic Languages and Civilizations* (Wiesbaden: Otto Harrassowitz, 1977), pp. 14ff. For an up-to-date and rigorous examination, see Harold R. (Chaim) Cohen, *Biblical Hapax Legomena in the Light of Akkadian and Ugaritic* (SBLDS 37; Missoula, Montana: Scholars Press, 1978). Since he accepts as *hapax legomena* only those words "*whose root occurs in but one context*" (p. 7), his lists contain approximately 450 items. It should be noted, however, that his lists would be longer if he had been less ready to adopt proposed emendations (cf. below, n. 19). Also note the valuable statistical analysis by Frederick E. Greenspahn, "The Number and Distribution of *Hapax Legomena* in Biblical Hebrew," *VT* 30 (1980): 8–19; and Benjamin Kedar, *Biblische Semantik. Eine Einführung* (Stuttgart: W. Kohlhammer, 1981), pp. 98–105.

[18]For example, *'amṣah* occurs only in Zech. 12:5, but the verb *'amaṣ* ('be strong') is very common and there can be no dispute that the noun means 'strength.' In the case of *šum* (occurring only in Num. 11:5), we can find no biblical word from which it is derived, but this noun was preserved in the living speech and occurs frequently enough in rabbinic literature with the meaning 'garlic.'

Understandably, a knowledge of related Semitic languages becomes essential in this case. Indeed, Old Testament scholars have expended a remarkable amount of energy searching for cognates and proposing new meanings. In some cases, the relationships can be established beyond reasonable doubt and the proposed meanings fit the contexts to the satisfaction of most scholars. For example, Job 40:12 reads: "Look on every proud man (and) humble him, and $h^a dok$ the wicked where they stand." Neither the verb *hadak* nor a derivative occurs elsewhere in the Bible; however, the Arabic *hadaka* conforms to the established phonological correspondences between Arabic and Hebrew, and its meaning 'tear down' fits the context perfectly. [19]

Etymological correspondences are also useful when examining passages that may have a frequently occurring word if the usual meaning of that word does not seem suitable in the context. For example, in Judges 18:7 we are told of a group of Danites who visited Laish and found the town in quietness and security. An additional descriptive clause has proven most difficult: "There was no one *maklim dabar* in the land." The verb *klm* commonly has the meaning 'disgrace, put to shame' (Hifil), but this meaning seems inappropriate here. Some scholars prefer to emend the text, while others appeal to the Arabic *kallama* ('speak') and thus translate, "No one uttered a word in the land," presumably a figure emphasizing the tranquility of Laish. Proposals of this type, however, because they are highly conjectural, seldom find acceptance. [20]

As a whole, then, the appeal to etymology is an indispensable element in Hebrew lexicography. Unfortunately, the method has received considerable abuse. Some proposals do not conform to the established phonological correspondences between the languages being compared, while others are made on the basis of an uncritical use of the evidence from the ancient versions; most of them are not

[19]This solution is accepted by a number of commentators and translations, but others prefer to emend the text. (An emendation must be presupposed by Cohen, *Biblical Hapax Legomena*, who does not mention this example.) Arabic plays an important role in the comparative method because of the extensive literature (with a rich and often archaic vocabulary) preserved in that language. For a general discussion of Old Testament etymology, see Kedar, *Biblische Semantik*, pp. 82–98.

[20]This example is treated by James Barr in *Comparative Philology and the Text of the Old Testament* (Oxford: Clarendon Press, 1968), pp. 14ff. Even more debatable, though admissible in principle, are etymological proposals used to emend the Massoretic text, as when *tirhu* (Isa. 44:8) is emended to *tidhu* on the basis of Arabic *dahā*; see Barr, ibid., chap. 8.

integrated into a coherent and linguistically sound view of Hebrew. We may illustrate this last point by noting the abundance of homonyms that would be created if we were to accept these proposals. James Barr, for example, has collected no fewer than six unrelated proposed meanings for the verb *yada'* ('to know').[21]

Although it would be a serious mistake to dismiss the method altogether, every proposal must be carefully scrutinized and evaluated on the basis of established semantic principles, such as the centrality of lexical structure and the determinative role of context. (These principles form the subject matter of part two of this work.) Even in the case of Ugaritic, for which etymological identifications are so important, de Moor can state the following rule: "An explanation which rests on the sole basis of etymology can never be anything more than a plausible hypothesis."[22]

ETYMOLOGY AND EXEGESIS

In the previous section we have examined the value of etymological science for the determination of otherwise unknown meanings. Ironically, however, etymology seems to occupy a more prominent place in the discussion of words whose meaning is already established! Also ironically, the use of etymology by ministers may be directly linked to a *lack* of genuine familiarity with the biblical languages.

This last point deserves some elaboration. One rarely finds a minister who can read a given piece of Hellenistic Greek at sight. The typical seminary graduate usually knows enough Greek to read most New Testament passages with relative ease (though for this he is more dependent than he realizes on his previous knowledge of the contents); he also is able to follow linguistic arguments and to discuss intelligently grammatical and lexical problems.

In the course of his sermon preparation, a minister may feel obligated to use his knowledge of Greek. If he is unable to draw from a true familiarity with the structure of the language, he may say, "The

[21]Ibid., pp. 19ff., 328.
[22]"Ugaritic Lexicography," p. 85. In his celebrated work, *Introducción a la lexicografía moderna* (Madrid: C.S.I.C., 1950), p. 33, Julio Casares argues that lexicography and etymology are as distinct from each other as the practice of medicine is distinct from the work of developing x-ray film: the lexicographer is concerned with collating *proven* linguistic facts, which means that he "should not get involved in the etymologist's investigation, a study never free of fantasy" (however, Casares has in view well-attested languages like Spanish).

original here means. . . ." But what *does* it mean? The congregation already knows what it means, for they have just read their English version. So the minister often makes comments on the etymology of the word. If the word happens to be ἁμαρτία, it means not just 'sin' but 'missing the mark'; if it is ὑπομένειν, it means not just 'to endure' but 'to remain under.' If the word is ἐκκλησία, it means not just 'church' but 'those who are called out.'

Less careful ministers give themselves over to excesses. It is not uncommon to hear sermons practically built on the etymology of some significant word. Sometimes this tendency goes beyond biblical words, as when the English *lord*, which in Old English meant 'keeper of the loaf,' is used to prove that Christianity has economic concerns.[23] An interesting twist, which we may call reverse etymologizing, consists of referring to English derivatives of a Greek word being discussed, as when a speaker commenting on the Holy Spirit's power (Acts 1:8) reminds us that "we get the English *dynamite* from the word used here"; or when the words *metamorphosis*[24] and *hilarious* are thought to shed light on Romans 12:2 and 2 Corinthians 9:7. These observations may seem innocuous enough, but, unless used with great caution, they tend to create certain associations in the mind of the modern Bible reader that might have been foreign to the original writers.

Ministers may be excused, however, for professional scholars themselves have set the pattern.[25] One of the longest chapters in Barr's

[23]Reported by Barr, *Semantics*, p. 110, n. 3.

[24]Cf. Donald Grey Barnhouse, *God's Discipline* (Grand Rapids: Eerdmans, 1964), p. 27, which specifically mentions the "abrupt change in the form and structure" of a tadpole or a grub. On p. 22, with reference to συσχηματίζεσθαι in Rom. 12:2, he appeals to the *Oxford English Dictionary* definition for the word *scheme*. See the valuable discussion by Louw, *Semantics*, chap. 4.

[25]Some of the blame must be placed on R. C. Trench; cf. *On the Study of Words* (London: Kegan Paul, Trench, and Co., 1888), p. 273. For him it was sincerely "a violation of truth" to use *congratulate* instead of *felicitate* when addressing a "stranger whose prosperity awoke no lively delight in my heart; for when I 'congratulate' a person (congratulor), I declare that I am a sharer in his joy . . ." (p. 277). For an example outside of biblical scholarship, we may note an observation by the nineteenth-century anthropologist, Edward B. Tylor, that "*kindred* and *kindness* go together—two words whose common derivation expresses in the happiest way one of the main principles of social life" (*Anthropology: An Introduction to the Study of Man and Civilization* [New York: Appleton, 1881], p. 405, referred to approvingly by Peter Farb, *Man's Rise to Civilization: The Cultural Ascent of the Indians of North America*, 2nd ed. [New York: Dutton, 1978], p. 60). It may be, of course, that Tylor saw the derivation as little more than an amusing coincidence.

Semantics is devoted to "Etymologies and Related Arguments." Take, for example, a well-known Old Testament scholar, Norman H. Snaith. Arguing that a word's "fundamental motif" tends to endure, no matter what changes occur, Snaith turns to a specific instance:

> Another word used in this connection, though less frequently, is *niham*, generally translated "repent" (in the passive form) and "comfort" (in the intensive form). Actually the word means "to take a breath of relief," the implication being "to breathe hard [as of a horse]," as is shown in Arabic. The word therefore has to do with "change of attitude," "change of mind," any other association being accidental.[26]

Snaith's argument is a complete reversal of things. If synchronic considerations are prior, then the *current associations* of the word are of the utmost importance; in fact, it is the (supposed) past history of a word that should be labelled "accidental"! Now even nineteenth-century commentators realized that usage is more important than etymology, and certainly Snaith himself was aware of this principle.[27] The least that can be said then is that his statements were unguarded and bound to have a regrettable influence on the readers. His defense that he was only trying to point out the survival of earlier meanings "side by side with later developments"[28] does not at all absolve him of this charge.

We may summarize the dangers of etymological work by quoting a highly regarded Indo-Europeanist, J. Vendryes, who sees the value of studying roots but is careful to add:

> Etymology, however, gives a false idea of the nature of a vocabulary for it is concerned only in showing how a vocabulary has been formed. Words are not used according to their historical value. The mind forgets—assuming that it ever knew—the semantic evolutions through which the words have passed. Words always have a *current* value, that is to say, limited to the moment when they are employed,

[26]*IB* 1:225. The question whether or not a word contains a permanent core of meaning ("fundamental motif") will occupy us in chap. 4.

[27]Cf. *The Distinctive Ideas of the Old Testament* (London: Epworth, 1944), p. 21.

[28]"The Meanings of a Word," *BT* 16 (1965): 44–48, p. 45. Even so, how can the idea of 'breathing hard' be said to have survived in Hebrew?

and a *particular* value relative to the momentary use made of them.[29]

The position adopted so far seems extreme. Does it mean that the history of a word is of no use at all? It is in this connection that we must qualify our earlier comments on the diachronic approach. Already in 1931 W. von Wartburg had made a case for the need to bring together the historical and descriptive methods, especially in dealing with vocabulary.[30] Ullmann has shown, however, that Wartburg's contribution is not irreconcilable with Saussure's.[31] Literature and philosophy, for example, are independent disciplines, but whenever they need each other for illumination they become interdependent. That some diachronic developments help explain certain synchronic facts, or vice versa, is no argument for fusing the two approaches into one. Sometimes, as Saussure argued, the past must be suppressed; at other times (something he did not point out) diachronic evidence is needed. In the present discussion then we should adopt Ullmann's plea for "some judicious combining of the two methods to the mutual advantage of both."

> This combination of the two perspectives is quite compatible with a somewhat liberal interpretation of the Saussurean principle, with the all-important proviso that combination does not lead to confusion and that the two methods are used side by side with the sole and unambiguously formulated purpose of throwing light on one another.[32]

The significance of Wartburg's ideas for etymological studies is simply that the root of a word *may* indeed be of value in determining its meaning. But in order to satisfy the principle of synchronic priority

[29]J. Vendryes, *Language: A Linguistic Introduction to History* (New York: Alfred A. Knopf, 1925), p. 176. Cf. Barr, *Semantics*, p. 109.

[30]See Wartburg's important synthesis, *Problems and Methods in Linguistics* (New York: Barnes & Noble, 1969), p. 139, n. 1. He exaggerates, however, when he denies any independence to each discipline and speaks of "the *profound* modifications . . . brought to the Saussurean dichotomy" (p. 194, my emphasis); Ullmann's formulation seems to me to be more reasonable.

[31]Ullmann, *Principles*, pp. 144ff.

[32]Ibid., pp. 145–46. An example of confusion, not legitimate integration, is this statement: "The meaning of any word is a function of its uses in language in the past up to the point of usage in question" (see the conclusion to George E. Mendenhall's remarkable review of Barr's *Comparative Philology* in *Int* 25 [1971]: 358–62).

it must be shown that the speaker's consciousness is stimulated by that root. In other words, *historical considerations may be of synchronic value, but only if we can demonstrate that the speaker was aware of them.*[33] For example, if a New Testament writer using the word ἐκκλησία could be shown to have made a conscious reference to the root of the word, then the idea of 'calling out' *must* be taken into consideration. This point is of course consonant with Vendryes's statement above.

But the incisive question may be asked, When *does* the root of a word in fact play a role in the writer's mind? One important clue is the relative *transparency* of the word.[34] The notion of transparency is applied rather broadly to all those words that are *motivated*, that is, words that have some natural relation to their meaning. *Splash*, for example, is phonologically motivated, because its sound recalls its sense. *Leader* is morphologically motivated, for someone who knows what *to lead* means and what the suffix *-er* stands for can easily arrive at the meaning of the word. Finally, we speak of semantic motivation in cases like *the foot of a hill*, where the figurative character of the phrase makes the meaning intelligible to someone who has not previously heard the expression. All of these words are transparent; whenever a word does *not* suggest a perceptible reason for having its form, then the relation between form and meaning is *arbitrary* and the word is *opaque*.

Whether the etymology of a word plays a part in its meaning is of

---

[33]N. W. Porteous, "The Present State of Old Testament Theology," *ExpT* 75 (1963–64): 70–74, may be correct in pointing out that Barr made "insufficient allowance for the overtones of language" that are sometimes exploited by careful writers (p. 71). Note, however, Barr's criticism of scholars who appeal to etymological associations "without any inquiry whether they existed in the minds of" the original writer and readers (*Semantics*, p. 116; see also Barr's reply to Porteous, "Did Isaiah Know About Hebrew 'Root Meanings'?" *ExpT* 75 [1963–64]: 242, and J. F. A. Sawyer, "Root-Meanings in Hebrew," *JSS* 12 [1967]: 37–50). The prominent linguist Dwight Bolinger, in a paper on "Semantic Overloading: A Restudy of the Word *Remind*," *Lg* 47 (1971): 522–47, speaks of the dangers of "excessive synchrony" and stresses that, since meaning changes very fast, "to understand a meaning now, it is necessary to know what it was yesterday" (p. 547). True enough, assuming that yesterday's meaning is also known to the speaker—but Saussure would not have denied that. To restrict synchrony to some mechanical (indeed, unreal) "present" fails to appreciate Saussure's concern for "the true and only reality to the community of speakers" (*Course*, p. 90).

[34]The following discussion is based on Ullmann, *Principles*, pp. 83ff., and on his *Semantics: An Introduction to the Science of Meaning* (Oxford: Blackwell, 1964), chap. 4.

course a question of morphological motivation. Now it should be noticed that languages differ greatly regarding the proportion of their vocabulary that may be considered transparent. Phonetic change may reduce considerably the number of transparent words; the classic example is French, where the etymologically related words *pied* ('foot'), *pion* ('usher'), *péage* ('toll'), *piètre* ('wretched'), etc., no longer call each other up. Analytic languages, like English, also will have relatively few transparent terms; the speaker will usually associate a word like *television* with a particular object directly, without a second thought about the etymology of the word.[35] In contrast German, which is highly synthetic, builds its own *Fernsehen*, 'far-seeing.' An extreme example of this German tendency is the word for *hammock*: an American Indian term, it was borrowed by Spanish and French *(hamaca, hamac)*, but when German sailors took it over from French, they Germanized to *Hängematte* ('hanging mat').[36]

What saves the etymologically minded minister from catastrophe is the fact that Greek—a rather synthetic language, which, in addition, has undergone little phonetic change—is relatively transparent. Thus ὑπομένειν, which does not "really" mean 'to remain under,' nevertheless was at one point associated with that idea and possibly recalled it even when 'endure' became its most important meaning. Even in the case of Greek, however, we must remember that some terms may be only *apparently* motivated. For this reason the following considerations cannot be ignored:

(1) In the first place, notice that

compounds and derivatives may lose their motivation if any of their elements falls into disuse. The days of the week are a case in point. Only *Sunday*, and, perhaps, *Monday* are fully analysable in English; the rest have become opaque since the disappearance of the names of pagan deities on which they were based.[37]

Thus we could imagine a situation where μένειν was no longer used by itself in New Testament times yet had survived in compounds such

---

[35]The word *television* is of course a synthetic term, but it was contrived by specialists who have some knowledge of classical languages and should not therefore be interpreted as reflecting an English tendency. In German, however, the pattern is against combining foreign (therefore opaque) words, as the example shows.

[36]Wartburg, *Problems*, p. 123.

[37]Ullmann, *Semantics*, p. 97.

as ὑπομένειν; if that had been the case, we could not regard the latter word as transparent.

(2) In some cases, a derivative that has not undergone phonetic changes may nevertheless undergo *semantic* changes and become unrelated to the original word. English *regard* was a derivative from *guard*, but the meanings of these words have drifted so far from each other that the speaker is not aware of their connection (as is reflected by the difference in spelling).[38] The Greek προκοπή had already in classical times developed the meaning of 'progress' and most likely did not normally call up its origin, κοπή; it would therefore be invalid to claim that in Philippians 1:25 Paul was making reference to the obstacles that must be "cut down, eliminated," if believers are to advance in their Christian life.

(3) In contrast to the first two cases, it is possible for a word to *acquire* a new motivation. That is, words may in time become associated (usually because of phonetic changes), even though genetically they have no connection; a good example is the French association of *décrepir* and *décrépit* (see p. 36). This phenomenon is known as "popular etymology," and is usually understood as "a reaction against the conventionality [arbitrariness] of signs. People want to explain at any cost what remains unexplained in language."[39] The synchronic character of this phenomenon underscores its importance in exegetical studies. For the lexicographer, Casares points out, popular etymology may often be of greater significance than true etymology.[40]

(4) Finally, we must reiterate the ultimate importance of the context. This point will be dealt with fully later, but it must be brought to bear in this connection. It would be unreasonable, for example, to appeal to the etymology of ὑπομένειν in a discussion of Luke 2:43. On the other hand, one could argue plausibly that ἁμαρτάνειν in Romans 3:23 evokes the earlier meaning, 'to miss the mark,' since the apostle describes the result of sin as a failing to obtain God's glory.[41]

---

[38]Ibid.

[39]Vendryes, quoted by Ullmann, *Semantics*, p. 102; cf. Wartburg, *Problems*, pp. 123ff. It is no doubt this impulse to discover what remains hidden that accounts for human interest in scientific, as well as popular, etymology; see the useful comments by Barr, "Etymology," p. 21, and his discussion of popular etymology in the biblical documents themselves, pp. 23ff.

[40]Casares, *Introducción*, p. 41.

[41]Here also belong literary puns; e.g., although we should resist the suggestion that ἀναγινώσκειν (in NT = 'to read') really means 'to know again,' Paul most surely exploits the verb's etymology in 2 Cor. 3:2 (cf. also 1:13).

To summarize, the idea that etymology provides what is essential to a word persisted through the nineteenth century; unfortunately, today we still hear comments concerning the "basic," "proper," even "real" meaning of a word when the reference is only to its etymology. Modern studies compel us to reject this attitude and distrust a word's history; at the same time, we must use the past history of a word in coordination with its present use by means of the notion of transparency. Even in the closest ties between historical and descriptive studies, however, the priority of synchrony, the *dominant* function of usage, must be maintained.

SUMMARY OF CHAPTER 2

GENERAL CONSIDERATIONS

Modern etymologists consider it their task to investigate not only the roots but also the history of words, a field best described as the study of semantic change. This type of study proves difficult in connection with Old Testament Hebrew words partly because of difficulties in dating the texts, and partly because the material is scarce.

SEPTUAGINT AND NEW TESTAMENT

All biblical scholars recognize the significance of the LXX for the study of New Testament words, but disagreement exists regarding the precise relation between these documents. E. Hatch emphasized the differences between New Testament and non-biblical Greek and attributed those differences to the influence of the LXX, which used Greek words to express Semitic ideas. Hatch's formulations were challenged by T. K. Abbott, who argued that the language of the New Testament is in some respects quite different from that of the LXX, and by H. A. A. Kennedy, who undertook a comprehensive study of the LXX and New Testament vocabularies. More recently there has been continued discussion regarding these questions, particularly as a result of papyrological discoveries and A. Deissmann's views. The influence of the LXX on New Testament language should be understood as largely restricted to stylistic elements.

USING THE SEPTUAGINT

The field of LXX studies is highly specialized due to the serious difficulties one encounters in trying to make use of the materials. Because mistakes are easily made, the student needs to use caution in two areas.

Ascertaining the Text. The textual transmission of the LXX is very complicated and use should be made of available critical editions. Awareness that the transmission of the LXX differs from book to book, that different techniques were used by different translators, that a consideration of the Hebrew text is essential, and that conjectural emendations are often necessary will help to prevent a misuse of this document.

Interpreting the Text. Before using a LXX passage as evidence for the meaning of a Greek word, the relation of that word to its corresponding Hebrew word must be responsibly determined, the meaning of the whole passage in the Greek text must be ascertained, and the possibility of distinctive ideas and methods in the Greek translation should be considered.

2 Semantic Change and the Role of the Septuagint

GENERAL CONSIDERATIONS

Our previous chapter examined etymology in its narrow, traditional sense. Modern scientific etymologists, however, consider this approach completely inadequate. The dean of Romance linguistics W. von Wartburg argues, for example, that it is not enough to say that Italian *ferire* ('to wound') comes from Latin *ferire* ('to strike'). The etymologist must go on to explain that when the word took on this new meaning, (1) it thereby supplanted *vulnerare*, which already meant 'to wound,' and (2) it was on the other hand replaced by *percuotere*, which previously had meant 'to knock against.'[1] Thus:

Several other questions—such as why French *ferir* retained the old meaning—call for an answer. Wartburg concludes that

> etymology must devote itself to the task of observing and describing all the changes a word undergoes, with a view to understanding and explaining them. . . . *Today the task of etymology is no longer solely to look for the root of a word or a*

[1]Wartburg, *Problems*, p. 115; I have simplified the data.

*group of words. It must follow the group in question through-
out the whole period during which it belongs to the language,
in all its ramifications and all its relations to other groups,
constantly asking the questions appropriate to etymology in
the strict sense of the word.* [2]

Although the last clause qualifies the statement somewhat, we
can see that for Wartburg (and many other scholars) etymological
science overlaps considerably with the study of semantic change.
Without necessarily denying that the etymologist should "paint for us
the broad scene of all the vicissitudes"[3] that words experience, we shall
continue to distinguish etymology—with its distinctive interest in origins, whether historical or prehistorical—from semantic change,
which focuses on *attested developments* in the meanings of words.

For fairly obvious reasons, the study of semantic change has considerably more relevance to the study of New Testament Greek than to
the study of Old Testament Hebrew. Before the New Testament was
written, there already existed a large corpus of Greek literature going
back several centuries. On the other hand, the Old Testament is itself
our oldest extant literature in the Hebrew language, and although a
study of postbiblical changes can prove rather fascinating,[4] and may
even throw indirect light on earlier periods, Old Testament scholars
have not traditionally occupied themselves with these later developments.[5]

To be sure, a very important qualification must be made: the Old
Testament literature spans several centuries and it is only to be expected that semantic changes during this period could be attested without recourse to either prebiblical or postbiblical stages. For example,
the poetic language of Judges 5 (the Song of Deborah) is universally

[2]Ibid., p. 121 (his emphasis). Note that Pierre Chantraine's *Dictionnaire
étymologique de la langue grecque* (Paris: Klincksieck, 1968–) carries the subtitle
Histoire des mots; cf. also his introductory comments.

[3]Wartburg, p. 121.

[4]This is particularly true of developments in Modern Hebrew, such as the use of
ḥašmal (found in Ezek. 1:4, 27 with reference to some shining object) for 'electricity.'
Cf. William Chomsky, *Hebrew: The Eternal Language* (Philadelphia: Jewish Publication Society, 1957), p. 200; also *EncJud* 16:1649–53.

[5]The importance of data from so-called Middle Hebrew has rightfully been
stressed by E. Y. Kutscher, "Mittelhebräisch und Jüdisch-Aramäisch im neuen
Köhler-Baumgartner," in *Hebräische Wortforschung* (VTSup 16; Leiden: Brill, 1967),
pp. 158–75.

recognized as archaic, doubtlessly taking us into the second millennium B.C., whereas the books of Chronicles are usually dated no earlier than the fourth century B.C. We can also distinguish between, say, eighth-century prophets (e.g., Isaiah, Hosea) and sixth-century prophets (e.g., Jeremiah, Ezekiel).

Using such evidence, as well as several other assumptions, William L. Holladay has made a detailed investigation of *The Root Šubh in the Old Testament*.[6] We may summarize some of his findings thus:

Early usages (spatial) ─────────▶	Covenantal applications
'return' to a person	'return' to God
'return' from a state	'return' from evil
'withdraw' from a person	'withdraw' from God

Holladay moreover finds that Jeremiah used the word frequently and innovatively, exploiting its twofold application so that it could actually mean, with deliberate ambiguity, 'to change one's loyalty.' Writers later than Jeremiah standardized the covenantal usage, thus approximating the meanings 'to convert' and 'to apostatize.'

Many comparable studies have been attempted, some fairly successful, but several obstacles stand in our way. To begin with, there is considerable uncertainty regarding the date of large portions of the material. For example, conservative scholars, who date the Pentateuch in the Mosaic period, generally recognize that its language must have been modernized in the course of transmission,[7] while scholars committed to the documentary hypothesis differ among themselves with regard to the date of the individual documents and admit the presence

---

[6]Subtitled, *With Particular Reference to Its Usages in Covenantal Contexts* (Leiden: Brill, 1958). Holladay does not always clearly distinguish between the linguistic usage and the theological associations. More satisfactory is Ingrid Riesener, *Der Stamm עבד im Alte Testament. Eine Wortuntersuchung unter Berücksichtung neuerer sprachwissenschaftlicher Methoden* (BZAW 149; Berlin and New York: Walter de Gruyter, 1979). There is some discussion of semantic change in Jean Margain, *Essais de sémantique sur l'hébreu ancien* (Etudes chamito-sémitiques, suppl. 4; Paris: Paul Geuthner, 1976).

[7]Cf. Edward J. Young, *An Introduction to the Old Testament*, rev. ed. (Grand Rapids: Eerdmans, 1964), p. 45: "Also, under divine inspiration, there may have been later minor additions and even revisions."

of old material in late documents.[8] So long as we are dependent on debatable source-critical theories, the study of semantic evolution will be greatly handicapped. Second, and more important, the material available to us for comparisons is very scarce. Scholars have often pointed out what a small percentage of the Hebrew vocabulary is preserved in the Old Testament.[9] In particular,

> it is highly hazardous to decide that a given word or usage is "late," because only fragments of ancient Hebrew literature are extant, so that the absence or rarity of a linguistic phenomenon may be purely accidental. To cite a familiar example. . . , the conjunction *še* was once confidently explained as a late form, reflecting Aramaic influence . . . and its presence in the "Song of Songs" was held to be *prima facie* evidence of its late date. It is today recognized as part of the north-Israelite dialect, and was probably used in southern Palestine as well.[10]

In view of these considerations, it will be more productive to devote the whole of this chapter and the next to the semantic evolution of Greek words that occur in the New Testament. Indeed, whereas a fragmented and superficial treatment of Old Testament words would be essentially unsatisfactory, a fairly comprehensive overview of the New Testament material will help us to establish certain principles and methods, most of which should also prove applicable to the Old Testament material. As is well known, however, most of the significant semantic changes attested for New Testament words can be traced back to LXX usages, and a preliminary review of the problems associated with that document demands our attention.

SEPTUAGINT AND NEW TESTAMENT

In the introduction to his *Greek-English Lexicon*, Walter Bauer claims: "As for the influence of the LXX, every page of this lexicon shows that it outweighs all other influences on our literature."[11] The

---

[8]Cf. Otto Kaiser, *Introduction to the Old Testament: A Presentation of Its Results and Problems*, tr. John Stanley (Minneapolis: Augsburg, 1975), pp. 33ff., 78ff.

[9]See especially Ullendorff, *Is Biblical Hebrew a Language?* pp. 3–4.

[10]Robert Gordis, *The Word and the Book: Studies in Biblical Language and Literature* (New York: Ktav, 1976), p. 159, from an article on "Studies in the Relationship of Biblical and Rabbinic Hebrew," originally published in 1946.

[11]Bauer, p. xviii.

New Testament authors, writing in Greek, had recourse to the LXX whenever they wished to quote or allude to Old Testament passages or topics, and thus Bauer's claim is not likely to be disputed by anyone. However, not every scholar has clearly formulated the relationship between the LXX and New Testament vocabularies, and those who have do not always agree among themselves. It would be profitable, therefore, to sketch some of the more important contributions to this topic.

We begin our survey with the year 1889, when the famed LXX scholar, Edwin Hatch, published a number of *Essays in Biblical Greek*. Our main interest is in the first of these essays, where the author complained that in his day there was very little concern with New Testament Greek for its own sake. This state of affairs, he believed, resulted from the assumption that the New Testament idiom was identical to that of Pericles or Plato; he therefore proceeded to set forth an adequate "appreciation of their points of difference."

One set of differences, he admitted, was due simply to the lapse of time, so that many of the linguistic changes manifested in the New Testament can be effectively compared with those found in contemporary secular writers. But Hatch's concern was that the lapse of time alone does not explain all of the differences, and that therefore we must take into account another set of causes, namely, the fact that biblical Greek was spoken in a different country and, more to the point, by a different race. The LXX and the New Testament, he claimed, "afford clear internal evidence that their writers, in most cases, were men whose thoughts were cast in a Semitic and not in a Hellenic mould."[12]

> The attitude of such men towards human life, towards nature, and towards God was so different that though Greek words were used they were the symbols of quite other than Greek ideas. For every race has its own mass and combinations of ideas; and when one race adopts the language of another, it cannot, from the very nature of the human mind, adopt with it the ideas of which that language is the expression. It takes the words but it cannot take their connotation: and it has ideas of its own for which it only finds in foreign phrases a rough and a partial covering.

[12]Edwin Hatch, *Essays in Biblical Greek* (Oxford: Clarendon Press, 1889), p. 10. The point had been strongly made by Bengel, who apparently had great influence on Cremer (so Duncan, *The Contribution of Hermann Cremer*, pp. 14ff.).

> Biblical Greek is thus a language which stands by itself.
> What we have to find out in studying it is what meaning
> certain Greek words conveyed to a Semitic mind.[13]

To achieve this aim, Hatch proposed to study the New Testament language anew, as though it were a recently discovered dialect. Although "it will probably be found that in a majority of cases the meaning which will result from such a new induction will not differ widely from that which has been generally accepted," nevertheless peculiar and important shades of meaning will be discovered.[14]

It is at this point that Hatch underlines the immense value of the LXX. Since it is the translation of an original that we possess, we can in fact refer to that Hebrew original "and in most cases frame inductions as to their meaning which are as certain as any philological induction can be."[15] The value of the LXX, he claims, is enhanced by the fact that it is largely Targumic in character: it often gives glosses and paraphrases, it does not always adhere to the original metaphors, and it even varies its own rendering of particular words and phrases.

Hatch makes much of this last point and calls special attention to those cases when the LXX uses a group of synonyms indiscriminately to translate a corresponding group of Hebrew terms. As an example he shows that six different Hebrew words are translated by ἐξαιρεῖν, λυτροῦν, ῥύεσθαι, or σῴζειν without apparent distinction.

> It is reasonable to infer that, in their Hellenistic use, the
> Greek words which one thus used interchangeably for the
> same Hebrew words did not differ, at least materially, from
> each other in meaning, and that no substantial argument
> can be founded upon the meaning of any one of them unless
> that meaning be common to it with the other members of
> the group.[16]

He feels his point is confirmed by the later Greek versions, which also use the terms interchangeably—"an evidence which almost amounts

---

[13]Hatch, p. 11. This passage is of great methodological significance, especially since it expresses assumptions still widely held; unfortunately, it raises more questions than it answers.

[14]Ibid., p. 12; but cf. below, n. 19.

[15]Ibid., p. 14.

[16]Ibid., p. 23.

to proof, that the words were in common use as synonyms."[17]

Hatch's general conclusion is that, although some words do not differ in meaning from their use in nonbiblical authors, "the great majority of New Testament words" are those that "express in their Biblical uses the conception of a Semitic race, and which must consequently be examined in the light of the cognate documents which form the LXX."[18] In fact, these words "are so numerous, and a student is so frequently misled by his familiarity with their classical use, that it is a safe rule to let no word, even the simplest, in the N.T. pass unchallenged."[19]

In his second essay, Hatch applies these general ideas to twenty-four words or groups of words, but not before recapitulating his results by laying down two "self-evident" canons for studying the relation of LXX words to the Hebrew terms they translate:

> (1) A word which is used uniformly, or with few and intelligible exceptions, as the translation of the same Hebrew word, must be held to have in Biblical Greek the same meaning as that Hebrew word.
>
> (2) Words which are used interchangeably as translations of the same Hebrew word, or group of cognate words, must be held to have in Biblical Greek an allied or virtually identical meaning.[20]

Two years after these essays were published, they were subjected

[17]Ibid., p. 30 (the New Testament, too, is supposed to reflect this semantic correspondence). This notion of determining the meaning of LXX words solely on the basis of Hebrew-Greek equivalences is characteristic of Hatch and has been adopted, at least in part, by subsequent workers, notably C. H. Dodd. The method is virtually worthless unless the following factors are carefully considered: (1) the context of each occurrence, since the choice of one of the synonyms may have been due to the general drift of the passage, to syntactical details or even to rhythmic considerations; (2) the stylistic preferences of individual translators; (3) polysemy in the Hebrew words themselves—the translator may have tried to reproduce the various shades of the original. Dodd's approach is best illustrated in his influential work, *The Bible and the Greeks* (London: Hodder & Stoughton, 1935), especially part one, "The Religious Vocabulary of Hellenistic Judaism," which discusses the names of God, law, and other theological terms. (See also below, p. 65 and n. 44.)

[18]Ibid., p. 34.

[19]Ibid. These opinions are somewhat inconsistent with his own earlier statement (quoted above, n. 14) that the investigation he proposed would not, "in a majority of cases," yield results not already accepted.

[20]Ibid., p. 35.

to a searching criticism by T. K. Abbott in a long review of recent publications on the subject of "New Testament Lexicography."[21] In my opinion, Abbott's work has not received anything like the attention it deserves; not only did Abbott cogently demolish the principles set forth by Hatch, but he also gave expression to opinions that, as we shall see, clearly placed him well ahead of his time.

From the very start, Abbott minimizes the importance of Hebraic influence on the New Testament: "This is, as far as the language is concerned, less than is sometimes supposed. Expressions characterized as Hebraisms may in not a few instances be paralleled in classical writers, *the difference being in their frequency*. As these Hebraisms, however, affect the phraseology more than the vocabulary, we shall not dwell on them."[22]

Neither is Abbott impressed with the idea that the LXX has greatly influenced New Testament Greek; after all, the Authorized Version, which was much more influential than the LXX, did not prevent the loss of old meanings (e.g., *quick* in the sense of 'living'). "For our part, when we read the Septuagint what strikes us is its unlikeness to the language of the New Testament." For example, Psalm 51, which was surely very familiar to the New Testament writers, contains five words that are not found at all in the New Testament and one word with a different meaning.[23] Even when considering the LXX and New Testament in general, Abbott finds relatively few "biblical meanings" common to both; further, there are numerous New Testament words and meanings *not* in the LXX, such as ὑπομονή (LXX 'expectation') and ἄφεσις (LXX 'release').[24] Contradicting Hatch's main principle, Abbott concludes: "Such facts as these show that the influence of the Septuagint version on the vocabulary of the New Testament was not predominant, and that to make the usage of the former determine the interpretation of the lat-

---

[21]*Essays, Chiefly on the Original Texts of the Old and New Testaments* (London: Longmans, Green & Co., 1891), chap. 3, pp. 65–109. The book was published after Hatch's death, but this particular review brought together three previously published articles.

[22]Abbott, p. 66 (my emphasis). Notice the similarity between this formulation and that of Moulton two decades—and many discoveries—later; J. H. Moulton, A *Grammar of New Testament Greek*, vol. 1, 3rd ed. (Edinburgh: T. & T. Clark, 1908), p. 11.

[23]Abbott, p. 69.

[24]Ibid., p. 71.

ter, except in the case of terms of Hebrew theology, is quite out of the question."[25]

After these general statements, Abbott goes on to criticize specific elements in the work of Hatch. For example, anticipating Barr's caveats against "illegitimate totality transfer,"[26] he has this to say concerning Hatch's treatment of ἀρετή: "It is, indeed, a grave fault in a lexicographer or interpreter to assume that because a word has a modified meaning when used in a particular connexion, therefore it may *per se* bear the same."[27] He even takes the LXX expert to task for a naïve understanding of the character of the LXX. Thus, in connection with the principle that the interchangeable translations of the same Hebrew word give a reliable clue to meaning, he comments:

> Apart from difference of judgment as to the rendering of a word, there are very few translators whose work can be safely taken as a standard of the usage of their own language. The English Version stands high in this respect, yet we find words incorrectly used in it: for example, 'soul,' where life is meant. We are not, however, to infer that 'soul,' 'life,' 'appetite,' 'person,' 'creature,' are synonymous because they translate the same word, *nephesh*, which has indeed a dozen other renderings in the English Bible. Yet the English Version is much more homogeneous than the Septuagint, which is really a collection of versions made by a series of independent translators, differing both in their knowledge of Hebrew and in their command of Greek.[28]

Abbott reviewed in detail the very examples Hatch had dealt with in his second essay, and came to the conclusion that where his examples are good, he had already been anticipated (e.g., by Grimm), and that where he "tries to apply to the N.T. a signification peculiar to the LXX, or ascertained according to the maxims he lays down, he is in no one instance successful."[29]

A work that followed Abbott's line of reasoning was H. A. A.

---

[25]Ibid., p. 71. The happy distinction between theological and nontheological terms—ignored by many, but especially by Hatch—is crucial.

[26]*Semantics*, p. 218.

[27]Abbott, p. 78.

[28]Ibid., p. 86.

[29]Ibid., p. 98. On p. 86 he speaks of Hatch's method of determining the meaning of New Testament words as unsound, and on p. 94, less kindly, as "utterly fallacious."

Kennedy's *Sources of New Testament Greek*, published four years later.[30] Ironically, Kennedy had been inspired to do his research precisely because of the work of Hatch, whose conclusions he had depended upon and even accepted. However, "the further the inquiry was pushed, the more decidedly was he compelled to doubt those conclusions, and finally to seek to establish the connection between the language of the LXX and that of the New Testament on a totally different basis."[31] Subtitled, *The Influence of the Septuagint on the Vocabulary of the New Testament*, this is apparently the only full-scale work devoted to a comprehensive analysis of that subject.

After a few introductory chapters on the evolution of Greek and the nature of the LXX, Kennedy devotes chapter 6 to a general discussion of the New Testament vocabulary. He emphasizes that the lexical stock cannot be termed "vulgar" (as is the case for most of the LXX), for it has too much in common with literary Greek. Rather, "the facts exhibited show clearly the existence of a language of popular intercourse from an early time, which verges on the borders of the literary language, but is excluded from composition except in the case of Comedy."[32]

He then proceeds to analyze those terms common to the LXX and the New Testament, but not found outside the Bible.[33] Kennedy realizes, however, that judgments concerning the relationship of the New Testament to the LXX must be made, *not for the vocabulary as a whole*, but for different types of words. He therefore classifies the vocabulary into (1) theological and religious terms, (2) actual Hebrew and Aramaic loan words, (3) technical terms for Jewish customs and ideas, (4) everyday words, (5) Alexandrian words, and (6) new compounds. Three of these categories (2, 5, 6) encompass new formations rather than words exhibiting semantic change, so we shall only notice Kennedy's evaluation of the other three groups.

Devoting the whole of chapter 8 to theological and religious terms, the author concludes that (apart from literal imitations of He-

---

[30]Edinburgh: T. & T. Clark, 1895.

[31]Ibid., p. v.

[32]Kennedy, p. 77. This evaluation, which probably could be defended even today (though Kennedy, like Abbott, could not have drawn from Deissmann's work), leads him, on p. 136, to deny Hatch's contention that the New Testament language stands by itself (quoted above, p. 58).

[33]His study was based on the list of terms provided in Grimm-Wilke's *Clavis Novi Testamenti* (see the Appendix to Thayer's *Lexicon*).

brew expressions) this class of words "is the clearest instance of a direct influence of the LXX on the vocabulary of the New Testament."[34] Another class consists of "words expressing ideas and customs especially Jewish, which were employed by the writers of the LXX. as literal translations of the Hebrew terms, or were formed by them on the analogy of these terms";[35] he finds twenty-six terms in this "very important" category. Third, he finds sixteen "everyday" words, but raises the question whether they found their way into the New Testament through the LXX or through the colloquial language of the time.

His conclusions concerning LXX influence on the New Testament vocabulary are summarized in chapter 10, and the concluding three chapters endeavor to confirm the colloquial character of New Testament Greek by references, for example, to Modern Greek. His final, general conclusions deserve to be quoted in full:

> The earliest Christian writers, in proclaiming the new faith, had to express in words deep theological ideas, unheard of in the old world. It was natural that, in making this attempt, they should take for their model a vocabulary already formed. These writers, moreover, were Jews. Their whole view of things was penetrated with Hebrew modes of thought. Accordingly, they could not fail to make copious use of a type of language already adapted to their special requirements.
>
> But the influence of the LXX. on the vocabulary of the New Testament must not be exaggerated. Caution is necessary in determining that which is to be regarded as *usage* in Biblical Greek, seeing that the LXX. is a translation done by unskilful hands, and that ignorance of Greek or ignorance of Hebrew is often responsible for phenomena of vocabulary which are peculiar to the Biblical language. When we con-

---

[34]Kennedy, p. 108. Even here, however, he remarks that some of these terms may have been common to the area, that the New Testament writers were bound to have a semiticized vocabulary regardless of the LXX, and that "the special theological terms of the New Testament are at the most *connected* with, not derived from, the usage of the LXX" (p. 109; he tells us that, as a rule, the LXX "simply affords a starting-point for the creation of the language of Christian theology"). Yet in spite of these reservations, Kennedy wants to "admit absolutely" that theological terms (and to a lesser extent those denoting Jewish customs) can be subjected to Hatch's canons concerning Hebrew-Greek equivalences (p. 136).

[35]Ibid., p. 111.

sider the exceptional importance of the Greek Bible to the New Testament writers, the astonishing fact is that its influence on their vocabulary is not incomparably greater than it is found to be.[36]

A work similar in character to Kennedy's was Theodor Nägeli's treatment of the Pauline vocabulary. Stimulated by the papyrological discoveries and convinced that Paul's letters were of utmost importance to the development of the Koine, Nägeli published some preliminary observations to a lexicon of Paul's writings in 1905.[37]

A detailed comparison with nonbiblical literature (Ionic, classical, contemporary, etc.) convinced him that Paul's language was neither literary nor vulgar.[38] He also dealt in detail with the LXX, noting Paul's strong dependence on it as well as some important deviations (coincidences with noncanonical LXX books), and concluding that Paul's lexical inheritance came from the Hellenistic colloquial language and from the LXX and, further, that Paul's Hebraisms—since almost all of them seem to have been mediated through the LXX—should be called "Septuagintalisms."[39]

Since the turn of the century, the question of linguistic relationships between the LXX and the New Testament has received attention from a variety of angles. Three issues in particular merit our consideration, namely, (1) the question of Hebrew-Greek lexical equivalences in the Old Testament, (2) the character of New Testament Greek, (3) Septuagintal influence on the New Testament vocabulary.

First, in direct opposition to Hatch, Adolf Deissmann argued against attributing to a LXX word the meaning of the Hebrew word it translated.[40] He illustrated his point with the term ἱλαστήριον, which

---

[36]Ibid., pp. 164–65.

[37]*Der Wortschatz des Apostels Paulus. Beitrag zur sprachgeschichtlichen Erforschung des Neuen Testaments* (Göttingen: Vandenhoeck & Ruprecht, 1905). The first part of the lexicon, which included the first five letters of the alphabet, was accepted for a doctoral degree at Basel in 1902; it contained an introduction that formed the basis for *Der Wortschatz*. The lexicon itself was never completed.

[38]Nägeli, p. 13.

[39]"Soviel ich sehe, liegen die meisten dieser Wendungen schon in den LXX vor und sind Paulus also nicht infolge eines hebräischen Sprachgefühls, sondern durch seine fleissige LXX-Lektüre zu eigen geworden; sie mögen im griechischen A. T. Hebraismen heissen; bei Paulus sollte man sie eher Septuagintismen oder ähnlich" (p. 74).

[40]*The Philology of the Greek Bible: Its Present and Future* (London: Hodder and Stoughton, 1908), pp. 88ff.

does not mean 'lid' (as *kapporet* does); the evidence from the papyri makes it clear that the LXX, instead of translating the Hebrew concept, "has replaced it by another concept which brings out the sacred purpose of the lid."[41]

Ottley, however, was not convinced by Deissmann's example and argued that *kapporet* itself implied 'propitiation'; in other words, the translators attempted, through the use of ἱλαστήριον, to capture the nuances of the Hebrew term.[42] Similarly, "had it been customary to translate the Hebrew *shophet* 'leader' or 'chief' instead of 'judge,' it would have been advisable to render κριτής in the same way when representing *shophet*: for the Greek translators meant whatever *shophet* meant."[43] Ottley is not here reverting to an uncritical acceptance of Hatch's principles; rather, he wishes to point out that there are two valid ways of approaching the LXX—by making use of the papyri and by considering the intention of the original. This judicious combination is also one of the more admirable qualities of David Hill's method.[44]

Second, attention has focused on a broader issue, the nature of New Testament Greek. Adolf Deissmann, on the basis of his momentous discoveries among the papyri, presented clear and convincing lexical evidence to confirm the conclusions to which Abbott and Kennedy, among others, had come: the language of the New Testament is neither a Semiticized jargon, nor a "Holy Ghost language," but contemporary, colloquial Greek. In contrast, the language of the LXX, though springing from the same source, was artificial and did not in fact represent the spoken Greek of Alexandrian Jews. Although Deissmann did not at all deny the existence of Semitisms in the New Testament, he strongly argued that they were not "sufficient reason for scholars to isolate the language" of the New Testament from the Koine of the time.[45] So-called Deissmannism has been criticized from vari-

[41]Ibid., p. 92.

[42]Richard R. Ottley, *A Handbook to the Septuagint* (London: Methuen & Co., 1920), pp. 167ff.

[43]Ibid., p. 171.

[44]In *Greek Words and Hebrew Meanings*. On p. 26 he states, in opposition to Dodd's method: "When we seek the meaning of a Greek word the meaning of the Hebrew word it renders on many occasions in the LXX is an important *guide*" (not conclusive evidence).

[45]*Philology*, p. 65. Other prominent exponents of this viewpoint were J. H. Moulton (see above, n. 22) and Albert Thumb, *Die griechische Sprache im Zeitalter des Hellenismus: Beitrage zur Geschichte und Bedeutung der* Κοινή (Strassburg: Karl J. Trübner, 1901).

ous angles,[46] but the basic formulation, when properly understood, has proved unassailable.[47]

The third area of concern is precisely the question, To what extent has the LXX, especially as a channel of Semitisms, influenced the New Testament writers? Hardly a book on New Testament studies fails to touch on the issue, even if only indirectly, yet concrete and well-defined formulations are surprisingly difficult to find.[48] A general consensus, however, can easily be detected: while rejecting the more extreme features of Hatch's position, most biblical scholars would surely agree with Swete that the New Testament student should

> make the LXX his starting-point in examining the sense of all words and phrases which, though they may have been used in classical Greek or by the κοινή, passed into Palestinian use through the Greek Old Testament, and in their passage received the impress of Semitic thought and life.[49]

The viewpoint adopted in this book follows closely along the lines laid down by Abbott and Kennedy. While the total impact of the LXX on the New Testament writers is so great as to defy measurement, its influence on the New Testament *language* must be defined within fairly clear bounds.[50] In particular, we must distinguish those uniform

[46]E.g., J. Vergote, "Grec biblique," *DBSup* 3:1320–69, especially 1361–68. More recently, Nigel Turner, "The Language of the New Testament," *Peake's Commentary on the Bible*, ed. Matthew Black and H. H. Rowley (London: Nelson, 1962), pp. 659–62.

[47]I have sought to defend Deissmann's views against recent criticisms in "Bilingualism and the Character of New Testament Greek," *Bib* 69 (1980): 198–219, which includes an assessment of LXX influence.

[48]Cf. James Barr's objections to the vague phrase, "lies behind," in *Biblical Words for Time*, p. 38.

[49]H. B. Swete, *An Introduction to the Old Testament in Greek* (New York: Ktav, 1968, originally published in 1902), p. 457; unfortunately, the statement begs the very question at issue, namely, how do we identify those particular words and phrases?

[50]It is worthwhile remembering that Deissmann himself, while emphasizing the *linguistic difference* between the LXX and New Testament, perceived with unusual force their *conceptual unity*. Though he may have allowed himself some exaggeration when he spoke of the LXX as "the sanctuary leading to the Holy of Holies, namely the New Testament," it was hardly an overstatement to point out the "hundreds of threads" that unite these two documents. And the following remarks, in my judgment, are an understatement: "All honour to the Hebrew original! But the proverbial *Novum in Vetere latet* cannot be fully understood without a knowledge of the Septuagint. A single hour lovingly directed to the text of the Septuagint will further our exegetical

elements of a language that form part of its very structure from those
variable elements that may be regarded as *stylistic*.[51] Literary monuments like the LXX or the English King James Version will affect the
latter, not the former; this is especially obvious if an author or speaker
wishes deliberately to imitate a style he or she regards highly,[52] but
more or less unconscious mannerisms are evidence of the same
phenomenon.

Now this distinction between regularity and variability cuts across
all levels of language (phonology, vocabulary, syntax, discourse), but
we are only interested here in its significance for assessing the New
Testament vocabulary. One need hardly document the fact that to a
very large extent lexical use is a matter of the writer's *choice*, a key
concept in linguistic stylistics (and one that will occupy us fully in part
two). On the other hand, that choice is limited by the lexical structure
of the writer's language. For example, in a particular context an author
needs to decide (and he may do this consciously or unconsciously)
between such adjectives as *living, alive, animate*, etc. Since the vast
majority of adjectives (to say nothing of other parts of speech) are not
even an option for him, his choice is severely restricted by the givens
(regularity) in his language. But these givens are part of what we mean
by structure, and for that we depend on the dynamic, spoken form of a
language, not on its written monuments. Thus, a writer of the present
day, even if he is immersed in the language of the King James Version,
will not consider using the word *quick* except in such idioms as *the
quick and the dead*. Conversely, an author may decide, under the
influence of the KJV, to use the word *soul* where another writer might
prefer, say, *life (Those gangsters went after the poor man's soul/life)*. In
this case the writer's literary tradition has affected his style, but only
because the present structure allows for it.

A crucial qualification, however, is needed here. As already indicated in the introduction (see above, pp. 30–31), not all items in the

knowledge of the Pauline Epistles more than a whole day spent over a commentary."
See pp. 7–15 in *The Philology of the Greek Bible* (quotations from pp. 12, 13, 15).

   [51]This distinction corresponds roughly with Saussure's dichotomy between
langue (the abstract system shared by all the speakers in a community) and *parole* (the
actualized speech of individuals). I have explored this subject in "Bilingualism" (see
above, n. 47), to which the reader is referred for the views on LXX influence espoused
here.

   [52]As in the case of Luke. See H. F. D. Sparks, "The Semitisms of St. Luke's
Gospel," *JTS* 44 (1943): 129–38.

vocabulary can be handled the same way. Technical terms, that is, words that serve as cultural tokens, must be distinguished from the rest. We need not discuss this issue fully here, since it will occupy us again in part two; nor do we need to worry about precise criteria for identifying technical terms. All that matters at this point is for us to recognize, with Abbott and Kennedy, that LXX words that appear to stand for cultural entities or theological reflection belong to a special class; no one cares to deny that, with reference to *this* class, the influence of the LXX on the New Testament vocabulary is very strong indeed.

It appears then that, in spite of all our reservations, research into the LXX vocabulary is of fundamental importance for New Testament lexicology, not only with regard to theological terms (though foremost here), but also in connection with more general usages that may have affected certain stylistic decisions. And beyond all that, quite apart from the question of *influence*, we must remember that the LXX is one of our most important sources of evidence for the Koine; that is, even if the New Testament writers had never read the LXX, that document would still have profound significance for New Testament lexicology.

USING THE SEPTUAGINT

Anyone acquainted with LXX studies will no doubt respond, "Easier said than done." The textual, linguistic, and conceptual problems associated with the LXX can probably be appreciated only by extensive and concentrated reflection on the text itself; even a careful reading of the standard introductions[53] fails to bring home the complex nature of these difficulties. Unhappily, courses on the LXX in theological schools are rare; where they *are* offered, few students opt for them, and frequently these courses are limited to the goal of increasing reading proficiency (a knowledge of Hebrew is usually not required) thus failing to provide skills in the proper use of the critical editions and other reference tools. These are the facts and they are not likely to change. It is certainly unrealistic to ask pastors, or even biblical and theological scholars whose main interest is not philological, to spend the time and effort necessary to master this field.

In other words, students of the Bible need to depend on the labor of those scholars who have chosen the LXX as their specialized inter-

---

[53]Especially Swete, *Introduction to the Old Testament in Greek*, and Sydney Jellicoe, *The Septuagint and Modern Study* (Oxford: The Clarendon Press, 1968; reprinted, Winona Lake, Indiana: Eisenbraun's, 1978).

est. What seriously complicates the problem, however, is that we lack the tools essential for a responsible handling of the material. An inexpensive, yet truly critical edition of the LXX text (as we shall see, Rahlfs's valuable edition does not really qualify), a basic lexicon, commentaries—no such materials are available. Until these tools are produced, the nonspecialist is severely handicapped. It would be a grave mistake, however, to set aside the LXX for fear of misusing it; while caution is indeed necessary, certain guidelines and checks can be suggested.

ASCERTAINING THE TEXT

Before using any passage in the LXX (or indeed in any other literature), we need to determine whether the text we are using is reliable. This first obstacle, unfortunately, will often prove insuperable. Because the LXX was produced by different translators at different stages, because it is a translation document, because of its popularity, because of its peculiar history of transmission—for these and other reasons, the textual criticism of the LXX probably ranks as the most difficult in all of ancient literature. To be sure, it is worthwhile remembering that even in the case of the LXX only a small proportion of the total text raises serious questions; the vast majority of variants can be easily and safely set aside. Without losing this general perspective, however, we still need to concentrate on the remaining variants, which are abundant and often important.

The modern student may well be grateful to Alfred Rahlfs, who shortly before his death completed an admirable edition of the LXX.[54] Previously, editors of the LXX had simply printed the text of a manuscript, normally Codex Vaticanus, which contains a large share of corruptions. Rahlfs's edition, in contrast, attempts to provide a critical text, that is, one that seeks to approximate the original. One must keep in mind, however, that Rahlfs did *not* intend to produce a definitive edition but only a temporary tool, since enormous work was still to be done in collating and grouping manuscripts as well as in analyzing the data. Since the late 1930s, fortunately, the Göttingen *Septuaginta* has

---

[54]*Septuaginta* (Stuttgart: Württembergische Bibelaustalt, 1935). For a critical appreciation of Rahlfs, see the important article by Peter Katz (W. P. M. Walters), "Septuagintal Studies in the Mid-Century: Their Links with the Past and Their Present Tendencies," originally published in 1956, reprinted in Sydney Jellicoe, ed., *Studies in the Septuagint: Origins, Recensions, and Interpretations* (New York: Ktav, 1974), pp. 21–53, especially pp. 34ff.

been appearing, so that today we can use magnificent, fully critical editions of all the prophets, parts of the Pentateuch, and several other books.[55] Perhaps in another decade or so the work will have been completed and a new, inexpensive edition of the Göttingen text (but with abbreviated apparatus, naturally) might become available. In the meantime, the following guidelines should prove helpful.

First of all, one must constantly keep in mind that the textual transmission of the LXX differs quite markedly from book to book (or group of books).[56] Relatively speaking, the text of the Pentateuch has been well preserved, so that Rahlfs's edition may be used with confidence; in contrast, the Greek Isaiah presents many complications that demand caution—to say nothing of the chaotic state in which we find the text of I–IV Kingdoms. In connection with this point, it should be emphasized that the value of an individual manuscript will also vary from book to book (and even between parts of the same book); thus, a student who learns that Codex Vaticanus generally preserves an ancient and reliable text is in danger of overlooking that he cannot trust it in Isaiah.

A related principle consists in recognizing that the LXX was produced by different translators using different methods. In other words, a solution that works in one book may not work in another. For example, it is recognized that, when deciding between two variants, a free rendering should be preferred to a literal one,[57] since the Greek text was more likely to be adjusted toward the Hebrew than away from it. However, whereas this principle might work regularly in such a freely rendered book as Job, it can prove treacherous in the literalistic, so-called καίγε sections of I–IV Kingdoms.[58]

Often, a textual decision in the LXX is inseparable from a decision regarding the corresponding Hebrew text. The principle that variants closer to the Massoretic text are suspect works most of the time but remains an oversimplification. No attempt can be made here to

[55]Note the brief report by John W. Wevers (editor of the LXX Pentateuch), "The Göttingen Septuagint," *BIOSCS* 8 (1975): 19–23.

[56]The reason is that only rarely was the LXX copied whole; instead, individual books circulated separately. According to Robert A. Kraft, "Only about one percent of the approximately twelve hundred known MSS of portions of OG [oldest recoverable Greek] contain a majority of OT writings." See *IDBSup*, p. 811.

[57]Cf. Swete, *Introduction*, p. 485.

[58]Cf. H. St. John Thackeray, *The Septuagint and Jewish Worship: A Study in Origins* (Schweich Lectures, 1920; London: British Academy, 1923), pp. 16ff.

sort out this most difficult subject; we can only refer the reader to standard works on Old Testament textual criticism[59] and advise the use of extreme caution when making a decision.

Finally, the LXX reader must be sensitive to the possibility that at many points the original reading has not been preserved in *any* manuscript, so that a conjectural emendation is necessary. Suppose, for example, that we are examining the verb ἀναγγέλλειν and come across Isaiah 53:2, ἀνηγγείλαμεν ἐναντίον αὐτοῦ ὡς παιδίον, which is a rather puzzling translation of the Hebrew *wayya'al kayyoneq l'panayw*, "and he grew up as a tender plant" (although *yoneq* may mean 'a suckling child'). Even if we are careful enough to examine Rahlfs's apparatus, we will find no help and thus might be tempted to suggest any of several possible but fanciful explanations. At this point a fully critical edition becomes essential. In his edition of Isaiah for the Göttingen LXX, Joseph Ziegler indicates that, although ἀνηγγείλαμεν is the reading found in the whole textual tradition, here we have a primitive corruption for the original ἀνέτειλε μέν, a conjectural emendation that few will dispute.[60]

INTERPRETING THE TEXT

It may seem unnecessary to stress the importance of exegeting the Greek text itself, but in fact many LXX users fail to do precisely that.

[59]Especially Emanuel Tov, *The Text-critical Use of the Septuagint in Biblical Research* (Jerusalem Biblical Studies 3; Jerusalem: Simor, 1981). One can still profit from Bleddyn J. Roberts, *The Old Testament Text and Versions: The Hebrew Text in Transmission and the History of the Ancient Versions* (Cardiff: University of Wales Press, 1951) if used in conjunction with recent studies, such as the relevant articles in the Supplement to *IDB* and Ralph W. Klein, *Textual Criticism of the Old Testament: The Septuagint After Qumran* (Philadelphia: Fortress, 1974). The pitfalls in this whole area have often been mentioned, most recently in John W. Wevers's criticism of the apparatus to Deuteronomy in *BHS*; see "Text History and Text Criticism of the Septuagint," in *Congress Volume: Göttingen 1977* (VTSup 29; Leiden: Brill, 1978), pp. 392–402.

[60]Joseph Ziegler, ed., *Isaias* (Septuaginta. Vetus Testamentum Graecum, 14; Göttingen: Vandenhoeck & Ruprecht, 1939), see p. 99. It may be worthwhile to point out, however, that even Ziegler may fail us. In v. 11 of the same chapter πλάσαι is probably a corruption of πλῆσαι, an old suggestion adopted by I. L. Seeligmann, *The Septuagint Version of Isaiah: A Discussion of Its Problems* (Medelingen en Verhandelingen 9; Leiden: Brill, 1948), p. 11, n. 8. The need for conjectural emendations was stressed very (perhaps too) forcefully by Peter Walters (Katz); cf. his posthumous work, *The Text of the Septuagint: Its Corruptions and Their Emendation*, ed. D. W. Gooding (Cambridge: The University Press, 1973) and my review in *WTJ* 36 (1973–74): 233–39.

Understandably, students surveying the use of some common word may feel they only have the time to look at the reference, check the Hebrew, and quickly deduce the meaning of the Greek word. But this is completely unsatisfactory. Again, we may call attention to a few guidelines.

One cannot assume, to begin with, that if we identify the Hebrew word corresponding to the Greek word being studied, the meaning of the latter is thereby established. It would of course be a mistake to ignore the Hebrew altogether, but we must maintain a sensitive balance between the meaning of a word in secular Greek and the desire of the translator to preserve the thrust of the original.[61] We have already alluded to this problem (see pp. 59n and 65). It remains to be pointed out that the very serviceable Oxford *Concordance* cannot always be relied upon for accuracy when searching for Hebrew equivalents.[62]

Second, one can hardly expect to do justice to the significance of a particular word apart from an examination of the whole passage in which it is found. In a different connection, M. Greenberg has rightly stressed that divergences between the Hebrew and Greek texts may indicate "alternative messages, each with its own validity."[63] For example, if we note the word $\dot{\alpha}\gamma\gamma\epsilon\lambda\dot{\iota}\alpha$ in Isaiah 28:9, it will hardly do to use the corresponding Hebrew *š^emu'ah* as a criterion (even if this is balanced by a proper assessment of the noun in secular Greek). In the Hebrew text, the false prophets are speaking of *Isaiah's* preaching: "To whom would he teach knowledge? And to whom would he explain the message?" In the Greek, on the other hand, these prophets *defend themselves*: "To whom have we reported evils? and to whom have we reported a message?"

This mistranslation of Isaiah 28:9 leads us to a final comment, namely, the need to interpret specific passages in the light of the LXX translator's characteristics, his theological emphasis, and his principles

---

[61]This latter point is particularly emphasized by Emanuel Tov in "Three Dimensions of LXX Words," *RB* 83 (1976): 529–44. For an emphasis on the LXX as a *Greek* literary work, see N. Fernández Marcos, "Hacia un léxico del griego de traducción," *REL* 9 (1979): 489–504, especially p. 491. On the need for a specific LXX lexicon, see the articles brought together in *Septuagintal Lexicography*, ed. Robert A. Kraft (SBLSCS 1; Missoula, Montana: Society of Biblical Literature, 1972).

[62]Note the very helpful evaluation by Emanuel Tov, "The Use of Concordances in the Reconstruction of the *Vorlage* of the LXX," *CBQ* 40 (1978): 29–36.

[63]"The Use of the Ancient Versions for Interpreting the Hebrew Text: A Sampling from Ezekiel II 1–III 11," *Congress Volume* (see above, n. 59), pp. 131–48, especially p. 140.

of translation. The discovery of such a blunder in the Greek Isaiah could lead some to dismiss this particular translator as an incompetent. We may indeed grant that he was not equal to his task, but a patient study of his work reveals a fertile (if fanciful) mind, wrestling with the text and seeking to bridge the gap between that text and his audience. Our consideration of these broader issues helps us to place the Greek text in its proper *context* (see chap. 6). Thus, if we read in the Hebrew that Jesse's stem "will strike the earth with the *rod* of his mouth" (Isa. 11:4), but the Greek uses λόγος instead of the Greek word for 'rod,' we will not merely dismiss the rendering as a banal rejection of Isaiah's bold metaphor but we will also consider the possibility that the translator may be giving expression to Stoic (pregnostic) ideas. [64]

---

[64] Cf. Seeligman, *Septuagint Version of Isaiah*, p. 119. Unfortunately, there are no readily accessible studies summarizing the characteristics of the various translators; indeed, many questions remain open for substantial portions of the LXX. The reader may be referred to A *Classified Bibliography of the Septuagint*, ed. Sebastian P. Brock et al. (ALGHJ 6; Leiden: Brill, 1973), especially pp. 98–142, for studies of individual books; for lexical studies see pp. 30–34 and add a recent and important contribution by the African scholar Laurent Monsengwo Pasinya, *La notion de 'nomos' dans le Pentateuque grec* (AnBib 52; Rome: Biblical Institute Press, 1973).

SUMMARY OF CHAPTER 3

CLASSIFYING SEMANTIC CHANGE

The several hundred words in the Greek New Testament that appear to have undergone semantic development can be grouped on the basis of a logical classification, according to which the new meanings may reflect expansion, reduction, or alteration. A more rigorous classification draws the following basic distinction.

Changes Due to Semantic Conservatism. These are cases of specialization of meaning (e.g., theological terms); they are caused by nonlinguistic factors and thus invite study according to the "word-and-thing" method, but they have little effect on linguistic structure.

Changes Due to Semantic Innovation. These changes include cases of ellipsis, when a word acts for a whole phrase; metonymy, when a word acquires the sense of another word because of a semantic relation other than similarity; and metaphor, when a word acquires the sense of another word because of semantic similarity.

SEMANTIC BORROWING

Many of the semantic changes found in the New Testament can also be traced back to Semitic influence on the Greek vocabulary. We take note of the following concepts.

Phonetic Resemblance. Most studies of semantic borrowing deal with languages that are genetically related; in these cases, semantic loans are usually based on similarity of sound between the native and foreign words. This factor has not played a role in New Testament semantic loans. Greater linguistic sophistication is necessary when semantic borrowing is *not* based on phonetic resemblance.

Semantic Similarity. The meaning of the native word and that of the foreign word may be similar (loan polysemy) or dissimilar (loan homonymy). No cases of loan homonymy are to be found in the New Testament; usually, the semantic changes are very slight.

The Causes of Semantic Borrowing. Semantic loans may result from consciously imitating a foreign usage, from overlooking the normal limitations of the native language, or from the pressures of cultural motivation.

THE STRUCTURAL PERSPECTIVE

Although our knowledge of Palestinian Greek is too limited to determine clearly how these semantic changes affected the vocabulary as a whole, some suggestions are possible. For example, the rich number of terms used for 'mind' in nonbiblical Greek is reduced in the LXX and in the New Testament due to the influence of the Hebrew. Structural considerations of this kind may affect exegetical problems.

3 Semantic Change in the New Testament

We have seen that the LXX, if used with caution, constitutes our most important source for establishing and explaining semantic changes in the New Testament. But it is not the *only* source, and thus we must deal with the distinctive elements of the New Testament vocabulary in the broadest possible terms. To be precise, we want to keep in mind *all* the Greek words that, while attested in nonbiblical literature, appear to be used in a unique fashion by the biblical writers.[1]

A useful and comprehensive list of such words is that of Grimm-Wilke, which was revised by Thayer and included as an appendix in his *Lexicon*.[2] Thayer himself gave expression to the difficul-

[1] We are not here concerned with coinages, such as new combinations of native Greek elements (e.g., ψευδαπόστολος) or loan words (e.g., ἀββά; for these see Bauer, pp. xix–xxi). I also regard παρακοή, 'unwillingness to hear,' a coinage, rather than a semantic development from its earlier meaning ('defect of hearing'); the pattern of παράβασις (cf. especially Heb. 2:2) plus the possibility of opposition to ὑπακοή (Rom. 5:19) facilitated this creation. At least from a diachronic perspective this would be an instance of homonymy. Cf. also αἱρετικός ('heretical'; previously 'able to choose'), δίλογος ('insincere'; previously 'repeating'), and perhaps ἔκβασις ('a way out,' if Heb. 13:7 is understood as 'issue, outcome,' rather than metaphorically of 'life's end').

[2] For what follows cf. the annotated list and analysis in my Ph.D. thesis, *Semantic Change and Semitic Influence in the Greek Bible* (University of Manchester, 1972). Note also Turner, *Christian Words*; various articles, such as the brief discussion by F. W. Gingrich, "The Greek New Testament as a Landmark in the Course of Semantic Change," *JBL* 73 (1954): 189–96; and, for Modern Greek, Procope S. Costas, *An Outline of the History of the Greek Language* (Chicago: Aries Publishers, 1979, originally published in 1936), pp. 109–23.

ties of compiling such a list;[3] indeed, anyone who has gone over it carefully must have been surprised at some of his selections—and omissions.[4] Thayer's list contains over 300 words and (since some words have more than one "biblical signification") almost 400 meanings. However, he rightly regarded the list as "a restricted rather than an inclusive one," since he would not accept figures of speech (such as πόλις, Heb. 13:14) or the "mere application of a word to spiritual or religious relations" (except for terms generally agreed to possess "characteristic or technical New Testament senses"). Quite a few of the meanings he did accept are now attested in nonbiblical sources; others are attested for derivatives.[5] Further, we should set aside a number of instances that belong to syntactical (rather than lexical) categories as well as entries that refer to whole phrases (usually loan translations, which are best treated separately).

On the other hand, the number can be almost doubled to well over 500 if we include (1) suggestions made over the past century regarding Semitisms for words that Thayer understood on the basis of secular Greek; (2) figures of speech and religious terms that, while not at all technical, could be regarded as in some sense "characteristic" of the New Testament; (3) a good many meanings that, though attested in nonbiblical sources, occur with such *frequency* in the New Testament (usually because of Septuagintal or other Semitic influence) that to ignore them would result in a completely false picture of the semantic distinctiveness of the New Testament.[6]

CLASSIFYING SEMANTIC CHANGE

Now whenever we happen to be studying one of these words and attempt to understand its semantic evolution, it is essential that we have some kind of framework to serve as the basis for our analysis. Fortunately, many scholars have dealt with this problem and thus a large number of classifications are available to us. The oldest and

[3]Thayer, p. 688.

[4]E.g., he explicitly rejects ἀπαρχή ('new convert'), whereas Bauer includes it in his very short list, p. xvii.

[5]E.g., it is surely misleading to include ὑποκριτής, 'pretender,' when both ὑποκρίνεσθαι and ὑπόκρισις are well attested with the meanings 'pretend' and 'pretense.' For other examples cf. my review of Turner's *Christian Words* (see above, introduction, n. 21).

[6]I have argued this point in "Semantic Borrowing in the New Testament," *NTS* 22 (1975–76): 104–10.

simplest of them—sometimes called the logical classification—is based on the results the changes produce, or, more specifically, on the range of the new meanings being considered. In comparison with the range of the old meaning, is it wider, narrower, or simply altered? To put it differently, has there been an expansion, a reduction, or a simple shift of the contexts where the word can be used?[7]

First, we may have expansion in the meaning of a word. A well-known example is Latin *causa* (as precise as English *cause*), which Romance languages now use in a wide variety of contexts (French *chose*, Italian and Spanish *cosa*, 'thing').[8] In the LXX the word ἄρτος, 'bread,' came under the influence of Hebrew *leḥem* which could mean more generally 'food' (Isa. 65:25); the influence from the LXX and/or the fact that Palestinian Greek speakers may have been influenced by Aramaic *laḥma* accounts for the use in Mark 3:20. Note that, from a different perspective, this can be interpreted as semantic impoverishment (greater *extension* entails diminished *intension*), for the word can now be freely used in many contexts where precision is not desired or unknown.[9]

Second, and much more frequently, we notice reduction in the meaning of words. The English word *undertaker*, which once could be used instead of *shepherd* in Psalm 23:1, has been greatly specialized. Of the numerous examples to be found in the New Testament, we may note εὐαγγέλιον, 'good news,' specialized to '*the* good news,' that is, the gospel. We must understand that once the semantic range of a term has been narrowed, we are less dependent on the context when we wish to grasp the meaning of the word. That is, the word becomes more precise: a more or less definite referent (what the word stands for) is automatically associated with the word itself. These are the terms that become technically charged at times, so that they serve as "shorthand" for considerable theological reflection.

[7]Cf. Winfred P. Lehmann, *Historical Linguistics: An Introduction* (New York: Holt, Rinehart and Winston, 1962), pp. 200ff., from which several of my examples are taken; the 2nd ed. (1973) differs markedly. Notice that in many instances the old meaning does not disappear and so the semantic range is wider, for it includes both meanings. For the purposes of this classification, the new meaning alone is set against the old (and the old is treated as no longer existing). The classic treatment is Michel Bréal, *Semantics: Studies in the Science of Meaning* (New York: Dover, 1964, originally published in 1900).

[8]Stephen Ullmann, *Semantics: An Introduction to the Science of Meaning* (New York: Barnes & Noble, 1962), pp. 227ff.

[9]Ibid.

Third, we may come across alterations in the contexts where the word can be used, as when we speak of *a climate of opinion*. Another example is the amusing case of *cheater*, which comes from the older form *escheater*, 'rent collector.' Metaphors and metonymies usually belong here, as in the case of μοιχαλίς, 'adulteress,' used in the sense of 'apostate' (e.g., Matt. 12:39).

This simple classification "introduces clarity and order into the chaotic realm of semantic processes"[10] and may be used with profit by biblical students. However, for a better understanding of the causes and linguistic significance of these changes a more rigorous system is needed. Choosing a scientific classification, to be sure, is not an easy thing, and past writers have candidly acknowledged their inability to deal adequately with all types of semantic change.[11] Ullmann's attempt, nonetheless, commends itself for its simplicity and comprehensiveness.

The clearest distinction in Ullmann's scheme is that between changes due to linguistic *innovation* and changes due to linguistic *conservatism*. He claims that the preservation of an old word (e.g., *ship*) to denote an object that has changed considerably is due to linguistic inertia, since the differences between the two referents have passed unnoticed by the language; in the same category belong cases where the speaker's knowledge of, or attitude toward, the referent has changed (e.g., *atom*, *Blacks*). All of these changes are the result of linguistic conservatism.[12]

[10]Ullmann, *Principles*, p. 205.

[11]E.g., Félix Restrepo, *El alma de las palabras: diseño de semántica general* (Barcelona: Imprenta Editorial Barcelonesa, 1917), who settles, like Nyrop in his treatment of French, for a practical and pedagogical scheme (see his preface). For an excellent survey of past efforts, see Ullmann, *Principles*, pp. 199–249, to be updated with W. P. Lehmann, "Diachronic Semantics," in *Semantics: Theory and Application*, ed. Cléa Rameh (Washington, D.C.: Georgetown University Press, 1976), pp. 1–13; for a summary of criteria for classification, Heinz Kronasser, *Handbuch der Semasiologie* (Heidelberg: Carl Winter, 1968), section 44; for a recent and informed treatment, Norbert Boretsky, *Einführung in die historische Linguistik* (Reinbek bei Hamburg: Rowohlt Taschenbuch Verlag, 1977), pp. 187–232; for an interesting summary with abundant examples, Leonard R. Palmer, *Descriptive and Comparative Linguistics: A Critical Introduction* (London: Faber and Faber, 1972), chap. 13; for a general discussion of semantic change in the Bible, G. B. Caird, *Language and Imagery*, chap. 3. I am particularly indebted to Gustaf Stern's classic work, *Meaning and Change of Meaning, with Special Reference to the English Language* (Westport, Conn.: Greenwood, 1975, originally published in 1931).

[12]*Principles*, pp. 210–11 (not even this classification, however, is free from difficulties). For the distinctions that follow cf. my diagram, p. 178.

CHANGES DUE TO SEMANTIC CONSERVATISM

This category includes all cases of (more or less technical) specializations, but further subdivisions are necessary. Some of the shifts have been caused by a factual change in the referent, particularly in Jewish culture:

ἀργύριον: 'silver coin' > 'shekel'
συναγωγή: 'place of meeting' > 'synagogue'
φυλακτήριον: 'amulet' > 'phylactery'

A few of these factual changes are peculiar to early Christianity:

ἐκκλησία: 'assembly' > 'church'
χήρα: 'widow' > of a special class of widows (1 Tim. 5:3)

Most of our specializations, however, are theological. Many of them are already attested in the LXX and may be considered semantic loans:

ἄγγελος: 'messenger' > 'angel'
διαθήκη: 'testament' > of the divine covenant
δόξα: 'opinion, appearance' > 'glory'
κύριος: 'lord' > of the only God

Even more terms are distinctive to the New Testament message:

ἀλήθεια: 'truth' > 'Christianity' (especially in John)
εὐαγγέλιον: 'good news' > 'gospel'
μετανοεῖν: 'repent' > of Christian conversion (cf. TDNT 4: 979–80)
χάρισμα: 'gift' > 'spiritual gift'

We should note that these theological examples usually involve, not a factual change in the referent, but a subjective change in the speaker's understanding: for example, once a Greek speaker identified true wisdom with the Old Testament conception, his use of σοφία must have changed.[13]

Now in order to understand these examples of conservatism, we must remember that we are dealing here with changes in history (technological, social, religious, etc.) that lead to changes in the meaning of words. These semantic shifts are so clearly different from the rest that they earn a specific category in most classifications.[14]

---

[13]Note cases where the change is in the speaker's attitude (e.g., Eng. *scholasticism*). For a somewhat different perspective see Stern, *Meaning*, p. 197.

[14]E.g., Wellander has the special niche *Bedeutungsunterscheibung* (Stern, p. 192n.); see also Antoine Meillet, *Linguistique historique et linguistique générale*, 2nd ed., 2 vols. (Paris: Librairie Ancienne Honoré Champion, 1926–36), 1:230ff.

G. Stern in particular uses the label *substitution*, since the change is caused by the substitution of a new referent. He goes on to say:

> The causes of substitution lie in the fact that referents change and that we require new names for them; these we get, in the present case, not by coining a new word, but by placing the referent in some known category, denoting it by the same name.[15]

It is most significant, however, that Stern draws a sharp dividing line between this category, as dealing with changes caused by *external, nonlinguistic* factors, and all other categories, which involve changes due to linguistic causes. While this formulation has not gained acceptance,[16] the distinction throws considerable light on our own discussion. For once we realize that (semi-) technical terms in the Bible have undergone this type of change, it becomes clear why *they are susceptible to little lexicographical investigation*. If the linguist ascertains that ἄγγελος is being used to cover the meaning of Hebrew *mal'ak*—that is, that further knowledge of the referent has issued in substitution, not in a new name—there his work ends: any further discussion of the meaning of ἄγγελος becomes a discussion of Hebrew theology, not of lexicography.

Some writers probably go too far when they claim that there is no change of meaning involved at all.[17] However, it is certainly true that these changes have little effect on the structure of language.

The structural approach, endeavoring to explain changes through the associative machinery provided by syn-

---

[15]Stern, pp. 192–93. He adds: "Substitution is an extremely frequent form of semantic change. There are few groups of synonymous or cognate words which have not been more or less affected by it. The stock of meanings in a language reflects in a thousand ways the momentary state of the material, intellectual and moral civilization of the speaking community. The constant progress and modification of all forms of human life and thought re-act on the meanings. In the course of time, such modifications of meaning amount to considerable sense-changes, even if the change is gradual and at any moment hardly perceptible." See also Ullmann, *Principles*, p. 209.

[16]See Ullmann, *Principles*, p. 210, who points out that euphemisms, e.g., are not due to linguistic causes either.

[17]So Schwietering, referred to by Ullmann (*Principles*, pp. 208–9). Cf. also Antal ("Meaning and Its Change," pp. 24, 26), who claims that this type of change "cannot occur in a really scientific form of semantics"; if it is the technical construction of a denotatum that determines the change of meaning, how can a linguist know when a shoe, e.g., has become different enough to produce a semantic shift?

chronous networks, is obviously confined to the second category, i.e., semantic changes due to linguistic innovation, since no such machinery comes into operation unless an actual innovation takes place.[18]

Another, perhaps more important reason, why this "machinery" does not come into operation is the fact that these are referential terms; being little more than labels for new referents, they are less easily susceptible to semantic field studies.[19]

These words, however, can be fruitfully investigated by the "word-and-thing" method.

For many philologists substitutions are the most interesting kind of sense-change because they help to throw light on the facts of human history. The development of meaning has followed the development of the referent, and if we can trace the former we can perhaps, at least in some cases, draw conclusions with regard to the latter, and vice versa. *Wörter und Sachen, ohne Sachforschung keine Wortforschung*, are well-known formulae.[20]

Here, TDNT can play an invaluable role. Of course, there must be a recognition that most of this type of research is not, strictly speaking, linguistic, but conceptual and historical. Second, what linguistic evidence is brought to bear must rest on solid research. Third, much caution is to be exercised in drawing parallels between lexical and conceptual facts, since they do not always correspond. Granted these conditions, the Kögel-Kittel method can yield substantial results, without which the study of biblical semantics would be impoverished "on a considerable scale."[21]

[18]Ullmann, *Principles*, p. 211, but his sharp dichotomy needs qualification.

[19]More on this topic below, chaps. 4, 6. It is worthwhile noticing an article by N. Rothwell, "Medieval French and Modern Semantics," in *MLR* 67 (1962): 25–30. Rothwell is suspicious of structural semantics because the vocabulary seems to be "a loose, largely fluid system of relationships between words, relationships able to absorb a new addition or accept the loss of an old element of vocabulary in due season without necessarily transmitting any disturbing influence to the other words in the same semantic field." However, his example is precisely a referential term: when the word *bureau* "is no longer used in its meaning of 'coarse cloth' there is no detectable chain reaction, *because the need for that term has disappeared*" (p. 29; my emphasis).

[20]Stern, pp. 104–5. Cf. Hope's formulation, quoted above, pp. 30–31.

[21]See Ullmann, *Principles*, p. 211.

CHANGES DUE TO SEMANTIC INNOVATION

We may deal satisfactorily with these changes by distinguishing between three types: ellipsis, metonymy, and metaphor.[22]

(1) Ellipsis

Ullmann describes this type of change as being due to associations that develop between words

> occurring frequently in the same context; so frequently in-deed that there is no need to pronounce the whole phrase: the sense of a contiguous word is, so to speak, transferred into its neighbour which, through a special kind of semantic ellipsis, will act for the complete construction.[23]

More specifically, ellipsis normally takes place when a term (headword) becomes closely associated with a qualifier. If the qualifier is omitted, the headword preserves its syntactical function while adopting a new meaning.[24] The headword may be a verb:

ἀναφέρειν: 'bring up' > 'offer (sacrifices),' qualifier θυσία
καταβαίνειν: 'go down' > 'leave Jerusalem' (cf. Luke 10:30, 31; Acts 24:1)

or a noun:

αἱ γραφαί = αἱ ἱεραὶ γραφαί
ἡ σκηνή = ἡ σκηνὴ τοῦ μαρτυρίου

In some cases, however, the headword is omitted. In English the

---

[22]Cf. Ullmann, *Principles*, pp. 220ff. A fourth type—changes due to phonetic similarity—is apparently absent in our literature. Note also our discussion of semantic borrowing below.

[23]Ibid., p. 238. The subject is treated by Bréal, *Semantics*, under the headings "abridgement" (pp. 146–54) and "contagion" (pp. 200–204), the latter dealing with particles. Stern (*Meaning*, chap. 10) prefers the label "shortening" and further distinguishes between "clippings" (*bus* for *omnibus*—no semantic change) and "omissions" (*fall* for *fall of the leaf*).

[24]Some of these instances can be understood as metonymies; still, the distinction should be maintained because "our psychic processes are so variable from person to person, and from occasion to occasion. A generic word with a particular meaning may, for one speaker, be a case of shortening, while for his hearer, it is a case of genus pro specie" (Stern, *Meaning*, p. 269; he fails to note, however, that his example, *fall of the leaf*, is itself a semantic unit which has undergone metonymy).

qualifier receives a new syntactical function (*private* = 'private soldier,' adj. to noun) and the same thing can happen in Greek:

οἱ δώδεκα = οἱ δώδεκα μαθηταί (1 Cor. 15:5)

More often, the Greek word simply changes its case, since a genitive acts as qualifier:

τὰ ἄζυμα (Mark 14:1) = ἡ ἑορτὴ τῶν ἀζύμων (Exod. 23:15)
ἀποστάσιον ('bill of divorce,' Matt. 5:31) = βιβλίον ἀποστασίου (Deut. 24:1)
παρασκευή = ἡμέρα παρασκευῆς (Luke 23:54; but cf. John 19:14)

(2) Metonymy

Following Ullmann,[25] we shall use this label to include all changes based on contiguity, that is any sense relationship (cause, time, space, etc.) *other* than that of sense similarity. When the relationship between two meanings is not one of similarity, the change, usually unintentional, will occur only if the word is used many times in an equivocal sense; for example, ἄρτος can often mean *either* 'bread' or 'food' as in Luke 15:17.

> When the association in question has been established, the way is open for the final stage of the shift: the use of the word in the new meaning without equivocation, and without implication of the primary meaning.[26]

This final stage in the case of ἄρτος can be seen in Mark 3:20, where the word cannot properly be translated 'bread.'

Metonymies can be further subdivided. For example, ἄρτος is a case of the part used for the whole. Other instances are:

κῶλον: 'limb' > 'corpse'
πούς: 'foot' > 'leg' (Rev. 10:1)

The whole is sometimes used for the part:

θάνατος: 'death' > 'pestilence' (e.g., Rev. 2:23)
παιδεία: 'upbringing' > 'chastisement' (Heb. 12:5ff.)

---

[25]*Semantics*, p. 218. Traditionally, *metonymy* has been used in a somewhat narrower sense, opposite *synecdoche*; cf. also Stern, p. 297n.
[26]Stern, p. 357. We may note that λειτουργία, 'service,' may be translated 'gift' in Phil. 2:30 and 2 Cor. 9:12, but since these passages are equivocal, it appears that the metonymy was not fully established.

The abstract is sometimes used for the concrete:

ἀνάπαυσις: 'rest' > 'resting place' (Matt. 12:43; Luke 11:24)
ἐξουσία: 'rule' > 'dominion' (cf. *TDNT* 2:565–66)
ἔπαινος: 'praise' > 'praiseworthy deed' (Phil. 4:8)

Only one example is found of the concrete for the abstract:

βασιλεία: 'dominion' > 'rule' (cf. ἐξουσία above!)

The effect may be given for the cause (in a loose sense of the words):

ἔλαιον: 'oil' > 'olive-tree' (Rev. 6:6)
κρίσις: 'judgment' > 'legal court' (? Matt. 5:21–22)

The cause may be given for the effect:

ῥαντίζεσθαι: 'sprinkle' >'cleanse' (Mark 7:4)
ῥίζα: 'root' > 'shoot' (cf. *TDNT* 6:987)

In many cases, the relationship between meanings is difficult to categorize and perhaps some general term like "accompaniment" will do:

ἀπειθεῖν: 'disobey' > 'disbelieve' (cf. Bauer s.v.)
ἐπισκέπτεσθαι: 'visit' > 'care for'

We may finally introduce another distinction that cuts across all metonymies: *simultaneous* vs. *successive*.[27] Most of our metonymies consist of a pair of meanings with a relationship that is temporally simultaneous. We do have, however, a few cases of successive contiguity, where the secondary meaning temporally follows the former meaning:

κλητός: 'called' > 'Christian' (one who has responded to God's call)
μάρτυς: 'witness' > 'martyr' (death results from witnessing)
ῥαντίζεσθαι (see above)

(3) Metaphor

Metaphors are like metonymies in that they both refer to words with a pair of related meanings; in the case of metaphors, however, the relationship between the meanings is one of *similarity*. For example, if a speaker becomes aware of the similarity between a leaf from a tree and a page from a book, he may "transfer" the word *leaf* and use it with

---

[27]Cf. Ullmann, *Principles*, pp. 232–33.

the meaning 'page'; this is a metaphor. In contrast, if we say *The White House issued a statement*, the transfer is based on a relationship (between the White House and the President) *other than* one of similarity; this latter figure is metonymy, and the meanings are contiguous rather than similar.

Metaphors are the most common type of semantic change and they present special problems of various kinds. We may, however, bring some order into our material by distinguishing between intentional and unintentional transfers.[28]

Although in many cases the decision is difficult, it is usually possible to detect whether or not a writer is using a figure deliberately for literary-aesthetic purposes. Some probable examples of *unintentional* metaphors are:

θάλασσα: 'sea' > 'lake' (Matt. 8:24)
καρδία: 'heart' > 'interior' (Matt. 12:40)
πρόσωπον: 'face' > 'surface' (Luke 21:35)

Most *intentional* figures are attested in the LXX as literal renderings of the Hebrew:

δοῦλος: 'slave' > 'God's servant'
ἔργον: 'deed' > 'moral deed'
μοιχαλίς: 'adulteress' > 'apostate'

Metaphors invite further scrutiny, but most studies of figures of speech belong rather to the literary and psychological fields and "are only indirectly relevant to a semantic inquiry proper."[29]

(4) Composite Changes

We may briefly note cases where more than one factor has operated. The verb συνάγειν ('gather') is used with the sense 'invite' in Matthew 25:35, 38, 43. Quite possibly this is a combination of ellipsis

---

[28]Ullmann (*Principles*, p. 222) acknowledges this distinction, but does not use it in his scheme. In contrast, the distinction is fundamental for Stern, who has a special niche (*nominations*) for *all* intentional transfers, whether metonymies or metaphors; note his criteria for deciding individual cases, pp. 284–87, 345–46.

[29]So Ullmann (*Principles*, p. 224), who nevertheless proposes a three-fold distinction between *substantial* (= cognitive), *emotive*, and *synaesthetic* similarities. Cf. also from a different perspective Derek Bickerton, "Prolegomena to a Linguistic Theory of Metaphor," *FL* 4 (1968): 34–52, and Robert J. Matthews's criticisms, *FL* 7 (1971): 413–25. For an extensive discussion of figurative language in the Bible, see part two of Caird, *Language and Imagery*.

(for συνάγειν εἰς τὴν οἰκίαν, Judg. 19:18) and metonymy (since 'gather' and 'invite' are related ideas; see Gen. 29:22). Particularly interesting is σταυρός ('cross'); by ellipsis or specialization we have 'the cross of Christ,' then by metonymy 'Christ's death' (Gal. 6:12, et al.).

SEMANTIC BORROWING

In the previous section we surveyed New Testament terms with distinctive meanings and classified them as developments *within the Greek language itself*. In other words, we did not consider the possibility that a foreign language might have influenced those developments. In fact, however, very many of these changes can be traced back to the influence of Old Testament Hebrew (via the LXX) or of Palestinian Aramaic. We may note the use of the English verb *to arrive* with the meaning 'to attain success'; this new meaning can certainly be understood as a simple metaphor, but historically it is a case of borrowing (French *arriver*).[30] In this section, therefore, we shall go over some of the words already discussed, but now from a quite different perspective.

To begin with, we should keep in mind that when two languages come in contact, linguistic "interference"[31] will leave its mark on all levels of language, such as the phonology, the grammar, and the vocabulary. Only the latter, *lexical interference* (or *lexical borrowing*), concerns us here, but even this field is too large,[32] and so we must

---

[30]Cf. Stern, p. 219. We should point out that all semantic loans, whatever else they are, belong under the category of "analogical (opp. direct) transfers based on sense-similarity" in Ullmann's scheme for semantic changes (*Principles*, p. 226; cf. Stern, chap. 9). Thus, if πούς came to mean 'leg' because of the influence of Hebrew *regel*, clearly the shift was due to semantic *similarity* (or overlap) between the Greek and Hebrew words. However, Greek speakers, particularly those not familiar with Hebrew, would have understood the new meaning as a case of metonymy (contiguity rather than similarity). Both approaches are valid.

[31]For objections to this term, see Joshua A. Fishman, *Bilingualism in the Barrio* (LSM 7; Bloomington: Indiana University, 1971), pp. 561–63. For a discussion of lexical Semitisms, see M. Black, *An Aramaic Approach to the Gospels and Acts*, 3rd ed. (Oxford: Clarendon Press, 1967), pp. 132–42; also Max Wilcox, *The Semitisms of Acts* (Oxford: Clarendon Press, 1965), chap. 4.

[32]"The vocabulary of a language, considerably more loosely structured than its phonemics and its grammar, is beyond question the domain of borrowing par excellence." See Uriel Weinreich, *Languages in Contact: Findings and Problems* (The Hague: Mouton, 1953), p. 56.

further delimit the scope of our discussion. Lexical loans belong to three distinct types:[33]

Loan words. In this case, whole words are borrowed, normally to designate foreign objects (or concepts) for which a word is missing in the native language; cf. *sombrero.* We find several loan words in the New Testament, such as ἀββᾶ and πάσχα. A subclass is that of *loan blend,* when only part of the word is imported; e.g., ἰουδαΐζειν combines a foreign term with a native ending.

Loan translations. When Spanish uses the term *rascacielo* in imitation of *skyscraper,* it is importing, not a foreign word, but a particular word combination. Similarly, λαμβάνειν πρόσωπον ('to be partial') is a loan translation of *naśa' panim.*[34]

Semantic loans. In this case, not even the morphemic arrangement is imported, but only the meaning. These loans are sometimes referred to as *extensions:* "If two languages have semantemes, or units of content, which are partly similar, the interference consists in the identification and adjustment of the semantemes to fuller congruence."[35] Thus, English *to introduce* and French *introduire* share the meaning 'to insert'; once this partial identification had been made by French speakers in Canada, *introduire* was extended to cover the meaning 'to cause to be acquainted.'

Our interest, then, is in this third type, *semantic borrowing.* Considerable progress has recently been made in understanding this phenomenon, particularly by T. E. Hope,[36] who makes two basic

[33]This classification owes most to Einar Haugen, *The Norwegian Language in America: A Study in Bilingual Behavior,* 2 vols. (Philadelphia: University of Pennsylvania, 1953), chap. 15. For a comparison of classifications see Els Oksaar, "Bilingualism," *CTL* 9:476–511, especially Table 2. More recently, J. Humbley, "Vers une typologie de l'emprunt linguistique," *CahLex* 25 (1974 no. 1): 46–70, continued in 28 (1976 no. 1) 18–42. See also Roberto Gusmani, *Aspetti del prestito linguistico* (Collana di studi classici 15; Napoli: Libreria Scientifica, 1973), and Umberto Rapallo, *Calchi ebraici nelle antiche versioni del "Levitico"* (StSem 39; Roma: Istituto di Studi sul Vicino Oriente, 1971).

[34]For a further subclassification of loan translations see Werner Betz, *Deutsch und Lateinisch. Die Lehnbildungen der althochdeutschen Benediktinerregel* (Bonn: H. Bouvier, 1949), p. 28.

[35]Weinreich, p. 48. Cf. also Kristian Sanfeld Jensen, "Notes sur les calques linguistique," *Festschrift Vilhelm Thomsen* (Leipzig: Otto Harrassowitz, 1912), pp. 166–73; and Louis Deroy, *L'Emprunt linguistique* (Paris: Les Belles Lettres, 1956), p. 93.

[36]See his article, "The Analysis of Semantic Borrowing," *Essays Presented to C. M. Girdlestone* (Durham: The University, 1960), pp. 125–41.

distinctions. In the first place the loan may or may not involve phonetic resemblance between the native and the foreign term. Second,
the borrowed meaning may or may not be similar to the old meaning.
We then have four possibilities:[37]

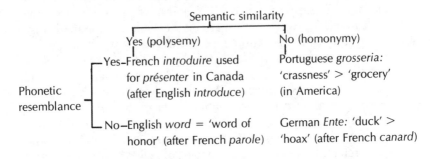

Semantic similarity

	Yes (polysemy)	No (homonymy)
Phonetic resemblance	Yes—French *introduire* used for *présenter* in Canada (after English *introduce*)	Portuguese *grosseria*: 'crassness' > 'grocery' (in America)
	No—English *word* = 'word of honor' (after French *parole*)	German *Ente*: 'duck' > 'hoax' (after French c*anard*)

PHONETIC RESEMBLANCE

It is essential to note that recent studies of semantic borrowing
usually treat contact between *related* languages, where phonetic similarity is likely to play a significant role. Haugen, for example, could
not find one instance of borrowing between phonetically dissimilar
words in American Norwegian.[38] Hope's comprehensive work on even
more closely related languages (French and Italian) disclosed very few
items of this kind. Hope concludes that "in the past lexicologists have
tended to ascribe undue importance to semantic calque [his term for
borrowing where there is *no* phonetic resemblance] at the expense of
other forms of semantic interference, presumably because it is superficially more striking and therefore more easily detected."[39]

In view of the characteristic morphology of the Semitic languages, phonetic resemblance becomes particularly significant when
considering linguistic contact between them. That is, a speaker of two
Semitic languages would very quickly identify similar sounds if they

[37]This diagram is modified from Hope's "Analysis," p. 131. Hope himself builds
on Haugen's distinction between *homophonous* (phonetic resemblance only),
synonymous (semantic resemblance only), and *homologous* (phonetic and semantic
resemblance). For a different, less useful classification, see Paul Schach, "Semantic
Borrowing in Pennsylvania German," *AmSp* 26 (1957): 257–67, which includes
many interesting examples.

[38]Haugen, *Norwegian Language*, p. 472.

[39]Hope, *Lexical Borrowing*, p. 644. But this statement needs qualification, since,
as we shall see, the situation is quite different for unrelated languages.

occurred in words that overlapped in meaning, but these two words would probably be related etymologically anyway. For example, a speaker of Hebrew would have readily identified his native *zakar* with Aramaic *dₑkar*, both meaning 'male.' Kutscher argues that the other meaning of the Aramaic word, 'ram,' was then borrowed by Hebrew.[40] We must counter, however, that these two words are etymologically the same (since proto-Semitic *ḏ* appears in Hebrew as *z* and in Aramaic as *d*) and one can seldom be sure whether borrowing, rather than parallel development, has taken place; in fact, one could argue that the word already had both meanings in "proto-Northwest Semitic" (that is, before the Canaanite/Aramaic split).

As we move away from related languages, however, the situation is altered radically. In particular, very few Greek words sound like any Hebrew or Aramaic words, and even this number is greatly reduced if we consider words that are both phonetically *and* semantically similar. To be sure, we must recognize the possibility that the LXX translators' choice of a word may have been facilitated by some kind of phonetic similarity (for example, note the use of ἐκκλησία for *qahal* and of ἐπισκέπτεσθαι for *paqad*),[41] but these cases belong in a separate category, namely, "translation technique." Apart from the use of σκηνοῦν in John 1:14, clearly intended to echo the Hebrew *šₑkinah* (but even here the Greek verb merely takes on a nuance—no new acceptation is created), phonetic resemblance has not played a role in the semantic loans found in the New Testament. In other words, all our cases of semantic borrowing belong to what Hope specifically calls *calque* (a term used more broadly by other writers).

Now we should perhaps stress that this criterion of phonetic simi-

[40]E. Y. Kutscher, "Aramaic Calque in Hebrew, " *Tarbiz* 33 (1963–64): 118–30, reprinted in *Hebrew and Aramaic Studies*, ed. Z. Ben-Hayyim et al. (Jerusalem: Magnes Press, 1977); the example assumes a late dating of Exod. 12:5, et al. Kutscher's only example of a loan where the phonetic resemblance is *not* due to etymological connection (Heb. *bhl* Nif., 'fear' > 'hurry,' after Syr. *rhb*) is not persuasive. See also below, n. 46. Professor T. E. Hope has suggested in a personal conversation that most semantic loans due to phonetic resemblance in *any* language involve etymological relationships (this is even true in the case of *glosseria/grocery*).

[41]For ἐκκλησία cf. TDNT 3:517. On the general question, see Walters, *The Text of the Septuagint*, chap. 9 (especially p. 196); G. B. Caird, "Homoeophony in the Septuagint," in *Jews, Greeks and Christians: Religious Cultures in Late Antiquity*, ed. Robert Hamerton-Kelly and Robin Scroggs (SJLA 21; Leiden: Brill, 1976), pp. 74–88; James Barr, *The Typology of Literalism in Ancient Biblical Translations* (MSU 15; Göttingen: Vandenhoeck & Ruprecht, 1979), p. 45; Jan de Waard, "'Homophony' in the Septuagint," *Bib* 62 (1982) 551–61.

larity helps us, not merely by sorting out the material in a formal way, but also by focusing on the different psychic processes involved. We may clarify this point by noting various degrees of difficulty in different types of borrowing. In the case of a *loan word* we have an elementary form of linguistic exchange, for which no real knowledge of the foreign language is needed (even though loan words are also common among fluent bilinguals). To imitate a foreign *usage*, however, some familiarity with both languages is necessary.[42] Now whereas the degree of familiarity required may be relatively low as long as there is strong phonetic resemblance between the native and the foreign word, the special case of calque demands "awareness of a semantic pattern in a foreign language as well as one's own combined with a perception of the semantic relationship that exists between the two languages."[43] Further, we should probably differentiate between apparently unconscious identifications (such as θάλασσα = 'lake' after Aramaic *yama*) and more sophisticated, deliberate imitations (such as διαθήκη = b$_e$rit). Thus:

Degree of linguistic sophistication			
low -- high			
		unconscious	deliberate
	phonetic resemblance	phonetic dissimilarity	
loan words	semantic loans		

[42]Cf. Bruno Migliorini, *Saggi linguistici* (Firenze: Felice de Monnier, n.d.), p. 12, who contrasts the loan words in the Old Latin Versions and the calques of the Vulgate. That a high degree of bilingualism constitutes a precondition of calque is especially stressed by Mirco Deanović, "Observazioni sulle origini dei calchi linguistici," *ArRom* 18 (1934): 129–42. For a useful sevenfold distinction in degrees of bilingualism, see Haugen, pp. 370–71.

[43]Hope, *Lexical Borrowing*, p. 643. In this passage Professor Hope stresses that "a high degree of intention" is characteristic of calque. However, many examples of semantic borrowing with phonetic dissimilarity are best explained as "confusions" originating in the speech of children and uneducated adults (so Haugen, p. 473, who nevertheless errs in understanding all calques in this way).

SEMANTIC SIMILARITY

Hope's second criterion of classification stems from a basic distinction in descriptive semantics (and will therefore occupy us again in chap. 4). If the native word is represented by A, the native meaning by X, and the borrowed meaning by Y, the resulting combination may be Axy (= polysemy, one word with two related meanings) or $A^1x + A^2y$ (= homonymy, for the speaker perceives two distinct words; cf. above, p. 37).

Cases of loan homonymy are relatively rare[44] and they nearly always involve phonetic similarity. In addition to *grosseria*, note American Portuguese *pinchar*, 'to jump' > 'to pinch'; American Norwegian *file*, 'file' > 'to feel'; Pennsylvania German *bieten*, 'to ask' > 'to beat' (in a contest).[45] Some cases of Aramaisms in Hebrew may belong here, such as *zaḥal*, 'to crawl' > 'to be afraid' (Job 32:6, after Aramaic *dᵉḥal*) and *kitter*, 'to surround' > 'to wait for' (Job 36:2, after Aramaic *katter*).[46]

As we might expect, no cases of loan homonyms are to be found in the New Testament; that is, the borrowings produced new acceptations for *old* words (the speakers did *not* perceive two different Greek words). All of our terms, then, can be understood as instances of loan polysemy. Unfortunately, this type of semantic borrowing presents "an acute problem of identification."

---

[44]Ullmann could say in 1951 that he knew "of no example where pure homonymy has been produced by foreign influence" (*Principles*, p. 130). The subject of loan homonymy is a complicated one and even Hope's treatment (*Lexical Borrowing*, pp. 641ff.) is not fully satisfactory. In my judgment, "loan homonyms" should be understood rather as a special category of loan words. Thus the use of *grosseria* for 'grocery' is not really a case of semantic "extension" but a wholesale borrowing of the English word (with certain modifications characteristic of loan blends) that happens to coincide with (or at most is facilitated by) an already existing word.

[45]Weinreich, p. 49; Haugen, p. 402; Schach, p. 265.

[46]The first example is from Kutscher (see above n. 40), the second from Max Wagner, *Die lexikalischen und grammatikalischen Aramaismen in alttestamentlichen Hebräisch* (BZAW 96; Berlin: Alfred Töpelmann, 1966), p. 70. (Wagner's work, in contrast to Kutscher's, lacks linguistic rigor and fails to distinguish between various kinds of borrowing phenomena.) The two examples chosen here may be disputed, since some semantic connection between the meanings is possible; however, they are given separate entries in KB3. We may note that even the LXX can alert us to some possibilities. In Isa. 53:10 the Hebrew *dakkᵉ'o*, 'to crush him,' is rendered καθαρίσαι αὐτόν, apparently through confusion of Heb. *dk'* with Aramaic *dk'* (Heb. *zkh*), 'to purify, (Seeligman, *Septuagint Version of Isaiah*, p. 50).

The difficulty is intrinsic. There is least doubt that a polysemic [as opposed to a homonymic] loan has occurred when the semantic innovation concerned is smallest: yet the more trivial the semantic divergence appears to be, the more likely it is to pass unnoticed.[47]

For example, δωρεάν means 'freely, gratis' in classical Greek, and the acceptations 'without reason' (John 15:25) and 'in vain' (Gal. 2:21) are usually understood as "slightly developed" meanings, similar to Latin *gratuitus*.[48] This is quite possible, but is it just a coincidence that these semantic developments are only attested in the LXX and the New Testament? May not Hebrew ḥinam (or Aramaic maggan) be responsible? Again, διακρίνεσθαι, 'to divide, distinguish, decide,' is used in the sense of 'to doubt' in the New Testament. Nägeli included this term among examples of natural development and Moulton-Milligan suggested that the new meaning "arises very naturally out of the general sense of 'making distinctions.'" But what gave rise to the change when Greek speakers could already use διστάζειν? Surely Büchsel[49] is right in understanding this usage as a calque of Aramaic pᵉlag ('to divide,' but in the passive, 'divided at heart, undecided').

There can be little question that a number of semantic loans in the New Testament remain unidentified. Joüon's numerous suggestions,[50] for example, have failed to establish themselves, but it is impossible to prove that the particular instances adduced by him are not true Semitisms.

THE CAUSES OF SEMANTIC BORROWING

We may conclude this section with a brief discussion of the factors that may give rise to borrowings; at least three of these can be distinguished.

[47]Hope, *Lexical Borrowing*, p. 645. Cf. Majed Farhan Saʻid, *Lexical Innovation Through Borrowing in Modern Standard Arabic* (Ph.D. dissertation, Princeton University, 1964), p. 103.

[48]Cf. MM, p. 174; also Nägeli, *Wortschatz*, p. 35. In contrast, Büchsel, *TDNT* 2:167. On this general question cf. Kronasser's handling of γινώσκειν, *Handbuch*, p. 142.

[49]*TDNT* 3:948–49. Büchsel, however, probably exaggerates the uniqueness of this usage.

[50]E.g., ὤφθη—'appear' (Matt. 17:3), φέρειν—'lead' (Mark 4:8); see *RSR* 17 (1927): 210–29, 537–40; 18 (1928): 345–59. Cf. also M. Silva, "New Lexical Semitisms?" *ZNW* 69 (1978): 253–57.

The first one we have already alluded to above (p. 90). A speaker or author may *consciously* seek to imitate a foreign usage for stylistic purposes. For example, when John uses the verb ὑψοῦσθαι ('to be lifted up') with reference to death, after the reflexive of Aramaic *s*ᵉ*leq*,[51] he is apparently making a play on words by echoing Isaiah 52:13 from the LXX (Ἰδοὺ συνήσει ὁ παῖς μου καὶ ὑψωθήσεται καὶ δοξασθήσεται σφόδρα). It may be argued that we should not classify such exceptional uses as cases of semantic borrowing, since they do not reflect the linguistic consciousness of a community. However, semantic loans (especially if polysemic) are in the very nature of the case relative and unstable;[52] it would therefore be a mistake to ignore individualistic usages altogether. At any rate, these loans may very well spread to the community as a whole.

A second and opposite cause is that of *oversight*.[53] This notion is not incompatible with our previous emphasis on the linguistic awareness that characterizes calques, for now we are not dealing with a speaker's failure to notice similarities between the native and foreign terms, but of his unconscious infringing on the limits of lexical distribution in the native language. This factor may explain why most semantic loans (other than technical specializations in meaning) can be understood as metonymies that result in expansion of meaning. The distribution of θάλασσα, for example, was normally limited to utterances where the meaning 'sea' was intended; an oversight of this limitation made it possible to equate this term more fully with the Semitic equivalent *(yama)*, leading to a lexical generalization (opp. differentiation), since now θάλασσα began to encroach on the context previously covered by λίμνη ('lake').[54]

There is a third factor, *cultural motivation*, that should perhaps be included as a subclass of the first; however, it requires special attention for a variety of reasons. With reference to loan words, Weinreich calls attention to the prestige (or disdain) that may be associated

---

[51]See Martin McNamara, *The New Testament and the Palestinian Targums to the Pentateuch* (AnBib 270; Rome: Pontifical Biblical Institute, 1966), pp. 145–49. If the occurrences in John 12:32, 34 do not imply a reference to 'exaltation,' this passage may be taken as evidence of an established semantic loan, that is, one that was part of Palestinian speech.

[52]Hope, *Lexical Borrowing*, p. 645.

[53]Cf. Weinreich, p. 60.

[54]The reader will note that the two causes mentioned so far correspond with our previous distinction between unconscious and deliberate loans.

with a particular language; this element often leads the bilingual to use a foreign term representative of positive (or negative) values.[55] This set of motivations cannot of course be transferred directly to the different category of semantic loans, but it calls our attention to the *external* considerations that affect linguistic borrowing. T. E. Hope informs us that in the course of his search, the borrowings with which he was dealing "began to fall into definite patterns," leading to a basic distinction between the linguistic (or semantic) and the extralinguistic (or cultural). The latter category included terms "which are essentially labels denoting a concrete object."[56] For example, the use of νόμος with reference to the Mosaic Law is a specialization of this kind, since the word acts as a label or referential term. The significance of this distinction is that, whereas terms like νόμος can be subjected to lexicocultural interpretation and the word-and-thing method, from a *linguistic* point of view our main interest is in the remaining terms, where

> lexical innovation is closely bound up with the semantic economy of the receiving language—with inherent tendencies to semantic change, the pressure exerted by related signs within a semantic field and the like. This is the sector in which the concept of semantic structure may be invoked.[57]

THE STRUCTURAL PERSPECTIVE

We began chapter 2 by noting Wartburg's concern, not only with the individual changes a word undergoes, but also with the other words that may in some way be affected by those changes. This perspective on historical semantics is informed by an understanding of the vo-

---

[55]Weinreich, pp. 59–60.

[56]Hope, *Lexical Borrowing*, p. 22; cf. pp. 724ff., 741. (See also the words from his preface, which I have quoted above, pp. 30–31. This whole subject will receive further elaboration in part two.) Readers may note that the distinction formulated here corresponds to our previous distinction between innovation and conservatism. Although semantic loans are certainly cases of innovation, one may argue that in the special instance of a native word used to denote a foreign entity, what we have is not really a semantic loan at all but an indigenous shift caused by cultural interference and thus to be treated as conservatism (indeed, note that earlier we treated ἄγγελος, used after *mal'ak*, as an example of conservatism). Hope feels this is going too far ("Analysis," p. 127), but it is surely significant that the issue can be raised. Cf. also B. F. Vidos, "Le bilinguisme et le mécanisme de l'emprunt," *RLR* 24 (1960): 1–19, especially p. 6.

[57]Hope, *Lexical Borrowing*, p. 724.

cabulary as a structured system. Although the significance of structural considerations will not be fully clear until we discuss this issue in part two, some brief comments are in order.

If we begin by asking what general consequences have resulted from the kinds of semantic changes discussed in this chapter, it will have to be admitted that our knowledge of Palestinian Greek is too limited to allow firm conclusions. We could speculate, for example, that the use of θάλασσα for 'lake' led to the disuse of λίμνη in Palestine, but we simply cannot prove it. Moreover, we are handicapped by lack of research into whole groups of semantically related terms. We may, however, take an example from the semantic field of 'mind' (= 'the seat of the mental faculties') to illustrate some of the subtle, but no less important, changes that the Greek vocabulary has undergone.[58]

In extrabiblical Greek literature we find a rather large number of words available with the general sense of 'mind'—νοῦς, διάνοια, φρήν, γνώμη, ψυχή, φρόνησις. The word καρδία had apparently been used in ancient times in this sense,[59] but no such usage is attested in Hellenistic literature. In fact, this word (with *any* meaning) had become relatively rare: Polybius uses it only once, Epictetus twice. However, even a cursory glance at the LXX reveals that in this document, because of the influence of Hebrew *leb*, καρδία has become the *standard* term for the seat of the mental faculties. A closer look at the LXX shows further that many of the passages where other Greek words for 'mind' occur also contain καρδία in the immediate context; this fact suggests that the other terms were used for stylistic variety, and that otherwise they played an insignificant role in the semantic structure of the language. These other terms, furthermore, are to a large extent confined to Genesis, Exodus, Chronicles, Sirach, Maccabees, and Proverbs. It is clear that the wealth of terms found in secular literature with reference to the mind—and the great variety of differentiations possible because of it—is lost in the language of the LXX. Of course, translation literature such as the LXX does not necessarily reflect the spoken language, but a look at Paul's letters shows an intermediate position between the LXX and, say, Epictetus. Whether Paul's usage is attributed primarily to the LXX or to the Aramaic of Palestine, one must emphasize the distinctively

[58]This example is taken from my Ph.D. thesis, *Semantic Change*, pp. 141ff.
[59]Perhaps by Hesiod; see Bauer, p. xxiii.

Semitic flavor conveyed by this semantic field in the New Testament.[60]

Structural considerations can have direct exegetical consequences as well. We may note as an example recent discussions of the Greek vocabulary for 'love.' It is still common to hear that, while the Greeks normally used φιλεῖν, this verb was considered inadequate by the LXX translators, who preferred the relatively rare term ἀγαπᾶν (and even coined a noun, ἀγάπη) and infused it with nobler meaning, leading to the New Testament use of this and cognate terms for 'divine love.' Quite apart from the fact that this reconstruction hardly fits the LXX's use of ἀγάπη and ἀγαπᾶν for incestuous lust (2 Sam. 13:15), we may well doubt the suggestion that the LXX translator's preference for ἀγαπᾶν over φιλεῖν was a complete innovation. In a careful study Robert Joly has brought forth considerable evidence that this preference is quite generally attested in Hellenistic times. More important for our purposes, however, Joly explains the change through structural considerations: ἀγαπᾶν was becoming the standard verb for 'to love' because φιλεῖν had acquired the meaning 'to kiss.' Furthermore, Joly explains that the change of φιλεῖν was itself due to the disappearance of the older word for 'to kiss' (κυνεῖν) and that this verb disappeared because of a homonymic clash (in the aorist ἔκυσα) with κύειν ('to impregnate').[61] Thus:

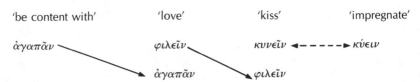

'be content with'   'love'   'kiss'   'impregnate'

---

[60]We should note incidentally that this example illustrates Moulton's view that biblical Semitisms consisted in the main of overdoing possible Greek usages (see above, chap. 2, n. 22). However, Moulton was wrong in underestimating the linguistic significance of these frequency changes. Cf. now Raija Sollamo, *Renderings of Hebrew Semiprepositions in the Septuagint* (AASF Diss. 19; Helsinki: Suomalainen Tiedakatemia, 1979), p. 299.

[61]Robert Joly, *Le vocabulaire chrétien de l'amour est il original? Φιλεῖν et Ἀγαπᾶν dans le grec antique* (Bruxelles: Presses Universitaires, 1968), p. 33. (The chart that follows is of course an oversimplification, since it does not, for example, bring καταφιλεῖν into consideration.) Joly's work is primarily a criticism of Ceslas Spicq's exaggerated claims for ἀγάπη; see most recently Spicq, *Notes de lexicographie néotestamentaire* I (Orbis biblicus et orientalis 22/1; Fribourg, Suisse: Éditions Universitaires, 1978), pp. 15ff. Cf. also Roy F. Butler, *The Meaning of "Agapao" and "Phileo" in the Greek New Testament* (Lawrence, Kansas: Coronado Press, 1977).

A recognition of these facts will not determine automatically, of course, how we shall interpret such disputed passages as John 21:15–17, but they should have a direct bearing on the linguistic perspective we bring to the text.

At any rate, if we recognize the need for structural considerations in historical semantics, we shall be well on our way toward a defensible integration of synchronic and diachronic linguistics:

> The time has come when our efforts to understand the evolution of languages, on the one hand, and their structure at a given period, on the other, can and must be co-ordinated. The aim must be to follow the whole structure of the language in its process of gradual transformation. Linguistic science, in a new phase of its evolution, will thus become *structural history*.[62]

---

[62]Wartburg, *Problems*, p. 178. E. Coseriu defines the aims of structural diachronic semantics thus: "C'est le developpement historique des 'champs conceptuels' considérés comme structures lexicales de contenu. Et, puisque structure veut dire avant tout opposition distinctive, la sémantique structurale diachronique aura à établir, à étudier et, si possible, à expliquer (motiver) le maintien, l'apparition, la disparition et la modification, au cours de l'histoire d'une langue, des oppositions lexicales distinctives." "Pour une sémantique diachronique structurale," *TLL* 2 (1964): 139–86, especially pp. 159–60. This article and five others, constituting Coseriu's most important essays on semantics, have been brought together in Spanish translation, with some revisions, in *Principios de semántica estructural* (BRE 2:259; Madrid: Editorial Gredos, 1977).

PART 2

DESCRIPTIVE
SEMANTICS

SUMMARY OF CHAPTER 4

DENOTATION

On the basis of the "Ogden-Richards triangle," we may analyze the claim that words inherently possess a certain basic meaning. Although most words have a stable semantic core, lexical meanings are largely arbitrary. Denotation views of meaning are fundamentally unsatisfactory, yet some vocabulary items can best be understood as denoting extralinguistic entities. This factor explains why theological terms can be profitably subjected to the word-and-thing method.

STRUCTURE

One of Saussure's important contributions was his emphasis on viewing languages as structural systems.

Phonology. Saussure's ideas have been successfully applied to the study of linguistic sound systems. After distinguishing the bare physical sounds from the (linguistically significant) phonemes, we recognize that these phonemes acquire their value through the relationship they sustain with one another.

Vocabulary. These structural principles are not as easily applied to the vocabulary as they are to the phonology, but significant advances have been made. While some words (those that denote) may have meaning of their own, most words depend for their meaning on their relation to one another.

Further Distinctions. Since these relations can take many forms, it is important to focus on those relations that primarily involve meaning. Most semantic studies treat the connection between one word and its meaning, but our own interest lies in the relation between the meanings of different words.

STYLE

Another important contribution by Saussure was his distinction between *langue* (the linguistic system) and *parole* (actual speech). Modern linguists have paid increasing attention to *parole*, which involves linguistic variation and therefore style. As opposed to grammar, style encompasses the area of linguistic choice.

4　Some Basic Concepts

It may be useful pointing out that when Michel Bréal[1] introduced and popularized the term *semantics (sémantique;* in German *Semasiologie,* more recently *Semantik),* he was designating with it a purely historical discipline. This approach dominated semantic research during the first half of the twentieth century. Indeed, Heinz Kronasser's standard introduction to the discipline, published as recently as 1951, deals almost exclusively with semantic change.[2]

To put it differently, intensive research in synchronically oriented semantics has been taking place for only about three decades. These circumstances, along with the perplexing difficulties inherent in any study of meaning, will help to explain why today we find so many competing approaches to the subject.[3] Particularly disturbing is the terminological confusion that reigns in the literature; and, not sur-

[1]First in a brief article in 1883; later in his book, *Semantics,* p. 8. See Eugenio Coseriu and Horst Geckeler, "Linguistics and Semantics," *CTL* 12:103–71, especially p. 104.

[2]His book is divided into two sections, the first dealing with the development of the discipline, and the second entitled, "Die Arten des Bedeutungswandels und ihre psychologischen Wurzeln" (*Handbuch,* pp. 82–197). Not surprisingly, the preface to the first edition of KB (1953) describes linguistic semantics as *Bedeutungsentwicklung* (p. viii.)

[3]For some excellent surveys, see the article by Coseriu and Geckeler mentioned in n. 1, pp. 103–39; Stephen Ullmann, "Some Recent Developments in Semantics," in *Meaning and Style: Collected Papers* (Oxford: B. Blackwell, 1973), pp. 1–39, and his fuller discussion, "Semantics," *CTL* 9:343–94. For a wide-ranging bibliography, not limited to linguistics, see W. Terrence Gordon, *Semantics: A Bibliography 1965–1978* (Metuchen, N.J., and London: Scarecrow Press, 1980).

prisingly, this confusion reveals substantial disagreements as well. Behind the confusion and the disagreements, however, stand a number of basic perspectives and even established principles that unite many contemporary researchers. I propose here to summarize and elucidate those areas that, in my judgment, appear most promising for biblical lexicology. To do this effectively, some compromises are necessary. In particular, the terminology used here is not intended as a model of scientific rigor, but as a temporary expedient that should prove intelligible to (and usable by) a fairly wide audience.[4]

The first distinction that we must make goes back to Ogden-Richards's famous triangle.[5] We may use the terms *symbol* (the word in its phonetic or written form), *sense*[6] (the mental content called up by the symbol), and *referent* (the extralinguistic thing denoted) to represent the three basic elements that will occupy us. We must note that the symbol, though usually a single word[7] (e.g., *tree*), may be composed of two or more words that constitute a single lexical unit

[4]The two other alternatives, of course, were the use of either a very ambiguous terminology (attractive to general readers but in the end disastrous) or a very rigorous terminology (attractive to the specialist, perhaps, but inevitably idiosyncratic as well as forbidding to my intended audience). My compromise consists primarily in using terminology only as rigorous as is necessary to clarify the basic concepts dealt with in *this* book. Since the work of John Lyons has proved particularly influential and is readily accessible to English readers, I have made a special, but only partially successful, effort to incorporate his terminology.

[5]C. K. Ogden and I. A. Richards, *The Meaning of Meaning* (New York: Harcourt, Brace and Co., 1945), p. 11. This work has had considerable impact, not only on linguistic semantics, but also on philosophical and literary thought and on the movement known as general semantics. The triangle was intended to stress the *indirect* relationship between a word and that to which it refers; hence the broken line between symbol and reference. For Klaus Heger's development of the triangle into a trapezium, see Kurt Baldinger, *Semantic Theory: Towards a Modern Semantics* (Oxford: B. Blackwell, 1980).

[6]Note that the contrast between symbol and sense is one of form vs. content. Instead of *sense*, Ogden and Richards used the terms *thought* and *reference*, which can prove very confusing. The term *sense* was used by Ullmann, who nevertheless preferred *name* instead of *symbol*; Ullmann (*Principles*, pp. 69ff.) also pointed out the parallel between Ogden-Richards's *symbol-thought-referent* and Saussure's *signifiant* ('signifier')—*signifié* ('signified')—*chose* ('thing'). It is important to stress at this point that my (and Ullmann's) use of *sense* differs from that of Lyons, even though there is some overlap (more on this problem below).

[7]We need not here be concerned with the theoretical problems involved in defining *word*; for our purposes, we may simply identify a word according to its orthographic representation (that is, those linguistic units that are written separately).

(e.g., the idioms *turn up, pain in the neck*). Further, we shall use the term *meaning* in a general, nontechnical way, bringing in other terms when more precision is necessary.[8] The resulting triangle:

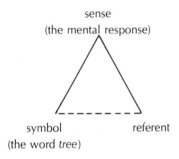

sense
(the mental response)

symbol   referent
(the word *tree*)

On the basis of this scheme, we may use three different approaches to lexical meaning. (1) We may focus on the relationship between symbol and referent; this approach (the "word-and-thing" method) consists primarily in analyzing the referent itself. (2) We may focus on the relationship between symbol and sense in individual words. (3) We may focus on the relationship between the sense of different words. This last approach will be our main concern in chapters 5–6.

DENOTATION

In our discussion of etymology (see above, p. 46) we took note of Norman H. Snaith's emphasis on the "fundamental motif" that each word tends to preserve. We can hardly doubt, of course, that most vocabulary items are linked to a more or less stable semantic core; indeed, without it, communication would be unimaginable.[9] The difficulty enters in when this simple fact is used to support misleading ideas regarding the supposedly "inherent" meaning of a word. Little genuine progress can be made in language study unless we recognize that, as a rule, the association of a particular word with a particular

[8]Cf. Lyons, *Semantics* 1: 4–5. For various attempts to classify meaning, see Ogden-Richards, *passim*; Geoffrey Leech, *Semantics* (Baltimore: Penguin, 1974), chaps. 1–2, especially p. 26; with special reference to biblical meaning, cf. Gerald Downing, "Meanings," in *What About the New Testament? Essays in Honour of Christopher Evans*, ed. Morna Hooker and Colin Hickling (London: SCM, 1975), pp. 127–42.

[9]Cf. Stern, *Meaning*, p. 85; Ullmann, Semantics, pp. 48–49.

meaning is *largely* arbitrary, a matter of convention.[10] For example, there is no *necessary* reason (i.e., inherent in language or in the nature of things) why the word *dog* rather than, say, *cat*, is used of canines; otherwise, we would not expect a Spanish speaker to be able to use a completely different symbol, *perro*, with the same meaning. The semantic core perceived by the speaker is therefore the result of convention and use.

Two other examples may serve to clarify the main issue. The word *bar* has quite a variety of meanings in modern American English, the most common of which seems to be, 'an establishment that serves alcoholic beverages.' The average speaker probably identifies this use as the semantic core of *bar* and fails to perceive a link between it and the straight metal object found in many windows. Historically, of course, there is a connection: 'obstructing object' (especially of the barrier in a courtroom, thence by metonymy, 'courtroom,' 'barristers,' etc.); then, by specialization, 'a counter where drinks are served'; then, by metonymy, of the whole establishment where such a counter is found.[11] It is further not at all inconceivable that *bar* may continue to be used in this sense even if such a counter is replaced by some other means of serving the drinks and even if all other meanings of the word should disappear.

This last step, though speculative for *bar*, is certainly real for many other words. Can the modern speaker of English sense a semantic relationship between *science* and *nice*? Hardly, though diachronically such a relationship exists. *Science* is derived from the present participle of Latin *scire*, 'to know'; its negative *nescire* yields the adjective *nescius*, 'ignorant,' whence (through Old French) we find Old English *nice*, 'foolish' (also 'lascivious,' 'lazy,' 'shy'!), later 'fastidious,'

---

[10]I emphasize the adverb *largely* to take into account Wartburg's qualifications (*Problems*, p. 134) and to recognize the significance, if not full persuasiveness, of the arguments marshalled in *Language, Context, and the Imagination: Essays by Paul Friedrich*, ed. Anwar S. Dil (Stanford: Stanford University Press, 1979), pp. 1–62. The usual theological objections to the position adopted here rest either on a misunderstanding of the biblical data or on the assumption that this position necessarily commits us to unwarranted philosophical viewpoints. This general discussion goes back to the Ancient Greek φύσις–νόμος controversy; see R. H. Robins, *A Short History of Linguistics* (Bloomington: Indiana University Press, 1967), pp. 17ff. Cf. also Ullmann, "Some Recent Developments," p. 17.

[11]The example is used in a somewhat different connection by Eugene A. Nida, *Componential Analysis of Meaning: An Introduction to Semantic Structures* (ApSem 57; The Hague: Mouton, 1975), pp. 11–12.

and finally 'pleasant.' This last acceptation is certainly the *present* semantic core of the word, yet it has nothing to do with its etymology or any supposed inherent meaning. To speak of the "basic" or "proper" meaning of a word invites confusion. We should specify whether we are referring to the word's etymology (in one of its several senses), its most frequent meaning, or that meaning that seems to account (historically or "logically") for the other meanings of the word.

Not infrequently, unwarranted ideas about the "basic" meaning of a word are associated with a *denotation* (or *reference*)[12] view of meaning, which is our primary topic of interest in this section. At a popular, unsophisticated level, we may simply call attention to the danger of positing a direct relation between symbol and referent *(denotatum)*. Ullmann points out that dictionaries encourage us to perceive words as independent entities with their own particular meanings.

> The vocabulary thus gives the impression of a vast filing system in which all items of our experience are docketed and classified. We are so convinced of the validity of our words that we automatically assume the existence of things behind the labels, and implicitly believe in the reality of abstract ideas.[13]

Here Ullmann is echoing the concerns of Ogden and Richards, who believe that such a simplification of the link "between words and things is the source of almost all the difficulties which thought encounters."[14]

However, what is usually meant by a denotation theory of meaning consists of a consciously philosophical understanding of language, such as that of John Stuart Mill, who sought to understand (virtually all kinds of) meaning as *naming*. The relationship between a thing and its name is so simple that most of us are in fact tempted to reduce all words to the same analysis. Thus we tend to assume that words merely denote (stand for, refer to) extralinguistic realities. But this assumption, though very old indeed, "is easy to demolish," as Ryle has done by pointing out that

---

[12]These two terms are, however, differentiated by Lyons in *semantics* 1, chap. 7. See also the philosophically astute discussion by Gibson, *Biblical Semantic Logic*, chap. 2.

[13]Ullmann, *Semantics*, p. 39.

[14]Ogden-Richards, p. 12. We need not pursue this issue, a dominant one in general semantics, for which note especially S. I. Hayakawa, et al., *Language in Thought and Action*, 4th ed. (New York: Harcourt Brace Jovanovich, 1978).

if every single word were a name, then a sentence composed of five words, say "three is a prime number" should be a list of five objects named by those five words. But a list, like "Plato, Aristotle, Aquinas, Locke, Berkeley" is not a sentence. . . . What a sentence means is not decomposable into the set of things which the words in it stand for, if they do stand for things. So the notion of *having meaning* is at least partly different from the notion of *standing for*.

More than this. I can use the two descriptive phrases "the Morning Star" and "the Evening Star," as different ways of referring to Venus. But it is quite clear that the two phrases are different in meaning. It would be incorrect to translate into French the phrase "the Morning Star" by "l'Etoile du Soir." But if the two phrases have different meanings, then Venus, the planet which we describe by the two different descriptions, cannot be what these descriptive phrases mean. For she, Venus, is one and the same, but what the two phrases signify are different.[15]

Drawing upon Ludwig Wittgenstein's ideas, Ryle insists that words do not denote, they are *used*. The meaning of a word "is a *functional* factor of a range of possible assertions, questions, commands and the rest."[16]

The point is a very important one, but it can be exaggerated. Some argue that the expression *This word means such and such* is inaccurate and should be replaced by *This word is used in such and such a way*. Apart from the pedantry of such a criticism, we should recognize that the expression sometimes *is* accurate. Words sometimes do stand for things. When A. Rosetti stated that "the word exists only through the context and is nothing in itself,"[17] he was making an unwarranted generalization.

Clearly, we must recognize that "at least certain items in the vocabularies of all languages can be put into correspondence with

[15]Gilbert Ryle, "The Theory of Meaning," p. 133.

[16]Ibid., p. 137. This development in (one school of) modern philosophy parallels an independent development in linguistics. Thus Ullmann developed his functional theory of meaning before becoming aware of Wittgenstein's work (cf. Ullmann, *Principles*, p. 303). Similarly, the views of James Barr, who drew on modern linguistics, were mistakenly associated with philosophical commitments (cf. *Biblical Words for Time*, 2nd ed., p. 197).

[17]Quoted by Ullmann, *Semantics*, p. 48.

'features' of the physical world."[18] In fact, the notion of reference cannot even be limited to *physical* entities. We need to appreciate, for example, that certain biblical terms denote *theological* entities. Unfortunately, we normally refer to these entities as *concepts*, which sounds as if we are discussing the apex of Ogden-Richards's triangle (i.e., the mental content, the sense). In our judgment, technical or semitechnical terms *refer to* or *stand for* defined concepts or ideas; e.g., νόμος, 'a body of commands'; ἁμαρτία, 'a violation of those commands.' To put it differently, these concepts are true referents. The recognition of this factor brings to a culmination our repeated emphasis on the distinction between technical and nontechnical terms.[19] Insofar as a word can be brought into a one-to-one correspondence with an extralinguistic object or entity, to that extent the word may be subjected to the concordance-based, word-and-thing, historico-conceptual method typified by *TDNT*.

However, certain qualifications must be kept in mind. Relatively few words in the biblical vocabulary can be understood as in some way technical. Furthermore, not all words can properly be understood as having reference of *any* kind. Words can seldom be classed in one clear-cut category. Thus, while proper names and a few other lexical units can be understood fully by invoking the notion of reference,[20] most of the vocabulary cannot be treated in such a way. Conversely, while some items in the vocabulary can hardly be said to have reference at all (What is the referent of *beautiful?*), most of the vocabulary, at least in some contexts, can be partially understood as referential. We may diagram the nature of the vocabulary as follows.

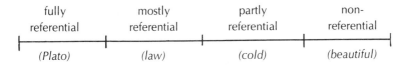

fully referential	mostly referential	partly referential	non-referential
(Plato)	(law)	(cold)	(beautiful)

[18]Lyons, *Introduction*, p. 425.

[19]See above, pp. 29–31, 62–63, 68, 79–81, 94. Note that Coseriu's "preliminary distinctions" begin with a distinction between extralinguistic reality and language and that they end with a distinction between designation *(Bezeichnung)* and signification *(Bedeutung)*; see Coseriu and Geckeler, "Linguistics and Semantics," pp. 140, 146. Note that in our use (contrary to the normal philosophical treatments) reference does not necessarily imply existence; Lyons acknowledges that even in the case of *unicorn* we can have "secondary" denotation *(Semantics* 1:211).

[20]Even proper names, from a certain perspective, require contextual interpretation, as Paul Friedrich has noted in *Language, Context, and the Imagination*, p. 450.

In conclusion, only a small number of words in the vocabulary can be fully understood by analyzing their referents; these words are susceptible to the word-and-thing approach but not to a structural approach. Among the remaining words, virtually all of them, to some degree, can be subjected to a structural analysis; and some of them, perhaps, can *only* be understood by means of such an analysis.[21]

STRUCTURE[22]

Anyone acquainted with a foreign language has probably felt that it is *systematically* different from his or her own. The famous American linguist Edward Sapir gave expression to this common "feeling" when he said that

> there is such a thing as a basic plan, a certain cut, to each language. This type of plan or structural "genius" of the language is something much more fundamental, much more pervasive, than any single feature of it that we can mention, nor can we gain an adequate idea of its nature by a mere recital of the sundry facts that make up the grammar of the language.[23]

Once again, however, it was Saussure who drew this point most sharply by comparing language with a game of chess. In chess "the respective value of the pieces depends on their position on the chessboard just as each linguistic term derives its value from its opposition to all other terms." Further, a move will have repercussions on the system as a whole and "resulting changes of value will be, according to the circumstances, either nil, very serious, or of average importance. A certain move can revolutionize the whole game and even

[21]This emphasis on the fluidity of lexical items distinguishes my approach from Coseriu's, which swiftly eliminates vast portions of the vocabulary as structurally insignificant (cf. Coseriu and Geckeler, p. 141).

[22]The term *structuralism* is used so freely in our day that we need to make certain distinctions. First of all, the present work is concerned with structure only as this applies to the *linguistic* system; out of consideration, therefore, lie anthropological, philosophical, and even literary approaches (such as the movement in biblical scholarship known as structural exegesis). Second, although in very general terms all major linguistic schools today operate with some concept of structure, we have adopted the Saussurean model in particular. See the valuable discussion in Lyons, *Semantics*, 1:230–38.

[23]Edward Sapir, *Language: An Introduction to the Study of Speech* (New York: Harcourt, Brace and World, 1957, originally published in 1921), p. 120.

affect pieces that are not immediately involved." Earlier Saussure had dealt with a specific phonetic change and made the remark that "one element in the first was changed, and this change was enough to give rise to another system." "It is as if one of the planets that revolve around the sun changed its dimension and weight; this isolated event would entail general consequences and would throw the whole system out of equilibrium."[24]

PHONOLOGY

The application of these ideas has had its most dramatic success in the area of phonology, and we would do well to become familiar with basic principles in this field.[25] The structural linguist begins by making a distinction between *phonetics* and *phonology*. The first discipline deals with the physical realities of sound, whether they are significant or not. With special instruments, for example, the phonetician confirms that such English occlusive consonants as [p], [k], [t] are accompanied by a puff of air (aspiration), but not if they follow [s]; thus the *t* in *top* and the one in *stop* are pronounced differently (although the speaker may not be aware of the difference). If the speaker were always aware of this distinction and used it deliberately, so that a word *stop* with aspirated [t] had a different meaning from *stop* with unaspirated [t], then we would be dealing with two different *phonemes*, not just with sounds.[26] The phonologist does not deal with the physical sounds merely, but only with those that are linguistically significant and can therefore be used to differentiate between words.

It is immediately clear that different languages have different phonological systems, so that their respective phonemes play different roles. For example, the sound [z] exists in Spanish when it is followed by a voiced consonant *(mismo, desde)*, but it is not a phoneme as in English, and for this reason the Spanish speaker is not normally aware of the distinction between [s] and [z] (a Latin American learning English may not even *discover* that distinction for years and even then may be unable to master it in his own speech). The phonologist would

---

[24]Saussure, *Course*, pp. 84–85, 88–89.

[25]Here we are concerned primarily with the so-called Prague School; the classic work is by N. S. Trubetzkoy, *Principles of Phonology* (Berkeley: University of California Press, 1969; originally published in 1939).

[26]It is customary to enclose speech sounds in square brackets and to enclose phonemes in obliques, / /. If the reference is to letters, not sounds, then italics are used.

say that the English voiced and unvoiced sibilants /z/ and /s/ are in *opposition*, and that the *distinctive features* of these phonemes—in this case the presence or absence of voice—permit that opposition. The principle in view may be formulated as follows:

> Phonemes are defined in a negative fashion by their differences between each other; the definition of a phoneme in a given language depends not on positive data . . . but on the place that it occupies over against the other phonemes in the same system. . . . It may be that a phoneme in one language presents an identical phonetical realization to that of a phoneme in another language; but the definition of this phoneme is different in each of the two languages, according to the relations that it presents in the respective systems.[27]

This last point deserves some further comments. English and Arabic share the phoneme /b/; in both languages the *phonetic* realization is identical (a voiced labial occlusive). But their *phonological* definition must be different, since English has other labial phonemes such as /p/, /v/ and /f/, whereas Arabic only has /f/. Because the relations of the phoneme /b/ with other phonemes will be vastly different in the respective languages, its significance or value (we might almost say its "meaning") will be different.

One further detail is of interest for us. The relationship that phonemes sustain with each other may be *paradigmatic* or *syntagmatic*. In the word *pet* the phoneme /p/ is in paradigmatic relation with, for example, /b/ and /v/ (*bet, vet*), but in syntagmatic relation with /e/ and /t/. The former indicates contrasting relations; the latter, combinatory relations.

The very significant point of this discussion is that phonemes are nothing in themselves, they "have no validity independently of their paradigmatic and syntagmatic relations with other" phonemes;[28] their value is completely determined by their place within the phonological system. What bearing does this have for semantic studies?

VOCABULARY

It is clear that in dealing with the vocabulary of a language some special problems appear. An obvious one is the fact that lexical items

---

[27] Emilio Alarcos Llorach, *Fonología española*, 4th rev. ed. (BRE 3:1; Madrid: Editorial Gredos, 1968), p. 46.
[28] Lyons, *Introduction*, p. 75.

are much more numerous than phonological items. Whereas languages usually manage with thirty or forty phonemes that remain fairly constant for centuries, a community of speakers uses thousands of words that are continually being replaced by other words. The methodological problems involved in handling so many items has been perhaps the greatest deterrent to the application of structural methods to the study of meaning.

But there is yet a more fundamental problem. We can assert confidently that phonemes have no value of their own. We cannot be that bold with words. Once we admit the existence of denotation we have to face the fact that many words do have their own value; even ✓ words depending mostly on their relationship with other words can occasionally *mean* something by themselves. A. Martinet argues that there are relatively few words "whose denotative value is imprecise and whose relational value is high," so that, in contrast to phonemes and morphemes, "the lexicon proper seems far less easily reducible to structural patterning."[29]

Martinet's pessimism should keep us on guard lest we overestimate the possibilities of a structural approach to semantics. But if we should not expect any vocabulary to be a tight system, neither should we expect it to be amorphous.[30] Lyons claimed two decades ago:

> It is now commonly accepted by linguists that a "structural approach" of the kind long practiced in the phonological and grammatical analysis of languages is required also for their semantic description: each language must be thought of as having its own semantic structure, just as it has its own phonological and grammatical structure.[31]

Saussure himself believed so, as the following example illustrates:

[29]Quoted by Ullmann, *Semantics*, p. 237.

[30]We may say that the vocabulary presents "incomplete patterns and half-finished designs" (Ullmann, *Semantics*, p. 238). Cf. also the "mitigated structuralism" of Francisco Rodríguez Adrados, *Estudios de lingüística general* (Barcelona: Editorial Planeta, 1969), pp. 22, 59.

[31]John Lyons, *Structural Semantics: An Analysis of Part of the Vocabulary of Plato* (PPS 20; Oxford: B. Blackwell, 1963), p. 37. According to Otto Ducháček, *Le champ conceptuel de la beauté en français moderne* (Praha: Státní Pedagogické Nakladatelství, 1960), p. 5, "Le lexique de n'importe quelle langue n'est pas la simple somme des mots de cette langue, mais un système où tout mot a sa place d'après ses acceptions et ses relations à d'autres mots."

> French *mouton* can have the same signification as English *sheep* but not the same value, and this for several reasons, particularly because in speaking of a piece of meat ready to be served on the table, English uses *mutton* and not *sheep*. The difference in value between *sheep* and *mouton* is due to the fact that *sheep* has beside it a second term while the French word does not.[32]

In summary, we may state that although some items in the vocabulary (the words that *denote*) have a low relational value, it is agreed that at least "part of the total meaning of many words in all languages is to be determined by their individual relations to other words, in both the basic dimensions of linguistic analysis, syntagmatic and paradigmatic."[33] But we can go further by pointing out, first, that the vast majority of words have at least *some* significant relational value and, second, that this relational value is of more basic importance than denotation—in Lyons's words, we must admit the "priority of sense-relations."[34]

FURTHER DISTINCTIONS

The relations that obtain between words can take many forms. As a point of departure we may take the following diagram, based on the relationships that the word *heat* may contract with other words in the vocabulary.[35]

We may note that the words in group I are related to each other only formally by having similar symbols, that is, they sound alike. The words in group V are related to each other "extralinguistically," that is, in the physical world the things (referents) denoted by these words have

[32]*Course*, pp. 115–16. (We need not concern ourselves with Saussure's term, *signification*.)

[33]R. H. Robins, *General Linguistics: An Introductory Survey*, 2nd ed. (London: Longman, 1971), p. 63.

[34]Lyons, *Introduction*, p. 443 (although the label *sense relations* is used by me as it is by Lyons, we must point out again that the same is not true of the term *sense* itself). Instead of sense relations, Coseriu prefers the appealing term *lexematics* (*lexeme* = 'unit of lexical content'); we have, with some reluctance, not followed Coseriu, primarily because the term *lexeme* is used quite differently by Lyons.

[35]The diagram is adapted from Eugenio de Bustos Tovar, "Anotaciones sobre el campo asociativo de la palabra," in *Problemas y principios del estructuralismo lingüístico* (PRFE 16; Madrid: C.S.I.C., 1967), p. 152. For other possible ways of diagramming associative fields, cf. Riesener, *Der Stamm* עבד, p. 73, and Kedar, *Biblische Semantik*, p. 45.

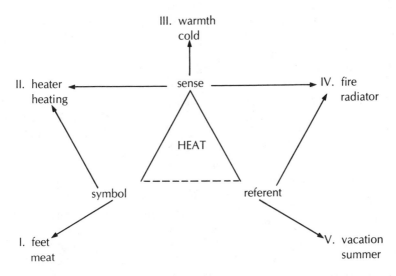

some kind of association. For our purposes we may dispense with both of these groups, even though formal and extralinguistic associations sometimes do have a bearing on semantic relations. The other three groups, however (and especially group III), contain words whose connection has a more direct semantic basis. In group II, the connection is both semantic *and* formal; group IV contains words that relate extralinguistically but whose semantic connection is more evident than in the case of group V. The words in group III are related exclusively on the basis of meaning, and so this set will become our major concern.

Now it should be pointed out that most semantic studies have been primarily concerned with the relationship between symbol (the word *heat*) and sense (the mental content evoked by that word).[36] Within this framework we can effectively distinguish between synonymy and polysemy.[37] Thus, synonymy could be understood as

---

[36]Cf. Ullmann, *Principles*, pp. 108ff.; and Leech, *Semantics*, p. 97. We shall not be concerned here with the further distinction between this branch of semantics, which in effect begins with the symbol and analyzes its sense(s), and another branch called *onomasiology*, which begins with semantic content and investigates the symbols used to designate that content (cf. Kronasser, *Handbuch*, pp. 69ff.). Usually, the semantic content that serves as the starting point of onomasiology is in fact a referent, not what we are calling sense.

[37]However, Hans-Martin Gauger argues cogently that the opposite of polysemy is not synonymy but what he calls *polymorphy*; see *Zum Problem der Synonyme* (TBL 9; Tübingen: no pub., 1972), pp. 133–34.

the phenomenon of *one* sense (the concept 'heat') with several symbols (the words *heat, warmth*); the subject of synonymy will occupy us again at various points. In contrast, polysemy would refer to the phenomenon of *one* symbol with several senses. We can however distinguish three gradations within polysemy. Sometimes we merely find a simple shift in application, as when the adjective *healthy* (normally used in combination with such a word as *climate*) is combined with, say, *complexion*; these shifts are so natural and frequent that dictionaries do not normally record them. Second, we may have a symbol with clearly different senses, as when *leaf* calls up not only the sense 'foliage,' but also 'sheet of paper'; a dictionary will normally list these as separate acceptations under one entry. Third, however, the senses may be so different that the speaker perceives two distinct symbols, in which case the dictionary should list them as two separate words; note the example of French *pas* mentioned earlier (p. 37). For this third category we have the term *homonymy* and therefore it is better to use the term *polysemy* only for the second category; however, it should be emphasized that the distinction between polysemy and homonymy is not always clear-cut.

Now our main interest, stemming from a structural understanding of the vocabulary, lies in the relationship, not between symbol and sense, but between the senses of different symbols. We shall therefore pay only incidental attention to polysemy-homonymy, a study that focuses on individual words. We cannot, however, dismiss the study of synonymy, for this field focuses on *groups* of related words. Furthermore, only exceptionally do different symbols call up exactly the same sense; that is, synonyms usually consist of symbols that have similar, but not identical, senses. In short, synonymy is more properly investigated from a structural perspective, which examines the relationship between the related senses of different symbols.

STYLE

Before proceeding any further, it will be profitable to introduce one more fundamental Saussurean distinction, that between *langue* ('language') and *parole* ('speech').[38] These two terms have become

[38]Cf. Lyons, *Semantics* 1:26ff., 239. Perhaps we should note here the view that dictionaries deal with *langue*, but commentaries with *parole*; see Gates, *Lexicographic Resources*, pp. 2–3. To the extent that this description is accurate, it may help to explain why lexicons sometimes create obstacles for interpretation. See below, chap. 6 and conclusions.

standard in linguistic literature and are intended to contrast the (abstract) linguistic system of a particular speech community with the actual utterances of individual speakers. We may illustrate most easily by recalling our previous comments on phonology. We mentioned that the sound represented by the letter *t* sometimes includes aspiration and sometimes it does not, a variation conditioned by the phonetic environment. As a matter of fact, very sensitive instruments can also detect a bewildering variety of different pronunciations by individual speakers. These phonetic variations belong to *parole*. A community of speakers, however, is able to ignore all of the nonsignificant variations and to abstract *one* phoneme /t/, which is then contrasted to a limited number of other phonemes. Phonemes are part of *langue*.

Now Saussure himself believed that linguistics is occupied only with *langue* rather than with *parole*, and in this judgment he was followed by most linguists.[39] During the past two decades, however, more and more attention has been devoted to the phenomenon of linguistic *variation*, particularly from the perspective of sociolinguistics.[40] It is probably no coincidence that during the same period a number of linguists have turned their attention to the study of style (whether social or literary), a subject that also focuses on group (or individual) variation.[41] Although it would be simplistic to equate *parole* and style, we need to recognize the fundamental connections that exist between them, particularly if individual style is under discussion.

The study of style, unfortunately, is plagued by many difficulties.[42] To begin with, one finds that most descriptions of individual styles are characterized by relatively vague, impressionistic terminology. How much do we really learn, for example, if we read that Paul's Greek is clumsy, flowing "straight out of the heart with impetuous

---

[39]Cf. Ullmann, *Principles*, p. 40; however, note Stern, *Meaning*, p. 17.

[40]See, e.g., William Labov, *Sociolinguistic Patterns* (Philadelphia: University of Pennsylvania Press, 1972), especially pp. 185–86.

[41]Cf. G. W. Turner, *Stylistics* (Harmondsworth: Penguin, 1973), pp. 7ff.; Nils Erik Enkvist, *Linguistic Stylistics* (JanL ser. crit. 5; The Hague: Mouton, 1973), pp. 16, 36ff., shows however the difficulties involved in identifying stylistics too simply with the study of *parole*. Cf. also above, chap. 2, n. 51.

[42]Some of the material that follows is taken from my article, "The Pauline Style as Lexical Choice: Γινώσκειν and Related Terms," in *Pauline Studies: Essays Presented to Professor F. F. Bruce*, ed. Donald A. Hagner and Murray J. Harris (Grand Rapids: Eerdmans, 1980), pp. 184–207. Used by permission of The Paternoster Press.

bubbling"?[43] For an extreme example, we may consider a certain writer who described Jonathan Swift's style as "hard, round, crystalline."[44] Subjective formulations and intuitive judgments, to be sure, often prove both valid and useful; indeed, we can hardly dispense with them in scientific research. But the intuitions of respectable scholars may lead to opposing conclusions. Might not linguistic science (itself hardly a panacea) provide certain objective checks?

Unsatisfactory descriptions, however, account for only part of the problem. Sooner or later one becomes aware that the very *concept* of style is surrounded by considerable ambiguity. The word has become so vague that a certain author decided to use it, he tells us, precisely because it would not bind him to a specific task![45] One is not altogether surprised to find writers who wish to deny the existence of style itself.[46]

For our purposes, however, we may draw a rough distinction between the patterns given by a language—that is, those rules, violations of which are regarded as "unacceptable" by the linguistic community—and the variability allowed by language, with *style* covering the latter of these. This unsophisticated concept of style as "what grammar leaves out"[47] may not do as a scientific description, but it is all we need here. Thus, *The executives ate tomorrow* is unacceptable,[48] since the rules of language require a future tense for the verb; that much is determined by language for the speaker. However, the language does not necessarily determine whether the speaker should say *will eat, shall eat,* or *are going to eat,* nor whether he must use the verb *to eat* rather than *to dine.* While there may be certain restrictions even in these matters, depending on the situation, we may say generally that here the speaker has a *choice*—and choice, as we

[43]Ulrich von Wilamowitz-Moellendorff, *Die griechische und lateinische Literatur und Sprache,* 2. Aufl. (KG 1:8; Berlin: Teubner, 1907), p. 159.

[44]Quoted by Louis T. Milic, A *Quantitative Approach to the Style of Jonathan Swift* (SEL 23; The Hague: Mouton, 1967), p. 30.

[45]Ibid., p. 40.

[46]Cf. Bennison Gray, *Style: The Problem and Its Solution* (DePrLit ser. mai. 3; The Hague: Mouton, 1969). Note also in this connection Talbot J. Taylor, *Linguistic Theory and Structural Stylistics* (Language and Communication Library 2; Oxford: Pergamon Press, 1980).

[47]Cf. Turner, *Stylistics,* p. 19.

[48]I am here using the term *unacceptable* in the somewhat technical sense it has in contemporary linguistics. Certain forms (e.g., *ain't*) may be socially unacceptable in certain situations, but this is a different issue.

shall see in chapter 6, is perhaps the fundamental concept of style.

Now style cuts across all levels of language: phonology, vocabulary, syntax, and discourse. Naturally, we are only interested in lexical style, but it is important to note that the vocabulary offers the greatest degree of choice to the speaker. Therefore, much of what we shall have to say in the next chapters properly belongs to stylistics. Further, we shall often be concerned with a matter that has serious exegetical significance, namely, deciding whether biblical writers have used particular words for semantic or for stylistic purposes.[49]

---

[49]It is only with reluctance that we shall contrast these two terms, *stylistic* and *semantic*. The distinction is adopted here purely for reasons of convenience; surely stylistic elements (e.g., emotive) should be regarded as part of meaning. Cf. Lyons, *Semantics* 2:613ff. On the relationship between linguistic and stylistic studies, see Ullmann, *Meaning and Style*, pp. 40–63.

SUMMARY OF CHAPTER 5

RELATIONS BASED ON SIMILARITY

Words may be semantically related because of similar or opposite meanings. We may distinguish three types under the former category.

Overlapping Relations (proper synonymy). Statements about synonymy often lack precision and so this section begins with some important distinctions. A number of scholars have sought to classify types of synonyms in detail, but the following three categories are basic: objective, emotive, sociological.

Contiguous Relations (improper synonymy). Although the sense of *walk* and *run* are similar, they are not interchangeable and therefore not to be regarded as proper synonyms.

Inclusive Relations (hyponymy). Some words are semantically similar only in the sense that one (e.g., *flower*) includes the other *(rose)*. Vocabularies contain large networks of such hierarchical patterns.

RELATIONS BASED ON OPPOSITENESS

The study of opposite terms has attracted the attention of logicians, but a simple linguistic classification consists of a twofold distinction.

Binary Relations (antonymy). Most sets of opposites come in pairs and these may be graded (those that indicate comparison) or nongraded. Nongraded opposites can be further grouped into complementary and noncomplementary.

Multiple Relations (incompatibility). These consist of oppositeness when it applies to more than two words.

COMPONENTIAL ANALYSIS

Phonologists use the concepts of distinctive feature and markedness for a detailed analysis of sound systems. These notions have been applied to the vocabulary by focusing on the sense components of words. Although controversial, this method has made an important contribution to the study of lexical meaning.

5 Sense Relations

The central observation of our previous chapter was that lexical meaning—which cannot be reduced to the concept of denotation—consists largely in the sets of (structural) relations obtaining between the senses of different symbols. We must now inquire into the nature of those relations by noting their various types.

Our most fundamental distinction, borrowed from phonological theory (see above, p. 110), is that between *paradigmatic* and *syntagmatic* relations. In the sentence, *The man is working slowly*, *man* is in paradigmatic relation with *woman*, *boy*, etc.; *working* with *running*, *walking*, etc; *slowly* with *fast*, *well*, etc. On the other hand, *man* is in syntagmatic relation with the other words in the sentence (e.g., *the*, *is*). To put it differently, we may say that words are in paradigmatic relation insofar as they can occupy the same slot in a particular context (or syntagm); they are in syntagmatic relation if they can enter into combinations *that form* a context (or syntagm). We should note that paradigmatic sense relations exploit the opposition[1] or contrast existing between words and thus may be referred to as *constrasting relations*, while √ syntagmatic sense relations may be called *combinatory relations*.[2]

[1]Strictly speaking, however, syntagmatic relations also involve opposition; the concept of *opposition* is an unusually rich one and will occupy us again. Note the broad discussion by C. K. Ogden, *Opposition: A Linguistic and Psychological Analysis* (Bloomington: Indiana University Press, 1967, originally published in 1932).

[2]"The theoretically important point is that the structure of the language-system depends at every level upon the complementary principles of selection and combination. . . . We identify units by virtue of their potentiality of occurrence in certain syntagms; and the selection of one element rather than another produces a different

Finally, it should be noted that the syntagmatic combinations play the determinative role in language.[3] While the paradigmatic relations alert us to the potential for lexical expression in a particular language, this potential becomes "actualized" only when words are in fact combined with one another by a specific speaker or writer to form sentences.[4] For this reason, we shall devote the present chapter to a study of paradigmatic relations and consider the syntagmatic perspective in the concluding chapter, "Determining Meaning." The reader should note, however, that this procedure renders the present chapter dependent on the next—*what is said here cannot be understood independently of the material discussed subsequently.*

RELATIONS BASED ON SIMILARITY

We may introduce this section by noting the following sentences:

John bought a *pretty/beautiful* car.

Mary *walks/runs* two miles every day.

I gave her some *flowers/roses.*

It should be immediately apparent that *pretty* is in paradigmatic relation to *beautiful; walks,* to *runs;* and *flowers,* to *roses.* It is also clear that these relations are distinct from the following three:

John is quite *short/tall.*

Mary's sister is *married/single.*

I own a *red/green* bicycle.

resultant syntagm. To describe a language-system is to specify both the membership of the paradigmatic sets and the possibilities of combination of one set with another in well-focused syntagms" (Lyons, *Semantics* 1:241).

[3] For a different perspective, see Paul Pupier, "A propos de la situation récente des études de sémantique en Allemagne," *Le français moderne* 39 (1971): 56–71; in the conclusion of the article, the author errs by claiming that syntagmatic semantics should be determined by paradigmatic facts. I admit with Lyons, however, that "we must not go from the one extreme of saying that the collocations of a lexeme are determined by its meaning or meanings (where meaning is defined independently of syntagmatic considerations) to the other extreme of defining the meaning of a lexeme to be no more than a set of its collocations" (*Semantics* 1:265).

[4] Such a formulation, which admittedly is lacking in precision, seems to bring together, rather smoothly, the two competing approaches to style suggested by Ch. Bally and L. Spitzer; see S. Ullmann, *Style in the French Novel* (Cambridge: University Press, 1957), pp. 4–5. Note also the views of V. V. Vinogradov, reported by Enkvist, *Linguistic Stylistics,* p. 38. The classification of sense relations in the present chapter owes much to Lyons and Nida, but a more detailed and rigorous attempt is that by Coseriu, "Vers une typologie des champs lexicaux," *CahLex* 27 (1975 no. 2): 30–51, also in his *Principios,* pp. 211–42.

In the latter three sentences we perceive each pair as consisting of opposites; that is, the paradigmatic relations exemplified by these sets are based on oppositeness, a topic that will be discussed later in this chapter. The relations exemplified in the first three sentences are based on semantic similarity.

OVERLAPPING RELATIONS (proper synonymy)

The first point to be stressed has to do with the symbol-sense-referent triangle; all of the relationships that concern us in this chapter ✻ *obtain only between senses*, not between symbols or referents. Thus, while we could, for the sake of convenience, say that πνεῦμα and ψυχή may be synonymous, we are not in fact referring to the words themselves (symbols) but to one of the senses of πνεῦμα and one of the senses of ψυχή; the sense 'corpse' for ψυχή (Lev. 19:28 LXX) is obviously not synonymous with *any* of the senses of πνεῦμα. Even more important, particularly when dealing with synonyms, is the need to avoid confusion between senses and referents. For example, take this sentence: *The "beloved disciple" and the author of the fourth Gospel are/are not synonymous.* This is a rather blatant example of sloppy word usage, but it appears frequently, even in serious works.[5] For the sake of clarity we should say, *The "beloved disciple" and the author of the fourth Gospel do/do not refer to (denote) the same person.* We can then reserve the term *synonym(ous)* for words that overlap in sense or (if we use a distributive model) in the sets of contexts where they may occur.

Our sample sentence, however, raises another issue that contributes to confusion when dealing with synonyms. When a speaker states that two terms are synonymous, he or she may intend to say merely that the terms are similar enough to be interchanged in some contexts, or that the terms are identical, no differences being discoverable (whether in a particular context or generally). The issue here is *not* whether absolute synonyms exist,[6] but whether the term *synonym*

[5]See the incisive discussion by Gibson, *Biblical Semantic Logic*, pp. 16–17, 199ff.

[6]This is a problem to which semanticists have devoted considerable energy. Cf. Ullmann, *Semantics*, pp. 141–42; differently, Lyons, *Introduction*, pp. 427–28. Much of the discussion, in my opinion, has not been productive. For the practical purposes of this book, we may assert that no two words are fully interchangeable in *all* the contexts where they may appear. However, we shall argue in the next chapter that distinctions between *any* synonyms may be fully neutralized in *some* contexts.

should be reserved for occasions when identity of meaning obtains. For example, in the sentence, *The words πνεῦμα and ψυχή are synonymous in 1 Thessalonians 5:23*, the speaker intends to say that in this particular passage there is no discernible difference between the terms—they overlap completely. Since this type of statement is extremely common and thus sanctioned by usage, attempting to stamp it out would be useless. However, such comments normally deal with referents, and thus it would be advisable to use different language, such as *They have the same referent* or *They refer to the same entity* (if the statement does not deal with referents, then one could say, for example, *Here the words have an identical connotation*). The point is that the particular *senses* of πνεῦμα and ψυχή in view (the immaterial aspect of man) are *always* "synonymous."[7] More precisely, it is *always* true that the relationship between *these* senses of πνεῦμα and ψυχή is of such a nature that the words may be used interchangeably in *some* contexts.

If these distinctions appear unnecessarily subtle, we need to remember that when scholars (biblical or otherwise) study synonyms, they do so precisely with a view to *discriminating* between them. Archbishop Trench put it this way:

> But what, you may ask, is meant when, comparing certain words with one another, we affirm of them that they are synonyms? We imply that, with great and essential resemblances of meaning, they have at the same time small, subordinate, and partial differences—these differences being such as either originally, and on the strength of their etymology, were born with them; or differences which they have by usage acquired; or such as, though nearly or altogether latent now, they are capable of receiving at the hands of wise and discreet masters of language. Synonyms are thus words of like significance in the main; with a large extent of ground which they occupy in common, but also with something of their own, private and peculiar, which they do not share with one another.[8]

[7] Part of our difficulty lies in the fact that, whereas the terms *synonym* and *synonymy* are normally used in the context of related words that must be differentiated, the adjective *synonymous* is used when the speaker wishes to deny the existence of any difference.

[8] Trench, *On the Study of Words*, pp. 248–49.

And in what became a standard hermeneutical manual at the turn of the century, Milton S. Terry argues that synonyms

> afford the biblical scholar a broad and most interesting field of study. It is a spiritual as well as an intellectual discipline to discriminate sharply between synonymous terms of Holy Writ, and trace the diverging lines of thought, and the far-reaching suggestions which often arise therefrom. . . . The exact import and the discriminative usage of words are all-important to the biblical interpreter.[9]

While these statements require a number of qualifications (see below, chap. 6), no one would contest their basic thrust; any interpreter of literature must develop those skills necessary for distinguishing between similar words. Can we, therefore, be more specific regarding *types* of overlapping relations? That is, can we construct a scheme that accounts for all the ways in which synonyms might differ? A number of semanticists have studied this question and proposed useful classifications. Unfortunately, the variety of possible distinctions can prove rather baffling.

We could take, for example, W. E. Collinson's scheme.[10] Collinson uses nine criteria: generality *(refuse/reject)*, intensity *(repudiate/refuse)*, emotivity *(reject/decline)*, approbation *(thrifty/economical)*, technicality *(decease/death)*, literary level *(passing/death)*, colloquialism *(turn down/refuse)*, geographical variation (Scots *flesher/butcher*), child-talk *(daddy/father)*. If we then turn to S. I. Hayakawa's informal arrangement,[11] we encounter approximately the same number of types, but these types do not always correspond to Collinson's. Thus:

> Some groups of words describe the same actions, but imply different relationships among the parties concerned. We *accompany* our equals; we *attend* or *follow* those to whom we

[9]Milton S. Terry, *Biblical Hermeneutics: A Treatise on the Interpretation of the Old and New Testaments*, rev. ed. (New York: Eaton and Mains, 1890), p. 100.

[10]W. E. Collinson, "Comparative Synonymics: Some Principles and Illustrations," *Transactions of the Philological Society* (1939), pp. 54–77; summarized in Ullmann, *Semantics*, pp. 142–43.

[11]S. I. Hayakawa, *Use the Right Word: A Modern Guide to Synonyms and Related Words* (n.p.: The Reader's Digest Association, 1968), pp. vi-vii. Cf. also F. R. Palmer, *Semantics: A New Outline* (Cambridge: University Press, 1976), pp. 60ff.

are subordinate; we *conduct* those who need guidance, *escort* those who need protection, and *chaperone* those who need supervision. . . .

Or again, note the following group: "*Feminine, effeminate, womanly,* and *womanish* are much alike in referring to female characteristics, but the second applies only to males, and then in a derogatory sense."

But that is not all. When studying specific groups of synonyms, one often encounters distinctions that seem to resist classification. For example, Trench's discussion of New Testament words for 'servant' suggests that three of the terms are distinguished on the basis of the relationship between the servant and the person served—δοῦλος (servility), οἰκέτης (familiarity), θεράπων (noble attitude)—one focuses on the activity (διάκονος) and another one on the official character of the servant (ὑπηρέτης).[12] An even more complicated instance is that of Hebrew terms for 'sin.' Girdlestone's treatment[13] implies that some of the terms could be brought together as focusing on the consequences of the action *(ra', 'awen),* others on the nature of the act *(ma'al, paša'),* still others on what we may call "accompanying circumstances" *('amal, 'ašam).* One might be tempted to conclude that there are as many *types* of synonyms as there are *sets* of synonyms![14]

On the other hand, Ullmann, arguing that even Collinson's scheme is unnecessarily subtle, seems to suggest a basic twofold dis-

---

[12]R. C. Trench, *Synonyms of the New Testament* (Grand Rapids: Eerdmans, 1963; reprint of 1880 ed.), pp. 30ff. We are not at this point concerned with the validity of these particular distinctions; how we arrive at such conclusions is the subject of the following chapter. A recent and useful work intended to supplement Trench is Stewart Custer, *A Treasury of New Testament Synonyms* (Greenville, S.C.: Bob Jones University Press, 1975). Note also George Ricker Berry, *A Dictionary of New Testament Greek Synonyms* (Grand Rapids: Zondervan, 1979, originally published in 1897, to which some helpful indexes have been added).

[13]Robert Baker Girdlestone, *Synonyms of the Old Testament: Their Bearing on Christian Doctrine* (Grand Rapids: Eerdmans, n.d.; reprint of 1897 ed.), chap. 6.

[14]No doubt the real nature of the problem lies in the difficulty of differentiating clearly between synonyms. Note Otto Jespersen, *Growth and Structure of the English Language,* 9th ed. (Oxford: Blackwell, 1938), p. 126: "It will be seen that it is not always easy to draw a line or to determine exactly the different shades of meaning attached to each word; indeed, a comparison of the definitions given in various essays on synonyms and in dictionaries, and especially a comparison of these definitions with the use as actually found in various writers, will show that it is *in many cases a hopeless task* to assign definite spheres of signification to these words. Sometimes the only real difference is that one term is preferred in certain collocations and another in others" (my emphasis). Cf. also Louw, *Semantics,* pp. 62–63.

tinction between objective and emotive differences,[15] and there is some value in this simplicity. However, the sociolinguistic advances of recent years force us to add at least a third category based on sociological distinctions (including formality, geographical variation, et al.).

Before concluding this section, we should note an important difference between modern languages such as English and ancient languages such as Hebrew or Greek. The enormous synonymic resources available to English are primarily due to the large influx of foreign words, especially French (after the Norman Conquest) and classical (with the revival of Greek and Latin learning). This is such a well-known phenomenon as to require no illustration.[16] But one needs to emphasize that the loan words attested for Hebrew and Greek, in addition to being very few in number, are not of such a nature as to provide synonyms (e.g., πάσχα is not a synonym for anything previously existing in Greek). In view of this fact, biblical interpreters should perhaps exercise caution when they see analogies between ancient and modern stylistic techniques.

CONTIGUOUS RELATIONS (improper synonymy)

All speakers of English recognize that the senses of *walk* and *run* are similar. Are they synonyms? We should note that Hayakawa treats *skip* and *hop* together as synonyms that need to be differentiated and gives *crawl* and *walk* as antonyms.[17] Interestingly, Eugene Nida lists *walk*, *run*, *hop*, *skip*, and *crawl* to illustrate a meaning relationship that he calls *contiguity*. He argues that these five words

> share the features of movement by an animate being, using the limbs; but the number of limbs, the order of movement, and the relation of the limbs to the supporting surface involve clearly definable contrasts.[18]

He illustrates the distinction between overlapping and contiguity thus:

[15]Ullmann, *Semantics*, p. 143.

[16]All histories of the English language devote considerable space to this subject. Note also Ullmann, *Semantics*, pp. 145ff., with regard to double and triple scale patterns (for the latter, compare native *time*, French *age*, Latin *epoch*).

[17]*Use the Right Word*, p. 558.

[18]*Componential Analysis*, p. 18. Louw (*Semantics*, p. 64) considers contiguity "the most important [relation], since it involves almost any word in its relation to other words."

overlapping   contiguity

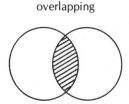   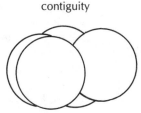

We shall follow Nida's approach; using the term *improper synonymy*, however, helps us to distinguish as clearly as possible between the two sense relations discussed so far. Now contiguous relations are most apparent in the case of referential terms, that is, terms whose meaning is best treated by pointing to the concrete extralinguistic entities to which they refer. Furthermore, no adequate explanation of contiguity can be attempted until we have discussed componential analysis, at the end of this chapter. We may, however, illustrate this relation from the biblical material by pointing to ἱμάτιον ('upper garment') and χιτών ('under garment'), treated together by Trench.[19]

If we then define overlapping relations as those that exist between words that may be interchanged in some contexts, contiguous relations must be understood as those existing between words that, while sharing some semantic features, *cannot* ever be interchanged (a speaker might use *skip* and *hop* interchangeably, but this would reflect an inaccurate use of the terms).

INCLUSIVE RELATIONS (hyponymy)

We stretch the notion of similarity to its limits when we say that it is the basis of the relationship between the senses of *flower* and *rose*. We deal with this relationship in the present section for the sake of simplicity, though it probably deserves a category all its own. Strictly speaking, then, it is not quite adequate to suggest that 'flower' and 'rose' are similar; we need to be more specific and state that 'flower' *includes* 'rose.' We may follow Lyons[20] in using the term *hyponymy* for this relation and in saying that 'rose' is a *hyponym* of 'flower,' that 'flower' is the *superordinate* of 'rose,' and that 'rose' and 'tulip' are *cohyponyms*.

[19]*Synonyms*, p. 184. We should note that ἱμάτιον can be used more generally of any garment, but this should be treated as a different acceptation (or sense) of the word. To put it differently, while the *narrower* sense of ἱμάτιον is contiguous to the sense of χιτών, the *general* sense of the former is inclusive (see below) of the sense of the latter.

[20]*Semantics* 1:291 (on the ambiguity of the term *inclusion*, see his *Introduction*, p. 454).

Now a number of points need to be made concerning this relationship. In the first place, we must distinguish between hyponymy and synonymy. The distinction becomes clearest by using Nida's diagrams:

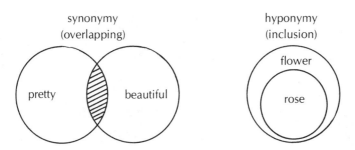

synonymy
(overlapping)

pretty   beautiful

hyponymy
(inclusion)

flower

rose

This representation helps us understand that while synonyms are *mutually* interchangeable in some contexts, the same is not true of a superordinate and its hyponym(s). *Flower* can take the place of *rose* in many sentences (ignoring stylistic considerations for a minute), whereas *rose* can take the place of *flower* only in sentences where another type of flower is not meant.

Second, a superordinate and its hyponym(s) are only a set in a larger network of hierarchical associations. For example:

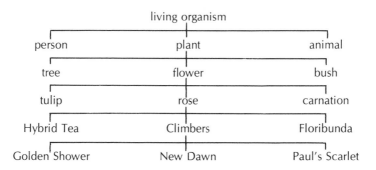

living organism

person   plant   animal

tree   flower   bush

tulip   rose   carnation

Hybrid Tea   Climbers   Floribunda

Golden Shower   New Dawn   Paul's Scarlet

It is an interesting question, but one that does not seriously concern us here, whether the whole vocabulary can be reduced to some such design.[21] Suffice it to recognize that most words we encounter probably belong to some comparable subset.

[21]Cf. ibid., 1:295–301.

Third, polysemous words may belong in more than one level of a hierarchical pattern. The generic sense of *man* (nowadays not highly regarded) belongs to a different level from that of its more common use:

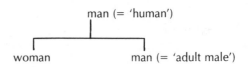

Similarly, the word *cat*, most commonly used of the 'domestic cat,' can also be used generically:

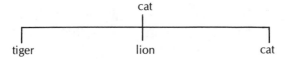

In our botanical example we face something of a conflict between ordinary and scientific terms. The more exact scientific taxonomy would require us to put the word *rose* (when the reference is to the rose order) higher up in the diagram (as including not only roses, but blackberries, hawthorns, etc.)—indeed, it would require us to restructure the diagram rather drastically.

Fourth, we must recognize the possibility of "holes in the pattern" on the one hand and duplicate superordinates on the other. An example of the latter is *feline* as an equivalent of the generic sense of *cat*. An example of the former is:

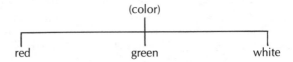

Here we need to use a noun rather than an adjective as the superordinate, though this limitation seems less a lexical deficiency than a necessity in the very nature of the case.[22]

[22]For a full discussion, see ibid., 1:301–5.

Fifth, cohyponyms themselves may be either overlapping or contiguous:

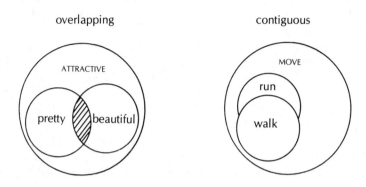

overlapping   contiguous

They may also be opposites:

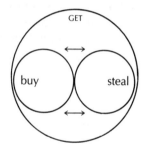

RELATIONS BASED ON OPPOSITENESS

All speakers of English recognize that *short* and *tall* are semantically related, but the nature of this relationship is certainly not one of similarity but of opposition. Here, unfortunately, we meet a terminological problem, for the term *opposition* is used broadly of all kinds of contrasts; we may even say that *pretty* and *beautiful* are in opposition insofar as they may be contrasted. We shall therefore use the less ambiguous term *oppositeness* here; further, we shall speak of *pretty* and *beautiful* as contrasting terms, while referring to *short* and *tall* as opposites (or contraries). It may be useful to note incidentally that the relationship now being considered can be described as one of exclusion, for the semantic area (or, viewed differently, the set of contexts) covered by one term excludes that covered by its opposite.

Now the task of identifying and classifying opposite terms (contraries) has fascinated logicians for centuries—"Aristotle himself was obsessed by the problem of opposition which appears in different forms in all his work."[23] As Ogden goes on to point out, people who have not reflected on the problem may well use the term *antonymy* to designate all examples of oppositeness, but it would not take long to persuade them that these examples are of very different types. Thus, while *black* and *white* are the extremes of a "scale," *hot* and *cold* refer to two sides of a "cut" (that is, we may use *hot* not in reference to an extreme but simply to one side of some neutral point). *Right* and *left* are directional opposites, whereas *before* and *after* are temporal (really a metaphor based on spatial direction). *Visible* and *invisible* are opposites by negation; *man* and *brute*, by negation of a definition (*man* must first be defined as 'rational creature'). Another instructive example is *kind*, which may be opposed, not only to *unkind*, but also to the extreme *cruel* and to the indifferent *not-kind*.

These distinctions and many others are interesting and useful for certain purposes, but they are not primarily linguistic—nor are they always necessary for proper biblical interpretation. Rather than attempt an exhaustive classification, therefore, we shall consider two major types and a few subtypes.

BINARY RELATIONS (antonymy)

Most sets of opposites, though not all, come in pairs. This phenomenon is so characteristic of, and fundamental to, lexical structure that some scholars have proposed reducing all lexical contrasts to binary sets.[24] For their part, general semanticists see in this phenomenon the root of "two-valued orientation," that is, the neat but simplistic compartmentalization of experience whereby everything is seen as either black or white, good or bad.[25]

Binary relations may be further subdivided into *graded* and *nongraded*. Graded opposites, such as *taller/shorter*, always indicate comparison: X *is taller than* Y. Nongraded opposites, such as *married/single*, do not permit comparison. *X *is more married than* Y. The point to note is that many binary opposites are not *explicitly* graded yet belong in this category. The statement *John is tall* gives the illusion of

[23]Ogden, *Opposition*, p. 21.
[24]Cf. Lyons, *Semantics* 1:322ff.
[25]Cf. Geoffrey Leech, *Semantics* (Baltimore: Penguin, 1974), pp. 38ff.

absolute value,[26] but as a matter of fact it *implies* comparison with some norm; the statement means one thing if John is four years old, but quite another if he is an adult. In other words, opposites such as *tall/short, good/bad,* and others are implicitly graded.

Nongraded opposites are of many kinds, but the most important distinction is between sets that are complementary and sets that are not.[27] In a complementary set, such as *married/single,* the assertion of one term implies the negation of the other. *Mary's sister is married* implies *Mary's sister is not single;* perhaps more important, the negation of one implies the assertion of the other: *Mary's sister is not single* implies *Mary's sister is married.* In contrast, we may note the distinction between *before* and *after.* These two terms are noncomplimentary and in many specific cases the assertion of one implies the negation of the other: *He came before lunch* usually (but not necessarily) implies *He did not come after lunch;* however, *He did not come after lunch* by no means implies *He came before lunch.* The looseness that characterizes noncomplementary sets can also be illustrated with *give/take:* an utterance containing *give* implies the notion of taking, but the action of taking by no means implies that someone has given. Among noncomplementary sets we have a special subgroup of conversives,[28] including such diverse pairs as *husband/wife* (kinship roles), *doctor/patient* (social roles), *come/go* (directional), *above/below* (spatial), *buy/sell, tie/untie, alienate/reconcile, killed/was killed.*

In some respects, relations between binary opposites may appear to be less significant than the ones previously discussed. Indeed, Nida argues that they are less valuable for semantic analysis. However, two comments are in order. First, Nida himself points out that these opposites help us greatly

> in sorting out the diverse meanings of polysemic lexical units (i.e., those having multiple meanings), since complementary contrasts highlight very quickly some of the important differences in domains. The fact that the form *good* stands in

---

[26]As pointed out by Sapir in a 1944 article in *Philosophy of Science,* reprinted in *Selected Writings of Edward Sapir in Language, Culture and Personality,* ed. David G. Mandelbaum (Berkeley: University of California, 1963), pp. 122–49. On p. 130 he draws some psychological conclusions of the type used by general semanticists.

[27]Nida (p. 107) uses the term *complementary* for all binary oppositions. I follow Lyons, *Semantics* (1:271–72), whose usage conforms to traditional logical categories.

[28]Cf. Lyons, *Semantics* 1:279–80. Nida (p. 109) distinguishes conversives *(buy/sell)* from reversives *(tie/untie).*

contrast to both *bad* and *poor* indicates immediately that the semantic unit *good* must belong to at least two different domains. . . .[29]

Second, we noted earlier the significance of opposite pairs in lexical structure and the view that this fact may reflect, in some way, a psychological need to polarize experience. As we shall see in the next chapter, a careful consideration of antonymy can prove most helpful in lexical-exegetical decisions.

MULTIPLE RELATIONS (incompatibility)

Only a few words are necessary here. We have already pointed out that the relation of oppositeness may be understood as exclusion of senses. Now if this exclusion applies to more than two terms, we have incompatibility. Thus the semantic area covered by *blue* excludes that covered by *yellow*, *red*, *black*, etc. Clearly, this is a relationship between species, or cohyponyms.

COMPONENTIAL ANALYSIS

In the previous chapter (see pp. 109–10) we noted that much of the inspiration to understand the vocabulary in structural fashion comes from the strides made in phonological analysis. It will now be necessary for us to consider briefly some further details of phonological theory before describing componential analysis.

The phonologist is not satisfied to say that /p/ and /b/ are contrasting phonemes. He wishes further to describe as accurately as possible the nature of that contrast.

The method used consists of identifying the *distinctive features* of these phonemes. We can say that /b/ is a consonant (rather than a vowel), that it is labial (articulated at the lips, rather than at the teeth, the palate, etc.), that it is occlusive (the air is momentarily blocked), and that it is voiced (the vocal chords vibrate when it is pronounced). The phoneme /p/ shares all these features except the last one: it is an occlusive, labial, *unvoiced* consonant. With the use of plus and minus signs, a useful notation has been devised to map our consonantal contrasts:

[29]Nida, pp. 109–10.

	p	b	t	d	m	n
nasal	−	−	−	−	+	+
voiced	−	+	−	+	+	+
occlusive	+	+	+	+	−	−
labial	+	+	−	−	+	−
dental	−	−	+	+	−	+

A further, very rich, concept suggested by the use of plus or minus signs is that of *markedness*. Phonologists could say, for instance, that in English the pair /p/ – /b/ consists of a marked member (/b/, voiced) and an unmarked member (/p/, unvoiced). One may use this analysis to compare the structure of different languages. For example, if we focus on occlusive labials, we note that English has a simple binary contrast: /p/ – /b/. Since aspiration was a phonemic feature in Ancient Greek, we find a threefold contrast:

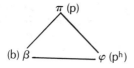

In some Oriental languages, aspiration is also phonemic in the voiced member, thus:

Now many structural semanticists believe that this approach is more or less directly applicable to the study of the vocabulary. We may illustrate the principle simply by considering the terms *chair, couch,* and *stool*.[30]

---

[30]This illustration (in more detailed form) has been used especially by B. Pottier, one of the pioneers of the method. Cf. his "Vers une sémantique moderne," *TLL* 2 (1964): 107–37. A very ambitious (but unnecessarily complicated) system is that developed by A. Greimas, *La sémantique structurale* (Paris: Larousse, 1965). In America, a similar approach has been used by anthropologists; see the early articles by W. H. Goodenough and F. G. Lounsbury in *Lg* 32 (1956): 158–216. This system has been broadened and developed most fully by Nida, *Componential Analysis*, especially chap. 2.

	chair	couch	stool
used for sitting	+	+	+
includes a back	+	+	−
seats more than one person	−	+	−

We may use another common example:

	man	woman	boy	girl
human	+	+	+	+
adult	+	+	−	−
male	+	−	+	−

Semanticists call 'human,' 'adult,' and 'male' *components of meaning* or *sense components* (equivalent to the distinctive features in phonemes). The thorough analysis of such components[31] is thought by many to be *the* goal of structural semantics.

Unfortunately, some problems arise in connection with this method. Perhaps the most serious question—at least with regard to the goals and principles informing the present work—is the emphasis of the method on referential categories. Componential analysis appears most convincing when illustrated with examples such as the ones above, but in these examples the analysis seems to consist of a description of external (rather than linguistic) features. Nida states that his componential analysis applies only to *referential meaning*, namely, meaning "based on the relation between the lexical unit and the referent"—again, "meaning based on cognitive, extralinguistic factors."[32] To be sure, he insists that meaning cannot be identified with the referent or "denotatum"; rather, "meaning consists of that particular structured bundle of cognitive features, associated with the lexical unit, which make possible the designation of all the denotata by the lexical unit in question."[33] Still, it would seem impossible for him to avoid what would be basically an encyclopedic approach to lexicology.

[31]That is, "determination of content," in the terminology of Coseriu and Geckeler ("Linguistics and Semantics," p. 129).

[32]Nida, pp. 25, 27.

[33]Ibid, p. 26; cf. also p. 203. I should also point out that Coseriu, who insists as strongly as anyone that designation (the relation of symbols to referents) cannot be a part of structural semantics, nevertheless subscribes to componential analysis (cf. Coseriu and Geckeler, p. 146–47). It appears to me that further clarification is needed.

Perhaps more fundamental is the criticism that different possible analyses of the material have been proposed and there are no means of choosing between them. Lyons points out:

> . . . it has yet to be demonstrated that sense-components of the kind that linguists have tended to invoke in their analysis of the meaning of lexemes play any part whatsoever in the production and interpretation of language-utterances; and if the allegedly more basic sense-components cannot be shown ✓ to have any psychological validity, much of the initial attraction of componential analysis disappears.[34]

Given the controversial nature of the topic, we shall not pursue componential analysis in any detail. However, it would be foolhardy to deny the contributions of this method. In some respects, the method simply formalizes the way in which we often distinguish terms from one another. If we say that *advise* and *notify* connote "more or less formal announcements," but that *notify* in addition "carries a note of urgency,"[35] we are in effect calling attention to sense components. As occasion permits, therefore, I shall make reference to the method. The question that concerns us here, nonetheless, is more fundamental, namely, how do we discover these sense components in the first place? More simply put, how do we go about establishing the meaning of words?

---

[34]*Semantics* 1:333. Lyons goes on to argue that even where componential analysis "looks relatively convincing, it leaves unexplained at least as much as it succeeds in explaining."

[35]Hayakawa, *Use the Right Word*, p. 306.

SUMMARY OF CHAPTER 6

CONTEXT

Syntagmatic Sense Relations. An analysis of the proper combinations of a word is an essential element of semantic description.

Literary Context. The concept should be widened to include more than a specific paragraph or section. Even the nature of the document is part of the literary context.

Context of Situation. A number of scholars have strongly emphasized the importance of the external surroundings within which language functions.

Other Levels of Context. Documents and situations subsequent to those of the original writing—including the presuppositions of the modern-day interpreter—form part of the total context.

AMBIGUITY

Deliberate Ambiguity. This technique is especially common in poetry, but we may have some examples of it in the Gospel of John and elsewhere.

Unintended Ambiguity. Occasionally we find it difficult to decide on the meaning of a specific word because we cannot determine with certainty the original context. In these cases we may appeal to the principle of maximal redundancy, which is based on data from communication engineering.

Contextual Circles. The closer contextual levels should take priority in interpretation, but broader theological concerns are not to be set aside in the exegetical process.

SYNONYMY

Lexical Choice. This concept is commonly used in discussions of style; evidence from communication theory has helped to clarify its significance.

Lexical Fields. A recognition of the importance of choice leads us to consider those groups of semantically related words from which a writer can choose the one most appropriate to the context. A number of biblical scholars have begun to exploit the potential of this approach.

Style. The various principles so far discussed are now applied to Paul's use of verbs sharing the lexical field of 'to know.'

6 Determining Meaning

The title of this chapter is not only presumptuous—it is also likely to raise unrealistic expectations, as though mastery of the contents of this book meant the end of uncertainty in the study of words. The truth of the matter is that, at least in some cases, our discussion will lead to *greater* uncertainty; I take comfort, however, in the fact that such a development could be interpreted, if we may trust Socrates, as the clearest proof of progress.

We may illustrate the nature of our dilemma in a very simple but practical way as follows. A student sits down to exegete a New Testament passage, in time wonders about the precise meaning of a particular word, and then looks it up in Bauer's *Lexicon* for guidance. Depending on his or her degree of sophistication, the student may simply adopt the information as authoritative or else weigh it as one suggestion among others. In either case, our student will eventually realize that while we are in some sense dependent on Bauer for our exegesis, Bauer himself was priorly dependent on the work of exegesis. This problem is but one more manifestation of the phenomenon we often dignify with the phrase, "the hermeneutical circle."

How did Bauer then come up with his meanings? We fool ourselves if we do not admit that, by and large, he got them from previous dictionaries. The earliest lexicographers in turn got their meanings from existing "implicit dictionaries"—information stored in grammar books and literal translations or simply preserved as a part of bilingual oral tradition. I wish to emphasize this somewhat obvious point to disabuse any readers of the tacit belief (possibly shared by some lexicographers) that dictionary makers approach their work completely from scratch, that is, without assuming knowledge of the meaning of any words.[1] No, their work consists largely of *refining* established knowledge and identifying a very small proportion of new words (or new meanings for old words).

That, to be sure, is no small task, as we shall soon discover, but such an appreciation of the lexicographical task helps us gain a better perspective on at least two issues. First, the problematic material comprises only a very small proportion of lexicographical work. I do not of course intend to deny that a number of unresolved questions—and fundamental questions at that—continue to plague the enterprise as a whole. Still, we need to recognize that the vast majority of lexical items in the vocabulary of most languages do not present a problem of *identification.* Second, as is generally recognized, lexicographers determine meaning by observing word usage, by examining contexts. This second point makes sense only because the first is true. Thus (to restrict ourselves to the most elementary level), if an unusual term x is found in a sentence (context) made up of seven words, and if the lexicographer depends on the sentence as a whole to interpret x, then obviously the lexicographer needs to be rather confident of what the other six words mean. Having made these preliminary (and in themselves inadequate)[2] remarks, we are in a better position to discuss the significance of context.

CONTEXT

The principle of contextual interpretation is, at least in theory, one of the few universally accepted hermeneutical guidelines, even though the consistent application of the principle is a notoriously difficult enterprise. Occasionally, however, one is left with the uncomfortable feeling that biblical scholars take exception to the principle itself. Even explicit reservations about the value of the context can be found, such as the following:

[1]Even in the case of a newly discovered language like Ugaritic, where many lexical problems remain after decades of intensive research, linguists do not exactly start from scratch, since they can rely on the information provided by cognate terms in related languages. On the lexicographer's work, cf. the popular description by S. I. Hayakawa, *Language in Thought and Action*, chap. 4; see also Allen Walker Read, "Dictionary," in the *New Encyclopaedia Britannica*, Macropaedia 5:713–22.

[2]For the sake of simplicity at this point we have left out of account a host of problems that arise in routine lexicographical work. Those that are particularly germane to our purposes will receive due attention in the course of this chapter.

To the linguist who lays emphasis on words and their forms and who treats them as units to be handled independent of context, the search for meaning in contexts only is not entirely satisfying. It may well be that, especially with the limited material at our disposal, we can only hope to say that a given word appears to be used in a given passage in a particular sense—and to relate this tentatively to other uses of the same word either in the same sense or in a readily relatable meaning. Context remains an untrustworthy guide —especially when some vital theological question is at issue—the uncertainty about the whole will inevitably lead to uncertainty about the parts.[3]

Leon Morris rejects a certain interpretation of λύτρον in Mark 10:45 on the grounds that it "seems to lean too heavily on the context"; in his understanding, the context "can indicate only in a general way the drift of a saying; it cannot finally determine its meaning in detail."[4]

Whatever these authors may have meant, their words, if taken at face value, stand in complete antithesis to those of linguists who would assign a *determinative* function to context; that is, the context does not ✓ merely help us understand meaning—it virtually *makes* meaning. A standard introduction to linguistic science informs us that "among the divers meanings a word possesses, the only one that will emerge into consciousness is the one determined by the context. All the others are abolished, extinguished, non-existent. This is true even of words whose significance appears to be firmly established."[5]

[3]Peter R. Ackroyd in *Words and Meanings: Essays Presented to David Winton Thomas*, ed. P. R. Ackroyd and B. Lindars (Cambridge: The University Press, 1968), p. 6. These reservations, of course, are valid when dealing with terms for which we cannot establish a semantic range, in which case etymology and other factors may play an important part (cf. James Barr, *Comparative Philology*, p. 282, and our discussion of ambiguity below). However, this can hardly be Ackroyd's point, since the example he adduces is a place name. As it stands, the statement seems to me misleading.

[4]*The Apostolic Preaching of the Cross* (London: Tyndale, 1955), pp. 33–34. In the third edition of this book (1965) Morris's statement is not found in his discussion of the meaning of λύτρον, but earlier, in a discussion of the authenticity of Mark 10:45. Furthermore, the author himself appeals elsewhere to the context in support of his interpretation (note p. 34 of the 3rd ed.). It may well be then that Morris means something other than what he seems to be saying; as in the previous example, I am objecting to the formulation. See also below, n. 25.

[5]Vendryes, *Language*, p. 177. See, however, the objections of E. D. Hirsch, Jr., *Validity in Interpretation* (New Haven: Yale University Press, 1967), p. 47.

Dealing also with words that have multiple meanings, B. Siertsema asserts that the "final interpretation" afforded by the context is what actually matters in communication. She adds that only those meanings "are called up, 'activated,' which are at that moment intended by the speaker or writer. The other aspects of meaning simply do not occur to us, neither to the speaker nor to the hearer."[6] Similar remarks could be multiplied, but the following passage provides a striking illustration:

> This relation between word and sentence, this dependence of the meaning of the word on the situation indicated by the sentence can go so far that the hearer no longer perceives the actual words of the speaker, but rather the meaning they were intended to have. . . . In volume 50 of *Philologus*, Polle has a whole article consisting entirely of linguistic mistakes in classical authors which had escaped the attention of the commentators. The most interesting case is perhaps Lessing's lapse in his *Emilia Gallotti*, where Emilia's mother says. . . : "My God! If your father knew that! How angry he was already merely to learn that the prince had lately seen you not without displeasure!" By confusing the two expressions *nicht mit Missfallen* and *nicht ohne Wohlgefallen* Lessing has said the exact opposite of what he meant to say. But the astonishing fact is that this mistake should have passed unnoticed for a whole century. The many thousands of earlier readers and theatre-goers had immediately inferred the correct meaning and had unconsciously taken the sentence in the sense Lessing intended.[7]

But now, what exactly do we mean by *context?* This term must be interpreted in the broadest sense possible, from the smallest syntactical detail to "the knowledge shared by speaker and hearer of all that has gone before."[8] Emphasis on the synchronic approach, incidentally, creates no conflict with this broad conception; on the contrary, such an

[6]B. Siertsema, "Language and World View (Semantics for Theologians)" in *BT* 20 (1969): 3–21, especially pp. 9–10. Cf. also Ullmann, *Principles*, p. 65; Stern, *Meaning*, p. 139. From time to time, of course, other aspects of meaning do occur to us and create misunderstanding; we shall address this problem of ambiguity below.

[7]Wartburg, *Problems*, p. 100. Cf. also J. P. Postgate, preface to Bréal, *Semantics*, p. lx.

[8]John Lyons, *Structural Semantics*, pp. 82–83 (my emphasis).

approach focuses precisely on "the true and only reality to the community of speakers."[9] Let us first discuss the nature of syntactic combinations.[10]

SYNTAGMATIC SENSE RELATIONS

We stressed at the beginning of chapter 5 that the paradigmatic contrasts discussed there could not be properly understood independently of syntagmatic considerations, since the former may be considered a linguistic potential that is actualized when words enter into combinations to form sentences. The fundamental significance of this topic can be illustrated with reference to the learning of foreign languages. An individual who immerses himself in a foreign culture can develop considerable fluency in a matter of months, but his failure to combine words "properly" (even words he can accurately define) will give him away for a good many years. During the writing of this chapter, the author received a letter from an organization representing a cultural group from the Middle East and offering the services of a certain speaker. The first sentence was written in impeccable English, but the second read: "If you wish to avail the opportunity of Mr. _____ free services then please intimate us of the topic. . . ." The letter then concluded by stating that although the speaker could present his religious viewpoint "on any essential aspect of human's life yet a few topics are given below to facilitate the issue." It is clear that the author of the letter had a basic command of English and even understood fairly well the very words he misused.[11] And, as anyone condemned to reading college papers knows, native speakers are hardly immune to comparable mistakes.

No group of scholars has done more to understand the nature of

[9]See above, chap. 1, n. 33.

[10]It is not my intent here to develop an exhaustive classification of context, but merely to make certain distinctions that appear particularly fruitful for biblical interpretation. The most comprehensive scheme is that of Eugenio Coseriu, who speaks of four basic environments: situation, region, context, and universe of discourse. All but the last of these include subcategories; for example, context is subdivided into idiomatic, verbal, and extraverbal, with further subdivisions (cf. Coseriu-Geckeler, "Linguistics and Semantics," pp. 132–33). For a full analysis of context, see chap. 14 in Lyons's recent work, *Semantics* 2:570–635.

[11]M. A. K. Halliday gives a number of other examples, such as "the situation of my stockings was a nightmare," "driving a bicycle," "a comprehensive traffic jam," "thoughts are under a strain"; see *Halliday: System and Function in Language*, selected papers edited by G. R. Kress (London: Oxford University Press, 1976), p. 82n.

syntagmatic relations than J. R. Firth[12] and those inspired by his work. In particular, M. A. K. Halliday has emphasized the value of determining the probability of a word's occurrence. He points out, for example, that while the words *strong* and *powerful* are in close paradigmatic relation, their contextual restrictions differ. Either adjective may be juxtaposed with *argument*, but we are not likely to say, *He drives a strong car*, nor *This tea's too powerful*. Grammatically, we would describe the phenomenon thus:

> first, *strong* and *powerful* are members of a class [=paradigmatic group] that enters into a certain structural [=syntagmatic] relation with a class of which *argument* is a member; second, *powerful* (but not *strong*) is a member of a class entering into this relation with a class of which *car* is a member; and third, *strong* (but not *powerful*) is a member of a class entering into this relation with a class of which *tea* is a member.[13]

All of this suggests that a proper description of the meaning of these adjectives cannot ignore their "collocations."

Traditionally, dictionaries have paid some attention to special syntactical combinations, but thorough and systematic treatments must be developed.[14] The importance of this point is best illustrated

---

[12]Note his article "Modes of Meaning," reprinted in *Papers in Linguistics 1934–1951* (London: Oxford University Press, 1957), especially pp. 194ff. While I find it inadequate to identify meaning with linguistic distribution—as though the meaning of a word consisted of its "collocability" (the contexts where it can occur)—the fact that such a position could be developed tells us a great deal about the fundamental importance of syntagmatic relations. It is unfortunate that Firth's ideas have not been as widely influential as they should have been. Cf. also n. 19 below.

[13]Halliday (see n. 11), p. 73. A different, but also insightful approach to syntagmatic relations was that of W. Porzig (cf. Lyons, *Semantics* 1:261ff., and Coseriu, *Principios*, pp. 143–61). See further S. Jones and J. McH. Sinclair, "English Lexical Collocations," *CahLex* 24 (1974 no. 1): 15–61.

[14]For a tentative outline of how the verb *get* could be described in a dictionary, see *Selected Papers of J. R. Firth 1952–59*, ed. F. R. Palmer (Bloomington: Indiana University Press, 1968), pp. 20ff. Note also J. Dubois, "Recherches lexicographiques: esquisse d'un dictionnaire structural," *EtLingAp* 1 (1962): 43–48; this article includes a folding chart with a tentative sample of the dictionary. Dubois emphasizes, for example, that sometimes a term must be defined by its opposition to terms which follow it; thus, *tourner* has quite different values in the sentences *il tourne* and *il tourne la tête*. Further, he distinguishes sharply between three types of syntagms: "le syntagme ferme (*hocher la tête*, *hocher* ne s'emploie pas sans l'object *tête*), le syntagme

with reference to bilingual dictionaries. Spanish-English dictionaries, for example, are normally content to give *eat* and *drink* as the respective equivalents of *comer* and *tomar*.[15] While this correspondence suggests that the terms "have the same meaning," the true facts emerge in the combination *to eat soup* (or *ice cream*), where Spanish does not tolerate *comer* but rather uses *tomar la sopa* (or *el helado*). This difference suggests that whereas the English terms should be defined with reference to the manner in which the food is taken to the mouth, the Spanish terms indicate the constitution of the food (i.e., whether or not mastication is necessary). In short, the meanings of these terms are, at least in part, a function of their possible syntagmatic combinations. Consequently, the definitions given in, say, a Greek-English dictionary of the New Testament must incorporate each word's collocability; moreover, since the New Testament itself is a very small corpus, the evidence must come from Hellenistic Greek as a whole.

LITERARY CONTEXT

When biblical exegetes appeal to the context in support of an interpretation, it is not the syntactical combinations that they usually have in mind, but rather the general tenor of the passage. It is useful to point out, however, that these two factors represent different gradations of the same phenomenon, not qualitatively different phenomena. In Luke 15:25, for example, the term ὁ πρεσβύτερος is used with reference to the older of the two sons in Jesus' parable. It does not occur to anyone that the term here means 'elder' in the technical religious sense because that meaning "does not fit the context." But another way of putting it is to say that the Greek term here is in "syntagmatic relation" with all the preceding words in the story, particularly ὁ νεώτερος in verse 11. Although it may not be a good idea to use the term "syntagmatic" beyond the area of syntactical combinations, we must emphasize the basic continuity between such combinations and the broader literary context.

While all interpreters recognize, at least in principle, the importance of our topic, one may need to emphasize that literary context

conditionné (*passer d'un lieu à un autre*, où l'emploie de la préposition *de* est lieé à l'emploi d'une autre préposition et où l'ensemble détermine une valeur d'emploi de *passer*) et le syntagme libre . . ." (pp. 45–46).

[15]The remarks that follow may not apply to all Spanish-speaking areas, particularly where *beber* is used in preference to *tomar*. I have used this illustration previously in "Describing Meaning in the LXX Lexicon," *BIOSCS* 11 (1978): 19–26.

cannot be identified narrowly as the specific paragraph or section being studied. All of us, I fear, tend to interpret, say, a verse in chapter 14 of Romans in the light of the immediate context without sufficient awareness that the first few chapters (or even other epistles) are, in the strictest possible sense, part of the context. There is of course a question regarding the relative weight to be placed on other passages—a subject that will occupy us shortly—but we must look at those other passages as more than just vague parallels or "background information."

Moreover, the *nature* of the literary work in question (a Pauline letter) is itself a determining contextual feature. Lyons argues that "the context of a sentence in a written work must be understood to include the conventions governing the literary genre of which the work in question is an example."[16] In other words, we have now moved from the usual understanding of context (the running text) to a broader category. Biblical scholars have shown themselves consistently sensitive to this issue. A great deal of effort has been placed, for example, on the task of determining the literary genre to which the Gospels belong. Or again, the current discussions regarding the purpose and meaning of Romans have sent scholars to a renewed search for the literary character of Paul's letters.[17]

CONTEXT OF SITUATION

Here we move from the linguistic to the *extra*linguistic features that also form part of context. A trivial but useful example, which I owe to a college teacher, is the utterance *djeet*. In isolation it is meaningless. However, let us imagine a student who notices his girlfriend near the dining commons around noon. If he asks her, "Djeet?" she has no trouble understanding him. In this case it is neither syntagmatic relations nor the larger linguistic context, but the life situation—informality, time, physical surroundings—that eliminates ambiguity.

The expression *context of situation* was coined many years ago by the famous anthropologist, Bronislaw Malinowski. On the basis of his work among natives in the Trobriand Islands (New Guinea), he argued that "the conception of context must be substantially widened, if it is to furnish us with its full utility. In fact it must burst the bonds of mere

[16]Lyons, *Structural Semantics*, pp. 82–83. See also Hirsch, *Validity*, p. 74.
[17]Cf. Karl P. Donfried, *The Romans Debate* (Minneapolis: Augsburg, 1977).

linguistics and be carried over into the analysis of the general conditions under which a language is spoken."[18] This idea was picked up and further developed by J. R. Firth in a somewhat peculiar fashion.[19] Without subscribing to "contextualism" as a theory of meaning, students of language generally have recognized the validity of Malinowski's emphasis.[20] One follower of Firth complains:

> It is easy enough to be scornful, as some scholars have been, of contextual theories and to dismiss them as totally unworkable. But it is difficult to see how we can dismiss them without denying the obvious fact that the meaning of words and sentences relate to the world of our experience.[21]

Indeed it would be difficult to find a modern treatment of meaning that does not take the external situation into account.

The term "grammatico-*historical* interpretation" and the immense efforts expended in modern times to reconstruct the historical background of Scripture demonstrate that biblical scholars have always ✓ been sensitive to the principle of situational context. To a large extent, the interpretation of ancient literature consists of bridging the temporal and cultural gaps that separate us from its authors. Even a relatively

[18]B. Malinowski, "The Problem of Meaning in Primitive Languages," a supplement to Ogden and Richards, *The Meaning of Meaning*, pp. 296–336, especially p. 306. On the same page, he unfortunately draws too sharp a distinction between living and dead languages, arguing that written documents are "torn out of any *context of situation*. In fact, written statements are set down with the purpose of being self-contained and self-explanatory." This is a great exaggeration, for an ancient author assumed, consciously or unconsciously, that his readers shared a considerable amount of knowledge with him.

[19]Cf. "Ethnographic Analysis and Language with Reference to Malinowski's Views," in *Selected Papers* (see above, n. 14), pp. 137–67; "The Technique of Semantics," in *Papers in Linguistics* (see above, n. 12), pp. 7–33. For a critical appreciation and evaluation, cf. John Lyons, "Firth's Theory of 'Meaning,'" *In Memory of J. R. Firth*, ed. C. E. Bazell et al. (London: Longman, 1966), pp. 288–302; also, more briefly, his *Semantics* 2:607–13.

[20]Geoffrey Leech, *Semantics*, pp. 71ff., strongly criticizes Firth's theory yet recognizes "that there is some degree of common sense on the side of the contextualists" (p. 76). In my judgment, Leech fails to do justice to context when he limits its function to one of "narrowing down the communicative possibilities" (p. 77). I suspect, however, that his very cautious statement simply reflects a concern not to construct a full theory of the nature of meaning based on context. As we shall see in our discussion of ambiguity, I have no difficulty with his regarding context as "a probabilistic weighting . . . of potential meanings" (p. 79).

[21]Palmer, *Semantics*, p. 51.

recent document belonging to our own culture, such as the American Declaration of Independence, may hide its meaning from us. How many of us, for example, appreciate what the word *course* ("When in the course of human events . . .") conveyed to a philosophically knowledgeable English speaker in the late eighteenth century?[22] Yet, all too often we read the biblical material with the tacit assumption that it is immediately intelligible to us. Few of us could imagine, for example, that the apparently trivial comment about the father's running (Luke 15:20) may hold a significant key to the interpretation of the parable of the lost son.[23]

Considerable difficulties, to be sure, stand in our way. Since our archaeological and literary resources are limited, the exegete is frequently dependent on the internal evidence of a document to reconstruct the historical situation. In other words, we encounter again the paradox of the hermeneutical circle. Paul's Epistle to the Galatians, for example, is universally admitted to have been written in the light of an urgent and specific need. The message of the letter cannot be properly interpreted in isolation from that historical context; but since that context can only be deduced from the letter itself, a certain degree of interpretation seems to require our priority. E. D. Hirsch has persuasively shown, however, that this is a paradox in appearances only—there *is* a way out of the circle.[24] But there may not be a way out of uncertainty at various points, such as whether the verb $\pi\acute{\alpha}\sigma\chi\epsilon\iota\nu$ refers to positive or negative experiences in Galatians 3:4 (see below p. 153).

Another difficulty is peculiar to historical narratives, namely, the tension between the literary context of a passage and the historical context of the event being described. This becomes a special problem

---

[22]Cf. the fascinating exegesis by Gary Wills, *Inventing America: Jefferson's Declaration of Independence* (Garden City, N.Y.: Doubleday, 1978), especially pp. 93ff. On p. 259 he says, "To understand any text remote from us in time, we must reassemble a world around that text. The preconceptions of the original audience, its tastes, its range of reference, must be recovered, so far as that is possible." I am less sure about Wills's next remark: "We must forget what was learned, or what occurred, in the interval between our time and the text's." What we bring to the text, if handled responsibly, is a necessary and valid element in the interpretive process (more of this below).

[23]In view of the cultural expectations that require an older man to walk slowly and with dignity, this parable may emphasize, more than anything else, God's humility. See Kenneth E. Bailey, *Poet and Peasant: A Literary-Cultural Approach to the Parables in Luke* (Grand Rapids: Eerdmans, 1976), p. 181.

[24]Hirsch, *Validity*, pp. 76–77 and *passim*.

when dealing with the Gospels, since exegetes are often concerned with what Jesus "really" said or meant, as opposed to what the evangelist intended to convey. For example, Cullmann dismisses Schweitzer's well-known interpretation of Matthew 10:23 with an indirect appeal to the original historical context: "But this thesis, uninformed by what we have learned from form criticism, is bound too much to the context in Matt. 10. . . ."[25] The recent renewed appreciation for the Gospels as literary wholes, a healthy development in my judgment, does not of course eliminate our problem—it intensifies the tension, since now we cannot with good conscience disregard the literary context on the grounds that what really matters is the historical event.

OTHER LEVELS OF CONTEXT

We may finally raise the issue of contextualizations that take place *subsequent* to the writing of the original document. In a useful discussion of this subject, Sawyer has stated:

> The meaning of OT traditions can be legitimately and rewardingly analysed on the basis of several, at times conflicting, but usually illuminating historical contexts in which they have been read and understood. Some of the fantastic interpretations of the early church fathers, for example, based on allegory and the like, are just as important for a complete description of the meaning of the text as the NT interpretations or those of the early Jewish rabbis. One may not agree with them, but this is not part of linguistic description. The writings of the Qumran sect, the Karaites, the Scottish Covenanters, the Seventh Day Adventists, the form-critics and the present writer all constitute contextualizations of OT words and passages, and all are therefore possible starting-points for semantic definition.[26]

This is true not only of interpretations deliberately worked out but of textual variants as well. The study of textual transmission should not be

[25]Oscar Cullmann, *Salvation in History* (London: SCM, 1967), p. 216. Possibly this tension between the historical and the literary context is behind Morris's statement quoted above (p. 139). In "Ned B. Stonehouse and Redaction Criticism," *WTJ* 40 (1977–78): 77–88, 281–303, I have tried to deal with the theological implications of overemphasizing the historical events narrated in the Gospels at the expense of appreciating the distinctive contribution of each evangelist.

[26]John F. A. Sawyer, *Semantics in Biblical Research: New Methods of Defining Hebrew Words for Salvation* (SBT 2nd series, 24; London: SCM, 1972), p. 9.

restricted to the recovery of the autograph. On the contrary, we must appreciate that to reconstruct the textual history of a passage is to produce something of intrinsic value, quite independent of its usefulness for establishing the original form.[27]

These considerations open up serious epistemological questions. Without attempting to deal with them in substance, I should briefly point out the lines along which our subsequent discussion is built. I take it as a valid assumption that the interpreter approaches any text with a multitude of experiences ("filed away" with some degree of coherence) that inform his or her understanding of that text. I further assume that it is impossible for the interpreter to evaluate the text without the point of reference provided by those presuppositions. But I believe just as strongly that the interpreter may *transcend*, though not eliminate, that point of reference. This can be done not by assuming that we can set aside our presuppositions in the interest of objectivity, but rather by a conscious *use* of them. The moment we look at a text we contextualize it, but a self-awareness of that fact opens up the possibility of modifying our point of reference in the light of contradictory data.

All of this means that the object of discovering authorial intent remains valid. That when we speak of the meaning of the text our primary concern should be authorial meaning.[28]

AMBIGUITY

We may now proceed to inquire how an appreciation for the

---

[27]It is quite an exaggeration, however, to suggest that the restoration of the autograph is a useless goal that would only occur to theologically motivated scholars; cf. M. M. Parvis, "The Goals of New Testament Textual Studies," in *SE* 6 (1973): 393–407. Why would a Thucydides scholar (who does not believe that the author was verbally inspired!) do textual criticism if not to determine as accurately as possible how the ancient historian *himself* interpreted the events of his time? Ironically, Parvis himself refers to Thucydides (p. 406), but claims that our task is different because "we are Churchmen; . . . we are concerned with the whole range of Church tradition."

[28]Again I refer the reader to E. D. Hirsch's persuasive discussion. Note, however, the qualifications entered by Vern S. Poythress, "Analysing a Biblical Text: Some Important Linguistic Distinctions," *SJT* 32 (1979): 113–37, especially p. 126n. It should be added that, since we stand at the end of a long line of interpreters who have directly or indirectly affected our preunderstanding, it is sheer folly to assume that we can skip twenty centuries of scholarship and have immediate access to the text. In this connection, see Anthony C. Thiselton, *The Two Horizons* (Grand Rapids: Eerdmans, 1980), p. 11 and passim.

significance of context can be brought to bear on concrete lexical problems. At the risk of oversimplification, we may view those problems as belonging to one of two basic types, semantic or stylistic. This distinction must not be drawn too sharply. As noted earlier,[29] style (connotation, emotive overtones, etc.) should probably be treated as a component of meaning; moreover, semantic anomalies are usually exploited for stylistic purposes. Nevertheless, there is an important difference between occasions when we simply *do not know the meaning* of a particular word and occasions where scholars may argue about the distinct nuance of words *whose meaning is established*. In the latter case, it is usually a question of synonymy; in the former, a matter of ambiguity. Now, since ambiguity may be deliberate or unintended, we must treat these two subtypes separately.

DELIBERATE AMBIGUITY

The topic of ambiguity necessarily looms large in any discussion of imaginative literature, particularly poetry, where an author will *deliberately* choose equivocal terms and constructions for a variety of purposes. In his classic analysis of this technique, William Empson distinguished a sevenfold gradation.[30] At the most elementary level, the author may simply leave unspecified the point of a comparison. Resolution of two alternative meanings and the simultaneous use of two unconnected meanings constitute the next two levels. The succeeding levels focus on progressive complications (the seventh type involves full contradictions in the author's mind). Much of this material is not directly applicable to biblical exegesis. Even Hebrew poetry, though it uses polysemy and homonymy frequently in word plays, does not seem to employ deliberate ambiguity as a standard technique.

For example, when we read in John 1:5 regarding the light, that ἡ σκοτία αὐτὸ οὐ κατέλαβεν, we naturally wonder whether the author meant 'seized' or 'comprehended.' If this were the only instance of ambiguity in John, we might simply choose one or the other. However, we learn from ἄνωθεν in 3:3 ('from above,' or 'again') and considerable other evidence that the author enjoyed word plays; we

---

[29]See above, chap. 4, n. 49.

[30]*Seven Types of Ambiguity: A Study of Its Effects in English Verse* (New York: Meridian, 1955). For a general discussion of ambiguity in Scripture see Caird, *Language and Imagery*, pp. 95–108. Note also David F. Payne, "O.T. Exegesis and the Problem of Ambiguity," *ASTI* 5 (1966–67): 48–69.

may therefore decide that 1:5 is a case of deliberate ambiguity. If so, it would be bad exegesis to choose one meaning to the exclusion of the other.

On the other hand, it is necessary to challenge the tendency, especially pronounced among elementary students, of avoiding decisions by including more than one meaning. This tendency manifests itself frequently at those points where the lexical element is inextricably tied to the grammatical, particularly in the use of the cases. When we read Jesus' statement, εἰ ἔχετε πίστιν θεοῦ . . . (Mark 11:22), it is difficult for most of us, having been taught that possession is the "primary meaning" of the genitive, to take the construction exclusively as an objective genitive, "have faith in God." We may therefore be tempted somehow to combine both ideas: "to have true faith in God means to have God's own faith." Some interpreters may even argue that such an approach is its own best confirmation—the fuller the meaning, the more valid the interpretation is likely to be. As we have seen, however, language works differently—context serves to *eliminate* multiple meanings.

Not all scholars will agree with these remarks. For example, M. Zerwick argues that ἡ γὰρ ἀγάπη τοῦ Χριστοῦ συνέχει ἡμᾶς (2 Cor. 5:14) must be taken as both subjective and objective.[31] Dealing with the same grammatical problem in Romans 3:3, Nigel Turner claims that "we need not sacrifice fullness of interpretation to an overprecise analysis of syntax." Turner is sensitive that such an approach smacks of "compromise," so he turns the tables by saying that, "with a mind like St. Paul's, quicker than his own pen or a scribe's, it will not be unreasonable to distil every ounce of richness from the simple genitives of abstract qualities which abound in his epistles."[32] Of course, no scholar enjoys being cast into the role of the villain. Who wants to suggest that Paul's mind is slow or superficial?

Oddly enough, it may be Zerwick's and Turner's position that robs these passages of semantic content.[33] We have noted earlier (pp. 77, 107) that semantic changes involving expansion go hand-in-

---

[31] *Biblical Greek, Illustrated by Examples*, ed. Joseph Smith (Rome: Pontifical Biblical Institute, 1963), p. 13. This particular example Zerwick defends with some plausibility by appealing to the immediate context. For a similar difficulty when dealing with prepositions, see Murray J. Harris's comments in *NIDNTT* 3:1177.

[32] Nigel Turner, *Grammatical Insights into the New Testament* (Edingurgh: T. & T. Clark, 1965), p. 111.

[33] I owe this observation to Dr. Vern S. Poythress.

hand with impoverishment; conversely, a narrowing of meaning by specialization entails greater intension.[34] What Turner represents as an admirable quality could be interpreted as sloppiness, since undisciplined minds prefer vagueness and ambiguity to precise expression. But this way of putting the matter is not any more helpful than Turner's. It may well be that a great mind occasionally and deliberately uses vague language for specific purposes. In view of the nature of language and communication, however, we should assume *one* meaning unless there are strong *exegetical* (literary, contextual) grounds to the contrary.

UNINTENDED AMBIGUITY

If we can establish that an author has used ambiguity for literary purposes, then our problem is resolved. On the other hand, if the ambiguity is accidental, we face the sometimes difficult task of deciding which meaning was intended by the author. To recognize that the decision *can* be difficult helps clarify and qualify our earlier insistence that context is determinative of meaning—we can hardly suggest that a quick look at the immediate context will resolve all doubtful cases. On the other hand, we cannot afford to ignore that these difficulties occur only *sometimes*. Since our attention is normally drawn, by the very nature of the case, to doubtful passages, we may be left with the impression that ambiguity is a pervasive phenomenon.[35] We need to remind ourselves, therefore, that while almost every word in Scripture is more or less polysemous *if considered in isolation*, that potential for ambiguity normally does not even occur to an individual in the course of reading substantive portions.

But now, what are the causes of unintended ambiguity? If we think of misunderstandings that take place during normal conversations, three basic categories stand out. In the first place, misunder-

[34]This suggests a qualification of our criticism. Zerwick argues that τὸ εὐαγγέλιον τοῦ θεοῦ may include three or four ideas. In this particular case Zerwick may be right, for here we are dealing with a technical expression, that is, one that has been *specialized* to act as shorthand for considerable doctrinal content.

[35]An analogy—not merely a trivial illustration, but a real analogy—is that of textual criticism. By necessity, any study of textual transmission deals with *variants*. After a while, the student could easily lose perspective and ignore the fact that the overwhelming majority of words in any text are not subject to reasonable doubt. It should perhaps be added that textual transmission is simply one more form of linguistic communication; the criteria used for textual decisions should probably be brought into closer correspondence with those used for semantic decisions.

standing may arise as a result of *noise*. I use this term in the somewhat specialized use it has acquired in communication theory. *Any* interference in the process of communication may be described as noise—a physical sound, static on the television screen, or even a smudge on the printed page. Textual variation is one manifestation of noise, but this form of ambiguity is dealt with by textual criticism rather than lexicology (although the connections between the two are quite important). Second, misunderstanding occurs when we hear a word with which we are not familiar; either the word is completely new to us or we have not heard it in a sufficient number of contexts to identify its sense. This situation corresponds to the problem of *hapax legomena* in the biblical text, especially in the Old Testament. It also corresponds to unusual occurrences of otherwise familiar words.

Third, confusion takes place occasionally, even in the case of words that are well understood, if the hearer's train of thought conflicts with the speaker's—that is, if the two *contexts* differ. The speaker is so absorbed in a particular point that he or she overlooks a potential ambiguity due to the capability of some words to acquire different values in similar or even identical syntagmatic combinations.[36] This problem corresponds to the distinction between authorial meaning and audience meaning. W. Bauer addressed this issue (from a slightly different perspective) in the introduction to his *Lexicon* and concluded "that sometimes there are two meanings for the same passage, one from the standpoint of the writer and another which becomes evident when one puts one's self in the place of the recipient, intellectually and spiritually."[37] What needs to be emphasized, however, is that twentieth-century scholars constitute one of many audiences that provide their own context in the interpretation of a passage. Indeed, the aim of grammatico-historical exegesis is to bring our context into congruence with that of the original author. It is therefore confusing to say, with reference to an ambiguous passage, that the context does not

---

[36]In Phil. 1:10, δοκιμάζειν τὰ διαφέροντα may mean either 'to test the things that differ' or 'to approve the things that excel.' In English, *he brought a suit* means one thing in a legal, another in a domestic, context (cf. Archibald A. Hill, "Laymen, Lexicographers, and Linguists," *Lg* 46 [1970]: 245–58, especially p. 254). Leech (*Semantics*, p. 79) gives the example, *put the electric blanket on,* which means either 'place it on the bed' or 'switch the current on.' Note the label "psychological noise," used by Peter K. Chow, "Analogical Applications of Information Theory to Semantic Problems," *BT* 31 (1980): 310–18.

[37]Bauer, p. xxiv.

help us; conceptually, it makes better sense to say that we are having difficulties *identifying* the original context.

A classic example of lexical ambiguity is Paul's question in Galatians 3:4, τοσαῦτα ἐπάθετε εἰκῇ; We may take the verb in its usual negative sense, "Did you suffer so many things in vain?" We may also translate it in a neutral sense, "experience," in which case the context would suggest a positive idea, that is, the blessings brought about by the Spirit. This ambiguity illustrates dramatically how two valid principles of interpretation can be brought into conflict. On the one hand, we could insist on choosing the predominant meaning of the verb. That is, since all other passages in the New Testament use πάσχειν *in malam partem*,[38] and since, with very few exceptions,[39] the same holds true for Hellenistic Greek in general, we should presume this negative sense unless the context prohibits it.[40] On the other hand, the principle of contextual interpretation would lead us to emphasize that nothing in the immediate context suggests suffering on the part of the Galatians—indeed, that nowhere in the letter is there an explicit reference to such suffering.

We are then at an exegetical impasse; no resolution is perhaps possible. However, there is an additional consideration that may throw light on our problem. In 1953 the prominent linguist Martin Joos delivered a paper, "Towards a First Theorem in Semantics." In it he suggested

the rule of maximal redundancy, "The best meaning is the least meaning," as the explicator's and defining lexicog-

---

[38]The variant reading in Matt. 17:15 (κακῶς πάσχει) is not really an exception, as Bauer suggests. Although the use of the adverb implies that the verb is used in a neutral sense, this conclusion is not necessary. The English *fall down* is simply pleonastic and does not imply that one may fall up.

[39]The clearest exception is Josephus, *Antiquities* 3:312. Retelling the story of Numbers 13–14, Josephus states that God reminded Moses of all the (good) experiences and benefits the Israelites had received from Him (ὅσα παθόντες ἐξ αὐτοῦ καὶ πηλίκων εὐεργεσιῶν μεταλαβόντες). As pointed out by W. Michaelis (*TDNT* 5:905, n. 3), "the preceding context, not the εὐεργεσίαι which only follows, fixes the meaning."

[40]One often hears or reads, incidentally, that a word cannot be said to have a certain meaning unless we can find occurrences where only *that* meaning is possible. This is a wise rule of thumb in that it prevents irresponsible interpretations; however, it can hardly be regarded as an absolute criterion for determining meaning, since the extant literature (particularly for Hebrew) does not reflect all the possible occurrences of every word, whether written or spoken.

rapher's rule of thumb for deciding what a hapax legomenon most probably means: he defines it in such fashion as *to make it contribute least to the total message derivable from the passsage where it is at home*, rather than, e.g., defining it according to some presumed etymology or semantic history.[41]

At first blush, this statement may appear strange or even unacceptable, for we tend "to assume that an odd word must have some odd sense, the odder the better."[42] However, a moment's reflection on the redundancy of natural language will persuade us that "Joos's Law" is eminently reasonable.

Research into communication engineering has had considerable impact on our understanding of language.[43] In particular, we have become aware of the *need* for redundancy in communication. When any piece of information is transmitted, considerable interference and distortion (*noise*) cannot be avoided; if the means of communication is one hundred percent efficient, the slightest interference will obliterate the information. In the course of a normal conversation, the hearer's reception is greatly distorted by a variety of causes: grammatical lapses on the part of the speaker, less than perfect enunciation, physical noises in the surroundings, momentary daydreaming on the part of the hearer. In the vast majority of cases, the hearers do receive the information because of the built-in redundancy of the language. Suppose, for example, that we hear a three-syllable word, but only understand the last two syllables -*terday*; not only are we able to guess that the word is *yesterday*, but we make the guess without any awareness that we failed to hear the first syllable. Similarly, missing a complete word seldom bothers us because the sentence as a whole normally discloses that word. Even if we fail to hear a complete sentence when listening

---

[41]The original paper was never published. The quotation is taken from "Semantic Axiom Number One," *Lg* 48 (1972): 257–65, p. 257 especially.

[42]Ibid., p. 263.

[43]The basic work is by Claude F. Shannon and Warren Weaver, *The Mathematical Theory of Communication* (Urbana: University of Illinois Press, 1949). Joshua Whatmough stressed the concept of mathematical probability in his famous work, *Language: A Modern Synthesis* (New York: Mentor, 1956). For a wide-ranging, detailed, and comprehensive treatment, cf. Gustav Herdan, *The Advanced Theory of Language as Choice and Chance* (Kommunikation und Kybernetik in Einzeldorstellungen 4; New York: Springer-Verlag, 1966). Note finally Lyons, *Semantics* 1, chap. 2, especially pp. 41–45; and Chow, "Analogical Applications."

to a speech, we are unlikely to miss anything that is not automatically deducible from the rest of the speech.

Joos illustrates his point by referring to *Webster's Third's* definition of *per contra*, which includes the supportive quotation, "the female is generally drab, the male, per contra, brilliant." Assuming the user of the dictionary has an adequate grasp of

> "the" and "is" and "generally" as discursive English, plus adequate background such as the ordinary or the technically biological and cultural pair "female" and "male," we imagine him to be in secure possession of *exactly two* of these three: *drab, per contra, brilliant*. (That is, *any two* of the three!) Then the third is "obvious" and the solution is child's play, both literally and figuratively.[44]

It is literally child's play, because as children we used precisely the method of maximal redundancy to learn a respectable number of words; indeed, that is the method that we *continue* to use when we are not consciously thinking about building our vocabulary.

Now while Joos's article addressed the problem of *hapax legomena* and other words whose meaning may be unknown, the principle is readily applicable to polysemy.[45] In the case of πάσχειν in Galatians 3:4, one could argue that the neutral sense 'experience' creates less disturbance in the passage than does 'suffer' because the former is more redundant—it is more supportive of, and more clearly supported by, the context. Such an argument is reasonable and this author finds it quite persuasive.[46] However, the principle must not be absolutized (Joos himself calls it a "rule of thumb"), nor can its application in Galatians 3:4 be regarded as conclusive. These reservations do not imply that the context does not give us the meaning; rather, as previously emphasized, it is that we are not fully cognizant of the context. For example, it may be argued (perhaps on the basis of Acts 14:22) that the Galatians had indeed undergone serious tribulation,

---

[44]Joos, p. 264.

[45]Hill has used it with reference to homonymy ("Laymen, Lexicographers, and Linguists," p. 255; his general discussion of context, beginning on p. 252, is quite relevant to our topic). Note also Hill's linguistic insights into the study of literature in *Constituent and Pattern in Poetry* (Austin: University of Texas Press, 1976).

[46]Hans Dieter Betz, *Galatians: A Commentary on Paul's Letter to the Churches in Galatia* (Hermeneia; Philadelphia: Fortress, 1979), p. 134, also appeals to the broader context of the mystery religions.

that their hope of avoiding persecution made them susceptible to the Judaizers' teachings (cf. Gal. 6:12), and that their conversations with Paul often dealt with this concern. If we therefore imagine that the subject was always in their mind, the sense 'suffer' in Galatians 3:4 would *not* create a disturbance in the (broader) context. Our uncertainty then is based on our inability to identify *that* context.

CONTEXTUAL CIRCLES

These last comments raise a question concerning the relative weight that we should attach to different levels of context. If we visualize the immediate context (verbal *or* nonverbal) as a small circle within a larger one (say, a whole chapter), both within a still larger circle (say, the whole book), and so on, which circle should receive priority? Without suggesting that we can come up with immutable laws to be applied mechanically, one must recognize that the smaller the circle, the more likely it is to affect the disputed passage.[47]

Building on the work of Quentin Quesnell,[48] Karl P. Donfried has applied this insight to Matthew 25:1–13.[49] We may focus on Donfried's treatment of the word ἔλαιον ('oil'), which clearly plays a basic role in the story. Possessing sufficient oil is indispensable to participating in the marriage feast. Step number one is looking at the immediate context, which however, in this case, tells us nothing about the meaning of the word. The next step consists of examining chapters 23–25 (the fifth Matthaean discourse), which begins and ends with emphasis on obedience (ποιήσατε καὶ τηρεῖτε, 23:3; οὐκ ἐποιήσατε, 25:45). This fact, in addition to some supporting details (e.g., ψυγήσεται ἡ ἀγάπη τῶν πολλῶν, 24:12) suggests the possibility that *oil* stands for 'good works.' Third, we turn to Matthew's teaching in general, recognizing some basic similarities between the first and fifth discourse and, more particularly, between 7:13–27 and

[47]Some time ago while reading a work on textual criticism, I was puzzled by this statement: "the names of the characters were frequently omitted." Since the "larger circle" was the subject of paleography, I took the word *characters* to mean 'letters,' but that made little sense in its narrower context. Further reflection made me realize that I had carelessly overlooked the specific illustration being used, namely, that in dramatic texts changes of *speaker* were not always indicated.

[48]*The Mind of Mark: Interpretation and Method Through the Exegesis of Mark 6,2* (AnBib 36; Rome: Pontifical Biblical Institute, 1969).

[49]Karl Paul Donfried, "The Allegory of the Ten Virgins (Matt. 25:1–13) as a Summary of Matthean Theology," *JBL* 93 (1974): 415–28.

25:1–13. The illustration of the wise man and the foolish man emphasizes the doing of Jesus' words (7:24), follows on the heels of the comment οὐδέποτε ἔγνων ὑμᾶς (7:23; in 25:12, οὐκ οἶδα ὑμᾶς), is part of a passage that uses the 'door' symbolism (7:13, 25:10), and concludes a discourse that began with an emphasis on the need for Jesus' disciples to shine like lamps through good works (5:14–16). In view of these parallels, the previous suggestion that *oil* equals 'good works' moves from the status of possibility to that of strong probability. The fourth step, the New Testament as a whole, gives us no help. Finally, when we look at the general religious environment, we find a midrashic comment on Numbers 7:19 where the grain offering (fine flour mixed with oil) is said to allude to "the Torah, the study of which must be mingled with *good deeds*"—a striking confirmation of the proposed exegesis.

Donfried's argument regarding method is that interpreters often begin with the fifth step, "immediately drawing parallels to Jewish literature. Our procedure has differed radically at this point by arguing that appeal to step five is only legitimate after one has worked through the preceding four steps."[50] One can hardly take exception to this proposal. If we return to our Galatians 3:4 problem, we could reasonably argue that the lack of reference or allusion to suffering in the immediate context takes precedence over what we may deduce from elsewhere (say, from Acts 14:22). Here again, however, we must stress that we are dealing only with a rule of thumb. If, as suggested earlier, we in the twentieth century are not privy to the Galatians' preoccupations, which may have been fully shared by Paul but which do not find explicit reference in the letter—if that is the case, those concerns form part of the *smaller*, that is, the immediate (though nonverbal) context.

Perhaps we can best illustrate this last point with an example that is not confined to lexical meaning. A recent commentator on Revelation 20:4 makes the following statement:

> If "they lived" in verse 4 means a spiritual resurrection to
> new life in Christ, then we are faced with the problem of
> discovering *within the context* some persuasive reason to

---

[50]Ibid., p. 428. Of course, it may well be that the exegete first thinks of this possible interpretation because he or she comes across the rabbinic statement, but how the idea *arises* is immaterial; what matters is the way in which the scholar seeks to establish that interpretation.

interpret the same verb differently within one concise unit. No such reason can be found.[51]

Again, with reference to Satan's binding, the author mentions that different interpreters appeal to different parallels in the New Testament to support their views. Then he adds: "The answer to the problem obviously does not lie in one's ability to support his interpretation by collecting verses *from other contexts* in Scripture. Careful attention needs to be given to *the text of Revelation itself.*" And as to whether the "thousand years" should be taken literally or not: "Nothing in *the immediate context* favors either interpretation. It is *the larger concern* to find a consistent millennial position which leads each exegete to commit himself on the meaning of the thousand years."[52]

All of these comments are well taken insofar as they call attention to the priority of the smaller contextual circles. As stated, however, his words leave the distinct impression that it is exegetically unsound to appeal to the broader contexts, as though such an appeal were little more than dogmatic bias. Contemporary biblical scholars, I fear, have too often overreacted against "dogmatism" in exegesis and in doing so they have ignored a valid and indeed essential element in the hermeneutical process. The (usually implicit) claim that proper exegesis may be done, or even can only be done, if one avoids commitments to broader issues seems to me not only to be a delusion, but to create an obstacle for interpretation.[53] I would therefore argue that "the larger concern to find a consistent millennial position" is a legitimate and necessary step in the interpretive process, since it focuses on one of the contextual circles. Surely the author of Revelation himself sought to instruct his readers along lines *consistent* with those general Christian

[51]Robert H. Mounce, *The Book of Revelation* (NICNT; Grand Rapids: Eerdmans, 1977), p. 356 (my emphasis).

[52]Ibid., p. 353 (my emphasis). For a comparable playing down of the broader context, see Robert L. Thomas, "A Hermeneutical Ambiguity of Eschatology: The Analogy of Faith," *JETS* 23 (1980) 45–53.

[53]C. E. B. Cranfield's otherwise superb work, A *Critical and Exegetical Commentary on the Epistle to the Romans*, 2 vols. (ICC; Edinburgh: T. & T. Clark, 1975–79), can be faulted at this point. Arguing against the advisability of presenting a (detailed) statement concerning the occasion of the letter at the beginning of the commentary, Cranfield says: "It is better to approach the detailed work of exegesis with as open a mind as possible on this matter" (1:24). By failing to state his views, however, he leaves the impression that the exegesis itself has been unaffected by what he considers more or less likely the occasion to have been. Cf. also my review of John Drane, *Paul: Libertine or Legalist?* in *WTJ* 40 (1977–78): 176–80, especially p. 179.

convictions that find expression in other parts of the New Testament. What must of course be avoided is the ignoring or violating of the smaller circles of context through excessive concern for the larger ones.

SYNONYMY

Although biblical (particularly Old Testament) exegesis must occupy itself with the problem of lexical ambiguity, more often than not lexical discussions involve words and phrases whose acceptation is universally agreed upon. There is no debate, for example, that ἀγαπᾶν is properly translated 'to love'—the disagreement begins when its relationship with φιλεῖν is considered; at this point, however, the discussion moves into the area of style.

In the previous chapter we considered some basic theoretical and terminological questions concerning synonyms. There we emphasized that synonymy should be understood as an overlapping relationship obtaining between *senses* (not between words nor between referents) and, further, that it should be clearly distinguished from "improper" synonymy (contiguous relations) and hyponymy (inclusive relations). More fundamentally, we advised the reader that these paradigmatic relations are context-dependent, that is, they represent only *potential* contrasts that must be defined in terms of actual syntagmatic combinations. We may now explore the significance of that claim.[54]

LEXICAL CHOICE

In the course of speaking or writing we are constantly faced with lexical choices, most of which we make without conscious deliberation. For example, we may begin thus: *The man is walking toward the* _____. While we must choose a word to end the sentence, the choice is greatly restricted by the context; a verb, for instance, will not do. After the various restrictions imposed by the whole situational context are taken into account, the nouns that remain available to fill that slot in the sentence will consist of more or less closely related terms, such as *building* or *house*.

Modern treatments of style, particularly by writers with some background in linguistics, make frequent use of the concept of choice.[55] To be sure, even ancient Greek writers were not ignorant of

---

[54]The section that follows is largely taken from my article, "The Pauline Style as Lexical Choice" (see above, chap. 4, n. 42.).

[55]"The pivot of the whole theory of expressiveness is the concept of *choice*. There can be no question of style unless the speaker or writer has the possibility of choosing

the role played by ἐκλογὴ ὀνομάτων in rhetoric. What characterizes recent treatments, however, is the use they have made of certain investigations in the area of communication (or information) theory. According to Warren Weaver's popularization, *information* is regarded as a measure of one's freedom of choice when selecting a message; indeed, it is a measure of uncertainty.[56] If there is no uncertainty whatever—if the message is totally predictable—there is no choice in the selection of the message and thus the message carries no information. To be more specific, information is said to vary inversely with probability.

It is not yet perfectly clear, in my judgment, just how far and under what precise circumstances we may transfer these results from communication engineering to the human linguistic system, but there can be no denying that some fundamental analogies are present. Thus Lyons states bluntly that "the more predictable a unit, the less meaning it has."[57] We may illustrate quite simply the principle by making reference to clichés: these are generally considered stylistically weak (they carry less "information" or "mean" less) precisely because they are frequent and relatively predictable. On the other hand, unpredictable terms can be used rather powerfully, as when a reviewer for *Time* magazine once said of a certain film that its producer "does not merely present truth—he inflicts it."

The reader will appreciate that although the term *inflict* is common enough, its particular collocation in that sentence (that is, with *truth* as its object) is quite unusual, probably unique. We can therefore understand why an analysis of lexical items, particularly for purposes of

---

between alternative forms of expression" (S. Ullmann, *Style in the French Novel*, p. 6). See also Ullmann's article, "Choice and Expressiveness," in *Language and Style: Collected Papers* (New York: Barnes and Noble, 1964), pp. 132–53. G. W. Turner, in *Stylistics*, p. 21, argues that the set of grammatical rules "is prior to style. It is given by the language, leaving no choice, and, though it does not appear in all definitions, an element of choice seems to be basic to all conceptions of style."

[56]Shannon and Weaver (see above, n. 43), pp. 8–9, 19.

[57]Lyons, *Introduction*, p. 89. For a fuller and more refined discussion, see his *Semantics* 1, chap. 2. This concept is readily applicable to the grammar as well. Consider the popular view that οὐχ ἁμαρτάνει in 1 John 3:6 must refer to *habitual* sin because the author has used a present tense. Whatever else may be said for or against this interpretation, the simple fact is that the author had no choice. Although a choice between aoristic and "imperfective" is available in the past indicative, the same is *not* true in the present indicative. The absence of a possible morphological opposition makes the present tense highly predictable and therefore relatively "meaningless."

stylistic evaluation, must pay special attention to syntagmatic combinations. Before pursuing this line of thought in detail, however, we need to consider its relation to previous studies of semantic (lexical) fields.

LEXICAL FIELDS

Although the concept of *Wortfeld* can be traced back to the mid-nineteenth century,[58] its development had to wait until Saussure's insights into the *structural* nature of language had made an impact. Although Saussure himself did not develop his views on semantics, he recognized the significance of lexical associations. For example: "Within the same language, all words used to express related ideas limit each other reciprocally; synonyms like French *redouter* 'dread,' *craindre* 'fear,' and *avoir peur* 'be afraid' have value only through their opposition: if *redouter* did not exist, all its content would go to its competitors."[59] This idea was picked up and applied in great detail by Jost Trier in his Marburg *Habilitationsschrift*. His starting point was clearly stated in what has become a classic formulation: "The value of a word is first known when we mark it off against the value of neighboring and opposing words. Only as part of the whole does the word have sense; for only in the field is there meaning."[60]

A number of scholars have made use of this concept for the analysis of the biblical vocabulary. One of the most useful is a study of 'image' terminology by James Barr. The author begins by questioning the assumption that "the image of God" in Genesis is a referential term for some entity or relation.

> Rather than concentrating on the one word *ṣelem* "image" and trying to squeeze from it alone a decisive oracle about its meaning . . . we look at a whole group of words and hope that meaning may be indicated by the choice of one word

[58]E. Coseriu, "Zur Vorgeschichte der strukturellen Semantik: Heyses Analyse des Wortfeldes 'Schall,'" in *To Honor Roman Jakobson: Essays on the Occasion of His Seventieth Birthday* (The Hague: Mouton, 1967), pp. 489–98.

[59]Saussure, *Course*, p. 116.

[60]Jost Trier, *Der deutsche Wortschatz im Sinnbezirk des Verstandes. Die Geschichte eines sprachlichen Feldes* (Heidelberg: Carl Winters, 1931), p. 6. The contributions and weaknesses of Trier and subsequent writers have been frequently discussed. Since most of the literature is readily accessible, I refer the reader to Lyons's valuable discussion with further bibliography in *Semantics* 1:250ff., and Ullmann, "Some Recent Developments," pp. 26–27.

rather than another within this group. The basis for procedure, then, is an approach to meanings not as direct relations
between one word and the referent which it indicates, but as
functions of choices within the lexical stock of a given language at a given time; it is the choice, rather than the word
itself, which signifies.[61]

In investigating the usage of related terms, Barr finds that several
of them were transparent and therefore probably unusable; e.g.,
mar'eh (from r'h, 'to see') might suggest that God could be seen.
Further considerations show that ṣelem was less likely to be misconstrued than the rest. It appears, however, that the term was rather
ambiguous and therefore in Genesis 1:26 "d'mut is added in order to
define and limit its meaning, by indicating that the sense intended for
ṣelem must lie within that part of its range which overlaps with the
range of d'mut."[62] After this first instance, either word could be used
alone without fear of confusion.

A more extensive work is Sawyer's analysis of hošia' ('to save') and
related terms.[63] After restricting his study to passages where God is
addressed, Sawyer pays special attention to the paradigmatic relations
obtaining between his terms and finally suggests that the best method
of defining the words is not by giving English equivalents but by
formulating those relations as clearly as possible. We can take the
criterion of frequency—hošia' is approximately five times more frequent (in language addressed to God) than either hiṣṣil or 'azar; or the
element of separation—hiṣṣil is almost always used with the preposition min, but hošia' only four times and 'azar only once. We may note
that hošia' is properly used only of God's activity or that this verb
occurs 50% of the time as one of four nominalizations (e.g., y'šu'a).
And so on. Sawyer's work can be criticized at a number of points,[64] but

[61]J. Barr, "The Image of God in the Book of Genesis—A Study of Terminology,"
BJRL 51 (1968–69): 11–26, especially pp. 14–15.

[62]Ibid., p. 24.

[63]John F. A. Sawyer, Semantics in Biblical Research.

[64]P. Wernberg-Møller's negative review in JTS 24 (1973): 215–17, though not in
every respect fair and accurate, asks some valid questions regarding Sawyer's selection
of terms (particularly the omission of antonyms). Sawyer's conclusions are largely
formalistic and tell us relatively little about semantic content. One can moreover fault
his playing down of the syntagmatic dimension (p. 78) and his treatment of nominalizations as though they were occurrences of the verb under discussion. Cf. further
Gibson's criticisms in Biblical Semantic Logic, pp. 14ff.

much can be learned by a proper assimilation of his main theses.

More recent is an ambitious work on the lexical field of 'separation' by Angelo Vivian.[65] Having limited his study to twelve verbs, the author applies componential analysis to them. We may summarize a small part of his results by describing through a chart three verbs used in biblical narrative. (The number 1 indicates the semantic component of 'separation' itself; 2 indicates that the verb may be used *without* reference to a spatial dimension; 3 indicates use *with* such a spatial dimension; 4 indicates a sacral component; 5 indicates that it is used absolutely.)

	1	2	3	4	5
bdl	+	+	+	−	−
ḥrm	+	+	−	+	+
qdš	+	+	−	+	−

Vivian's extensive researches constitute the most thorough application of structural principles (particularly as formulated by E. Coseriu) to a portion of the biblical vocabulary.[66] We have good reason to anticipate significant developments in this approach to lexicography.

STYLE

Strictly speaking, a lexical field includes *all* of the lexical relations discussed in chapter 5 and all of them, therefore, must play a role in

[65]*I campi lessicali della "separazione" nell'ebraico biblico, di Qumran e della Mishna: ovvero, applicabilità della teoria dei campi lessicali all'ebraico* (QSem 4; Firenze: Istituto di Linguistica e di Lingue Orientali, 1978). Along similar lines, see no. 7 in the same series: I. Zatelli, *Il campo lessicale degli aggettivi di purità in ebraico biblico* (1978).

[66]Unfortunately, Vivian does not explain how one determines what semantic components are shared by specific verbs. See my review, *WTJ* 43 (1980–81): 392–95. We should at this point note studies of lexical fields which attempt, not merely to sharpen lexicographical description, but to reach some understanding of the theological concept reflected by the field. This approach falls somewhere in between that of *TDNT* on the one hand and the purely linguistic concerns of the present book on the other. The following dissertations are good examples: Kenneth L. Burres, *Structural Semantics in the Study of the Pauline Understanding of Revelation* (Northwestern University, 1970); Erickson, *Biblical Semantics*; Vern S. Poythress, *Structural Approaches to Understanding the Theology of the Apostle Paul* (University of Stellenbosch, 1981), which discusses the semantic field of 'holiness.' Other important contributions to the study of biblical semantic fields are Riesener, *Der Stamm* עבד, and Matthys Klemm, *EIPHNH im neutestamentlichen Sprachsystem* (FTL 8; Bonn: Linguistica Biblica, 1977).

one's determination of meaning. We must emphasize again, however, that exegetical decisions focus most frequently on *stylistic* variations and that such variations are possible because of the *synonymic* resources available in language.[67] We may therefore conclude this chapter by exploring the exegetical value of the principles discussed so far. For a variety of reasons, Paul's use of verbal expressions within the field of 'to know' provides an excellent example.[68]

Numerous biblical scholars have offered their opinions as to whether γινώσκειν and εἰδέναι in the New Testament preserve their Attic distinctions. One cannot help but be perplexed, and even amused, at the diametrically opposed conclusions drawn by capable scholars, and even more at the great confidence with which they express their views. Can the methods suggested in this chapter throw any light on this disagreement?

It will be convenient to take as a base for our discussion a recent and sober summary by Donald W. Burdick.[69] The author begins with the assumption (which we will grant for our purposes) that classical writers used εἰδέναι of knowledge that is grasped directly or intuitively, or of knowledge characterized by assurance, or of common knowledge of facts; whereas γινώσκειν draws attention to the acquisition of knowledge (the process of knowledge obtained by experience, instruction, etc.) rather than to its possession.[70] Burdick then examines all occurrences of these two words in Paul, taking special note of passages where the verbs are used in close proximity and of pairs of syntagmatically similar passages. He concludes that

> of the 103 occurrences of οἶδα in the Pauline epistles, 90 were used with the classical meaning, 5 were judged to be

[67]Cf. Ullmann, *Style,* p. 6.

[68]For what follows, see my article, "The Pauline Style as Lexical Choice," and Erickson, *Biblical Semantics,* pp. 294–307.

[69]"Οἶδα and Γινώσκω in the Pauline Epistles," in Richard N. Longenecker and Merrill C. Tenney, eds., *New Dimensions in New Testament Study* (Grand Rapids: Zondervan, 1974), pp. 344–56.

[70]Cf. also Thayer's note s.v. γινώσκω: "γινώσκειν . . . denotes a discriminating apprehension of external impressions, a knowledge grounded in personal experience. εἰδέναι . . . signifies a clear and purely mental perception, in contrast both to conjecture and to knowledge derived from others. ἐπίστασθαι primarily expresses the knowledge obtained by proximity to the things known . . . ; then knowledge viewed as the result of prolonged practice, in opposition to the process of learning on the one hand, and to the uncertain knowledge of a dilettante on the other. συνιέναι . . . implies native insight. . . ."

equivocal, and 8 were used with the same meaning as the classical γινώσκω. Of the 50 occurrences of γινώσκω, 32 were used with the classical meaning, 8 were judged to be equivocal, and 10 were used with the same meaning as classical οἶδα.

In his judgment, then, "there is no room to question" the view "that Paul normally followed the classical pattern," though he adds that each occurrence must be evaluated on its own merits.[71]

We may begin by making a general observation about discussions of synonymy. When a writer states that *x and y are* (or *are not*) *synonymous*, he implies (and is generally taken to mean) that in the linguistic system as such, more or less independently of actual occurrences, these terms are (or are not) synonymous. In other words, even though a writer may grant in principle that exceptions could be found, one seldom finds a recognition that semantic relationships are "established for particular contexts or sets of context."[72] Semantic distinctions that are drawn on the basis of convincing examples must not be generalized, as is usually done, without paying due attention to the possibility of semantic *neutralization*.[73]

An instructive example from English style may be noted in the summary by Thayer, quoted above in footnote 70. In that passage Thayer uses the words *denotes, signifies, expresses,* and *implies* respectively when summarizing the distinctive meanings of four Greek words.

Now we all know, and Thayer knew, that these four English words "mean different things"; but it is also quite clear that at least the first three could have been interchanged by him with no semantic loss whatever. We may also suspect that even the fourth term, *implies*, was not intended by Thayer to suggest that his description of

---

[71]Burdick, p. 354.

[72]John Lyons, *Structural Semantics*, p. 80. In *Introduction*, p. 452, Lyons argues that synonymy in particular is *context-dependent*. It may be that Lyons has taken his position a bit too far; cf. the exaggerated criticisms of Francisco Rodríguez Adrados in *Estudios de lingüística general* (Barcelona: Editorial Planeta, 1969), p. 42, and the technical discussion by Roy Harris, *Synonymy and Linguistic Analysis* (Oxford: B. Blackwell, 1973), p. 123ff. Incidentally, a specific context may even create unexpected paradigmatic contrasts (see above, chap. 1, n. 41).

[73]The term is borrowed from phonology: the opposition between voiced and unvoiced stops in some languages, for example, is said to become neutralized in final position (German *Rad* and *Rat* are both pronounced with a final [t]).

συνιέναι dealt with a different aspect of meaning.[74]

Francisco Rodríguez Adrados[75] argues that neutralization is an "omni-present phenomenon" of the most fundamental significance and that a failure to recognize it is responsible for one of the main defects of traditional dictionaries (i.e., giving definitions that do not apply in some specific contexts). Archbishop Trench's famous work on *Synonyms of the New Testament*, in spite of its obvious and enduring value, is vitiated by the same failure.[76] No scholar, of course, not even Trench, absolutizes all distinctions; Burdick himself shows commendable caution in his article. I hope to show, however, that we need considerably more sensitivity to, and a deeper understanding of, the issue at stake.

How do we then approach γινώσκειν and εἰδέναι? On the assumption that an investigation limited to the two verbs in question would be inadequate, our first order of business is to survey the Pauline corpus in search of terms that make up the lexical field as a whole. A number of verbs are immediately obvious, such as ἐπιγινώσκειν, ἐπίστασθαι, καταλαμβάνεσθαι, κατανοεῖν, νοεῖν, and προγινώσκειν. Furthermore, certain contextual considerations—such as the parallelism between ἰδόντες and γνόντες in Galatians 2:7, 9—suggest the inclusion of at least some occurrences of ἰδεῖν, βλέπειν, ἀκούειν, et al. Since we cannot restrict our study to single verbs, we also include such expressions as γνῶσιν ἔχειν, νοῦν ἔχειν, σοφὸς εἶναι, φρόνιμος γίνεσθαι, ἐν γνώσει πλουτίζεσθαι, et al. Finally, we take note of opposites, such as ἀγνοεῖν, μωραίνειν, ἀγνωσίαν ἔχειν, and μωρὸς γίνεσθαι. There might also be some value in a preliminary classification of these terms according to the five sense relations described in chapter 5.

---

[74]For a persuasive discussion by a literary critic, note E. D. Hirsch, Jr., *Validity*, pp. 117–20, and *The Aims of Interpretation* (Chicago: University of Chicago Press, 1976), pp. 60–61, where he argues that even the lexical units *bachelors* and *unmarried men*, which in isolation are certainly perceived as semantically distinct, may become completely interchangeable in a club charter. See also Gauger, *Zum Problem*, pp. 103–17.

[75]*Estudios*, p. 52.

[76]In defense of Trench, one could argue that much of his work was an attempt to refute the exaggerated denials that semantic distinctions might be present even occasionally. Further, Trench recognized from time to time the possibility of neutralization. Nevertheless, the practical effect of the book has been to mislead its users, who normally look up his discussion and apply it to whatever passage they are considering. For an instructive discussion of Trench's method, particularly his excessive regard for etymology, note his popular book, *On the Study of Words*, especially lecture 7.

The next step is to group the actual occurrences of the terms according to syntagmatic principles. For example, which of these verbs does Paul use with a direct object? Which does he use ruling a clause, such as a verb plus ὅτι? Which does he use in the passive? and so on. A listing of the passages along these lines will inevitably reveal Pauline patterns, some clearer than others.

One such pattern of relevance to our problem is the predominance of εἰδέναι followed by ὅτι. Perhaps a better way to appreciate the significance of this fact is to note that even though εἰδέναι occurs more than twice as many times as γινώσκειν in Paul's letters, it occurs *less* frequently in the pattern of verb plus direct object (twenty-three times as against thirty-three for γινώσκειν). Probably the difference is even greater than that, since in eight of those instances (as opposed to three for γινώσκειν) εἰδέναι is followed by ὅτι as well.[77] The inference seems inescapable that the combination εἰδέναι ὅτι, being largely predictable, should not be pressed. This simple syntactic factor, however, has not played a role in modern discussions. Thus, Burdick appeals to Romans 8:28 (οἴδαμεν δὲ ὅτι τοῖς ἀγαπῶσιν τὸν θεὸν πάντα συνεργεῖ εἰς ἀγαθόν) and 1 Corinthians 15:58 (ἑδραῖοι γίνεσθε . . . , εἰδότες ὅτι ὁ κόπος ὑμῶν οὐκ ἔστιν κενὸς ἐν κυρίῳ) as evidence that Paul uses εἰδέναι in the classical sense of knowledge characterized by assurance. It seems more reasonable to suggest that the choice of the verb in these and similar cases was dictated by stylistic, rather than semantic, reasons.[78] In any case, the note of assurance is provided by the whole context in these verses, as Burdick himself seems to recognize; but if so, the context is no proof that the verb itself (in contrast to, say, πεποιθέναι) conveys that nuance.[79]

[77] In an additional seven instances γινώσκειν happens to be present in the context and one wonders how that factor may have influenced the choice of one term over the other. Cf. also the use of οἶδ' ὅτι ('surely') in classical writers; see H. W. Smyth's *Greek Grammar* (Cambridge, Mass.: Harvard University Press, 1956), par. 2585.

[78] I should emphasize that the terms *stylistic* and *semantic* are here contrasted purely for the sake of convenience (see above, chap. 4, n. 49).

[79] In other words, even if the syntax were not a factor in these two passages, we could only say that the verb is more often or more naturally found in contexts of assurance. Note also Burdick's view that γινώσκειν with the nuance 'acquisition of knowledge' is confirmed by 1 Cor. 1:21, even though that nuance is found primarily in the accompanying phrase, διὰ τῆς σοφίας (p. 348); similarly, the idea of 'thorough knowledge' is borne by ἀκριβῶς, not by the verb in 1 Thess. 5:2 (p. 354). I do not wish to deny, of course, that individual words sustain a mutual relationship with their contexts.

One may also argue that the tendency to use εἰδέναι with ὅτι has misled scholars to view this verb as denoting knowledge of facts. Note that although in English we can say, *I know that fact* (i.e., using a verb plus a direct object), we normally *describe* the fact, for which indirect discourse becomes the pattern: *I know* (the fact) *that he went to the park*. Similarly, it appears that the parallel *structure* in Greek, not the semantic distinctiveness of εἰδέναι, accounts for the use under consideration.

But now, if εἰδέναι plus ὅτι should not be pressed as carrying a distinctive meaning, we should certainly pay attention to breaks in the pattern, for these deviations[80] may suggest (though even here not necessarily) the presence of semantic motivation. For example, we find eight instances of γινώσκειν plus ὅτι. How shall we explain them? To begin with, four of these instances (Rom. 6:6; 1 Cor. 3:20; 2 Cor. 8:9; 2 Tim. 3:1) do not strictly belong here, since in them the verb is ruling a direct object as well. Incidentally, the first of those references (Rom. 6:6) is particularly interesting, for Burdick, who notes the use of εἰδότες in verse 9, can find "no adequate reason for the change from one term to the other."[81] But the reason appears to be, quite simply and unsensationally, the presence of the direct object τοῦτο in verse 6.[82] A fifth passage, Ephesians 5:5, may be accounted for by noting the presence of ἴστε or by recognizing the distinctive style of this epistle (one of the factors leading many scholars to deny its Pauline authorship). The other three passages, however, should probably be interpreted on semantic grounds (2 Cor. 13:6; Gal. 3:7; Phil. 1:12). In all three of them Paul wants his readers to know something they did not know before. Although εἰδέναι can be used this way,[83] we notice a decided preference for γινώσκειν with the nuance 'find out.' Burdick's treatment of this aspect is more satisfactory.

---

[80]For this topic of deviation, cf. more generally Enkvist, *Linguistic Stylistics*, pp. 24–26, 98ff.

[81]Burdick, p. 350.

[82]Perhaps this is also the reason for the κρίναντος τοῦτο of 2 Cor. 5:14. I suspect that very few scholars would be happy with the suggestion that κρίνειν may be interchanged with εἰδέναι in this passage, but is it possible that we are not sufficiently sensitive to the phenomenon of neutralization?

[83]1 Cor. 2:12; 11:3; Eph. 1:18; 6:21; Col. 2:1. (According to Smyth's *Grammar*, par. 795, the verb stem itself means 'find out,' but this has nothing to do with the point being made here.) Note also instances of ἐπιγινώσκειν plus ὅτι (Rom. 1:32; 1 Cor. 14:37; 2 Cor. 1:13b, 14; 13:5); with the apparent exception of 2 Cor. 1:13b (and even this instance can be understood differently) the references include a direct object.

Finally, we may note that although as many as eleven verbs are used by Paul in the passive, εἰδέναι of course occurs only in the active voice.[84] This information can help us in certain situations. Take, for example, Galatians 4:8–9 (τότε μὲν οὐκ εἰδότες θεὸν . . . νῦν δε γνόντες θεόν, μᾶλλον δὲ γνωσθέντες ὑπὸ θεοῦ). One may argue that the change from εἰδότες to γνόντες, rather than being a mere stylistic variation, is semantically motivated insofar as the latter verb is often used when speaking of someone or something not known before.[85] But now, how about the following instance of γνωσθέντες? Burdick wonders why, if God knows directly without the process of observation, Paul should employ this verb, rather than εἰδέναι, when referring to divine knowledge. The question is almost meaningless, however, since εἰδέναι, not being used in the passive, was not a choice available to Paul.[86]

It appears, then, that sensitivity to lexical structure—paradigmatic resources, syntagmatic patterns, neutralization—can have a direct and significant effect on exegetical decisions.

---

[84]It may be worthwhile to note that among verbs used in the passive εὑρίσκεσθαι heads the list in number of occurrences (ten), even though this verb occurs only a total of seventeen times in Paul. The verb was included in this study because γινώσκειν often suggests the idea of 'find out'; further, εὑρίσκειν may acquire the nuance 'to perceive' (cf. Rom. 7:21, parallel to vs. 23). Note also that five of the passive occurrences (Rom. 7:10; 1 Cor. 15:15; 2 Cor. 11:12; 12:20b; Gal. 2:17) approach the sense of 'appear, turn out' (a meaning regarded by some as a Hebraism) and this is very close to 'to come to be known.'

[85]This is not to say that the verb necessarily means 'to acquire knowledge,' for in Rom. 1:21 it is used of the pre-Christian stage, just as εἰδότες is used in the Galatians passage (cf. 2 Thess. 1:8). Still, we may grant the appropriateness of Paul's language in v. 9. J. B. Lightfoot (The Epistle of St. Paul to the Galatians [Grand Rapids: Zondervan, 1962, originally published 1865], p. 171) suggests that since γινώσκειν "gives prominence either to the attainment or the manifestation of the knowledge," it is used more naturally "where there is reference to some earlier state of ignorance. . . ." Bultmann (TDNT 1:703, n. 61) implies that we can find no distinction here between the two verbs, but possibly he is only interested in denying that one verb denotes more thorough knowledge than the other; perhaps he would not have objected to the distinction suggested by Lightfoot.

[86]Burdick's answer to his own question is that Paul was describing the knowledge of persons, not of facts; however, this distinction does not seem to hold up (cf. 1 Cor. 2:2; 2 Cor. 12:2–3; 1 Thess. 5:12; Titus 1:16).

Conclusions

Students of the biblical languages have at their disposal a wealth of publications designed to help them reach responsible exegetical decisions. With such aids as critical commentaries, lexicons, concordances, as well as innumerable articles and monographs on biblical words, no other literature can boast a comparable expenditure of effort and research. It must not be thought, however, that the work has been completed—nor that such work as *has* been done can be used uncriti- ✓ cally. We may therefore summarize the contents of this book by pointing out specifically how our standard works of reference may be used with greatest profit and furthermore how they can be supplemented.

We may focus our attention on Walter Bauer's great achievement, *A Greek-English Lexicon of the New Testament and Other Early Christian Literature*. It may be stated categorically that this is the best specialized dictionary available for any ancient literature. Anyone who exploits the resources modestly tucked away by Bauer in his articles must surely marvel at the extraordinary competence needed to have accomplished this feat. In particular, one must point out several qualities—following the best tradition of classical scholarship—that establish the work as a solid and enduring lexicographical contribution. By a careful use of italics and parentheses, for instance, Bauer distinguishes actual acceptations of the Greek word from meanings otherwise associated with it; thus, under κατaλείπω 1.b., "die and *leave (behind)*" for Mark 12:19, 21 and Luke 20:31. Second, Bauer pays great attention to syntactical and grammatical details that are essential for the proper handling of the material; thus, he usually specifies whether, say, a verb occurs absolutely or with an object or with a preposition, etc. Often, Bauer gives indications regarding terms that stand both in syntagmatic relationship (e.g., under καταλαμ-βάνω 1.a., with reference to Phil. 3:12a, 13, he tells us, "As a result of διώκειν") and in paradigmatic relationship (e.g., under κρίσις 1.a.β. he specifies that in John 5:24 the noun is used in opposition to ζωή). Finally, Bauer was fully sensitive to the need *not* to isolate the New Testament language from the contemporary speech and thus his work abounds with thousands of invaluable references to secular literature where parallel constructions occur—these references alone make Bauer's *Lexicon* a veritable treasure.

All of this and more must be emphasized lest my criticisms be misconstrued. For indeed criticisms are in order. We have already noted[1] that occasionally Bauer goes beyond the lexicographer's task, as when he tells us (s.v. σάρξ 7.), "In Paul's thought esp., the *flesh* is the willing instrument of sin, and is subject to sin to such a degree that wherever flesh is, all forms of sin are likewise present, and no good thing can live in the σάρξ." Usually this move from the linguistic to the theological is not so explicit, a factor that may, however, intensify the danger of confusion.

The failure to distinguish carefully between language and theology is often linked to a more serious problem, namely, Bauer's inconsistency in the arrangement of his articles. The author was no doubt torn between the ideal of scientific consistency and the practical needs of New Testament students. His compromise, in my opinion, tends to distort the data. Take the following examples chosen randomly from the first letter of the alphabet.

αἷμα *blood*
1. literally: a. of human blood; b. of the blood of animals
2. figuratively: a. as the seat of life; b. blood and life as an expiatory sacrifice
3. of the (apocalyptic) red color

[1]See above, introduction, n. 51. If the criticisms that follow are valid for Bauer's rigorous work, the reader may deduce how such problems are intensified in other publications (*TDNT, TDOT, NIDNTT*, et al.) that demonstrate less sensitivity to careful lexicographical method. For a comparable criticism of BDB, note Gates, *Lexicographical Resources*, p. 79 (cf. pp. 85–88 on the lexicon's use of semantically related terms). See also Eugene A. Nida, "Implications of Contemporary Linguistics for Biblical Scholarship," *JBL* 91 (1972): 73–89, especially p. 85, and Louw, *Semantics*, p. 2.

αἴρω
1. *lift up, take up, pick up.* a. literally. b. figuratively.
2. *(lift up and) take* or *carry (along)*
3. *(lift up and) carry away, remove*
4. *take away, remove* with no suggestion of lifting up

ἁμαρτάνω *do wrong, sin*
1. absolutely
2. with fuller indication of that in which the sin consists, by means of a supplementary participle
3. with indication of the manner of sinning
4. with indication of the person against whom the sin is committed
5. with indication of the result

ἁμαρτία *sin*
1. the action itself
2. in Johannine usage ἁ. is conceived as a condition or characteristic quality, *sinfulness*
3. Paul thinks of sin almost in personal terms
4. in Hebrews sin appears as the power that deceives men . . .
5. special sins

ἀνήρ *man*
1. in contrast to woman
2. in contrast to boy
3. used with a word indicating national or local origin . . .
4. used with adjective to emphasize the dominant character of a man
5. with special emphasis on manliness
6. equivalent to τίς
7. *a figure of a man*
8. of Jesus as the judge of the world

ἀφίστημι
1. transitive: *cause to revolt, mislead*
2. intransitive: a. *go away, withdraw;* b. *keep away;* c. fig. *depart, withdraw*

Even a superficial look at these arrangements shows that different criteria of classification have been used, making it very difficult, if not impossible, to compare different words. Sometimes the main distinction arises from grammatical factors (ἀφίστημι), sometimes from the need for different translation equivalents (αἴρω), sometimes from the semantic content of the *sentences* in which the word is used (ἁμαρτάνω), sometimes from the distinction between literal and figurative meanings. And in the case of ἁμαρτία, Bauer actually gives us a miniature biblical theology.

More significantly, we occasionally find inconsistency within the article itself. His treatment of ἁμαρτάνω, for example, begins with what appears to be a syntactical criterion (1. absolutely. 2. with a participle), but soon it becomes clear that the article is intended merely to save the user time by grouping together the various kinds of things said *about* sinning in the New Testament—a subtle move from the linguistic to the theological. In the article on ἀνήρ, the first two items are based on paradigmatic oppositions, the next two on syntagmatic combinations, the last four on special uses. Needless to emphasize, however, syntagmatic combinations are important for the occurrences listed under 1. and 2., while the paradigmatic dimension does not disappear after the second category!

We need not here decide whether Bauer was right or wrong in sacrificing consistency for the sake of usefulness. We do need to recognize, however, that the inconsistencies are there and that the user of the *Lexicon* must not allow them to distort his understanding of the vocabulary. The simplest and most effective way to deal with this problem is to ask ourselves *precisely* what we are after. For example, if we are interested in determining how many acceptations the verb ἁμαρτάνω has, we will not be misled by Bauer's article into thinking that the verb has five meanings or acceptations; apparently, it has only one, for which two English equivalents are given, *sin* and *do wrong*.

But these last remarks alert us to the most basic problem at hand: What is the relationship between acceptations and translation equivalents? Are *sin* and *do wrong* two distinct senses of the Greek verb or, as we have suggested, two possible ways of translating a word that should be regarded as having only one sense? To put it differently, What is the most accurate way of describing meaning? Even lexicographers involved with monolingual dictionaries must face this fundamental question. Should they define an English word with a (relatively long) English phrase or sentence? or by using English synonyms (equivalents)? or by contrasting it with members of its paradigmatic field? or by tabulating its (syntagmatic) distribution?[2]

Such questions become more pressing in bilingual dictionaries, for even closely related languages are *not* isomorphic—equivalences between them (lexical, grammatical, etc.) are rarely complete. Earlier[3] we called attention to the English verbs *to eat* and *to drink* and their Spanish equivalents *comer* and *tomar*. From the perspective of both cultural and linguistic similarities, one would expect these equivalences to be rather straightforward. Given their differences in distribution, however, we cannot quite say that *to eat* is the same as *comer*. But now, suppose that we give *tomar* as an alternate translation equivalent for *to eat* (in such contexts as *to eat soup*). A Spanish speaker learning English would probably deduce that "*to eat* can mean either *comer* or *tomar*," suggesting that the English verb has two distinct acceptations—a fundamental misunderstanding!

Yet similar misconceptions arise frequently when students see two different English translation equivalents for one Greek word. Occasionally, this may have theological repercussions, as when some modern scholars have latched on to *person, human being* as possible translation equivalents for σῶμα (see LSJ), have further assumed that these constitute distinct acceptations, and have therefore used them as evidence that Paul understood σῶμα with reference to the whole person, not to the physical body. As Robert H. Gundry has shown, however, the very examples given in LSJ indicate that the physical existence is in

---

[2]During the past two decades, and especially since 1970, a great deal of attention has been paid to these and related questions. Among the more useful works, note Josette Rey-Debove, *La lexicographie* (Langues 19; Paris: Didier & Larousse, 1970); Jean Dubois and Claude Dubois, *Introduction à la lexicographie: le dictionnaire* (Paris: Larousse, 1971); M. H. Goshen-Gottstein, *Introduction to the Lexicography of Modern Hebrew* (in Hebrew with English summary; Jerusalem: Schocken, 1971); Ladislav Zgusta, *Manual of Lexicography* (JanL ser. mai. 39; The Hague: Mouton, 1971); *Probleme der Lexikologie und Lexikographie. Jahrbuch 1975 des Instituts für deutsche Sprache* (Sprache der Gegenwart 39; Düsseldorf: Pädagogischen Verlagschwann, 1976); and particularly useful, Ali. M. Al-Kasimi, *Linguistics and Bilingual Dictionaries* (Leiden: Brill, 1977). Some of these works, plus many others, are surveyed by Demetrius J. Georgacas, "The Present State of Lexicography and Zgusta's *Manual of Lexicography*," *Orbis* 25 (1976): 359–400. It should be added that Casares's older work, *Introducción*, remains very valuable.

[3]See above, pp. 142–43. Note in this connection James E. Ianucci, "Meaning Discrimination in Bilingual Dictionaries," in *Problems in Lexicography*, ed. Fred W. Householder and Sol Saporta (Bloomington: Indiana University, 1976), pp. 201–16; and Gates, *Lexicographical Resources*, pp. 79–80.

view;[4] the apparent discrepancy arises simply because in those contexts the English *body* is not as suitable as *person*.

It is not our intent here to solve this serious lexicographical dilemma.[5] We simply wish to alert the reader to the existence of these problems with a view to overcoming them. In short, students of the biblical languages must use their valuable tools critically—and they must also supplement them. In the light of the large number of topics touched on in this book, how *can* we supplement those tools? The diagram at the end of this chapter summarizes in the middle column those lexical phenomena that are of greatest interest to biblical exegetes. The following steps are offered as a suggestion for determining the meaning and the proper English equivalents of specific words in specific contexts:

1. First, the student should determine, insofar as this is possible, to what extent the term is or is not referential. The more referential it is—particularly if it appears to have a (semi-) technical force—the less susceptible it is to structural analysis, and the student should consider whether a conceptual (as in *TDNT*), rather than a linguistic, approach would be more profitable. See pages 22–31, 62–63, 79–81, 105–8. If a linguistic approach seems appropriate, the following steps should be included.

2. Using the standard lexicons, determine the attested semantic range of the term, paying special attention to the distinction between acceptations and translation equivalents. This step lays out the options available to the exegete.

3. Consider the paradigmatic relations of the term. Using works on synonymy and other lexical helps, determine the opposition of the term to other related terms by drawing up a tentative classification along the lines suggested in chapter 5.

4. Consider the syntagmatic combination and broader contextual levels in which the term is found. How does it compare with

---

[4]*Sōma in Biblical Theology, with Emphasis on Pauline Anthropology* (SNTSMS 29; Cambridge: Cambridge University Press, 1976), chap. 2. Should we relate these kinds of difficulties to the comments above, chap. 4, n. 38?

[5]The reader may be referred to Francisco Rodríguez Adrados's contributions to *Introducción*, ed. Gangutia, especially the last two chapters, and to his later article, "La lexicografía griega: su estado actual y el diccionario griego-español," *REL* 9 (1979): 413–39. It would be going too far to suggest that translation equivalents should not be used at all.

the combinations in which related terms appear? Apply the principle of maximal redundancy, giving preference to the "smaller contextual circles." See pages 141–48, 153–59.

5. Consider the historical (diachronic) dimension. Can the term's etymology (in at least one of its senses) be determined? Is the term transparent? If its meaning has changed, identify the nature of the change. If foreign influence has been at work, identify the form of interference. See pages 39–41, 48–51, 76–88.

6. A final decision should focus on the consciousness and intention of the writer. Thus, if it seems improbable that the author would have been acquainted with or interested in one of the historical factors discovered, such a factor should not influence one's decision. The probabilities of deliberate ambiguity, choice of a term against its synonyms, and neutralization should then be weighed in the light of the preliminary conclusions in step 4. See pages 139–41, 149–51, 159–63, 165–66.

None of these considerations should be applied mechanically. A sense for the fluidity of language—its suppleness, if we prefer—must dominate our thinking from beginning to end. Therefore, we need not be disturbed when complete precision and certainty elude us; responsible uncertainty will take us considerably further than baseless assurance.

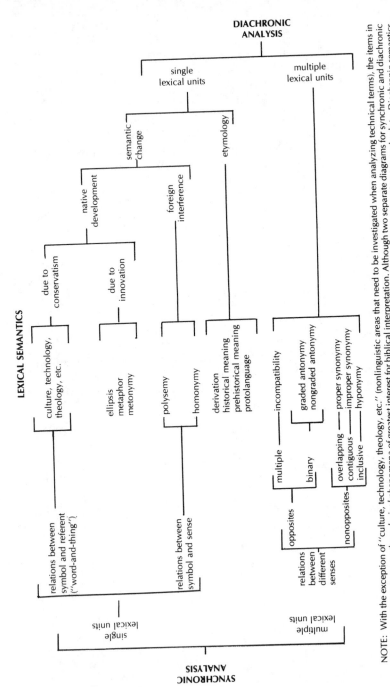

LEXICAL SEMANTICS

DIACHRONIC ANALYSIS

single lexical units
- semantic change
  - native development
    - due to conservatism — culture, technology, theology, etc.
    - due to innovation — ellipsis / metaphor / metonymy
  - foreign interference — polysemy / homonymy
- etymology — derivation / historical meaning / prehistorical meaning / protolanguage

multiple lexical units
- relations between different senses
  - opposites
    - incompatibility — multiple
    - binary — graded antonymy / nongraded antonymy
  - nonopposites — overlapping / contiguous / inclusive — proper synonymy / improper synonymy / hyponymy

SYNCHRONIC ANALYSIS

single lexical units
- relations between symbol and referent ("word-and-thing")

multiple lexical units
- relations between symbol and sense

NOTE: With the exception of "culture, technology, theology, etc." (nonlinguistic areas that need to be investigated when analyzing technical terms), the items in the center column represent those *lexical phenomena* of greatest interest for biblical interpretation. Although two separate diagrams for synchronic and diachronic analysis might prove less confusing, the present diagram helps to show that the distinction between those two approaches is not absolute. Diachronic semantics should ideally be the application of synchronic semantics to different stages (incidentally, the inclusion of semantic change and etymology under the study of "single lexical units" does not mean that those two types of investigation cannot be applied to groups of words). Finally note that although the syntagmatic dimension is not explicit in the diagram, it cuts across the whole of the center column.

Annotated Bibliography

A complete list of works cited may be found in the index of authors and titles (full bibliographic information is given upon first mention of each work). The selection of titles below is merely intended as a guide for students who are interested in general discussions and surveys of the areas covered in this book. With only two important exceptions, the selection is restricted to works in English. Books issued in paperback are marked "pb." after the date.

GENERAL LINGUISTICS

Among popularizations of linguistic study, one of the best is Peter Farb, *Word Play: What Happens When People Talk* (New York: Bantam Books, 1975, pb.), with emphasis on the sociological dimension. Numerous college texts are available and most of them are adequate, but perhaps the most successful is by Victoria Fromkin and Robert Rodman, *An Introduction to Language*, 2nd ed. (New York: Holt, Rinehart and Winston, 1978, pb.). Less entertaining, but closer to the perspective incorporated in the present work, is John Lyons, *Language and Linguistics* (Cambridge: Cambridge University Press, 1981, pb.). Any of these books will lead the reader to works intended for advanced students.

SEMANTICS

Although the movement known as general semantics represents concerns not covered in the present work, students of linguistic semantics should become acquainted with it; most popular is S. I.

Hayakawa et al., *Language in Thought and Action*, 4th ed. (New York: Harcourt Brace Jovanovich, 1978, pb.). Readers interested in what scholars other than linguists are saying about meaning will profit from *Semantics: An Interdisciplinary Reader in Philosophy, Linguistics, and Psychology*, ed. D. D. Steinberg and L. A. Jacobovitz (Cambridge: Cambridge University Press, 1971, pb.).

A brief and relatively simple introduction to the linguistic study of meaning is F. R. Palmer, *Semantics: A New Outline* (Cambridge: Cambridge University Press, 1976, pb.). More demanding is Ruth M. Kempson, *Semantic Theory* (Cambridge Textbooks in Linguistics; Cambridge: Cambridge University Press, 1977, pb.), which also introduces the reader to relevant areas from the philosophy of language. The very valuable book by Geoffrey Leech, *Semantics* (Harmondsworth: Penguin Books, 1974, pb.) begins at a somewhat elementary level but becomes difficult in the later chapters. The most comprehensive synthesis is John Lyons's two-volume work, *Semantics* (Cambridge: Cambridge University Press, 1977, pb.).

The four titles just mentioned discuss meaning on all linguistic levels. Among books that focus exclusively on lexical meaning, the most readable and literate is Stephen Ullmann, *Semantics: An Introduction to the Science of Meaning* (New York: Barnes & Noble, 1978, pb., originally published in 1962). Ullmann's earlier work, *The Principles of Semantics*, 2nd ed. (New York: Philosophical Library, 1957) is more theoretical and difficult but very rewarding. Eugene A. Nida, *Componential Analysis of Meaning: An Introduction to Semantic Structures* (Approaches to Semiotics, 57; The Hague: Mouton, 1975, pb.) is the most thorough description of lexical meaning available in English; it includes sets of problems that provide "illustrative data required for full comprehension of the procedures and the acquisition of skills in dealing with semantic structures" (p. 8).

BIBLICAL SEMANTICS

Some treatment of word meanings is to be found in most hermeneutics manuals, such as A. Berkeley Mickelsen, *Interpreting the Bible* (Grand Rapids: Eerdmans, 1963). The significance of James Barr, *The Semantics of Biblical Language* (Oxford: Oxford University Press, 1961), has been discussed at some length in the present book; his later work, *Comparative Philology and the Text of the Old Testament* (Oxford: Oxford University Press, 1968), which is addressed to Old Testament specialists and has a narrower focus, constitutes a major advance in sharpening the scholar's approach to lexical questions.

Johannes P. Louw, *Semantics of New Testament Greek* (Semeia Studies; Philadelphia: Fortress Press, 1982, pb.), not confined to lexical meaning, is the most satisfactory attempt to integrate contemporary linguistics into biblical exegesis. The best treatment of Old Testament semantics is in German: Benjamin Kedar, *Biblische Semantik. Eine Einführung* (Stuttgart: W. Kohlhammer, 1981, pb.); unfortunately, it devotes only a brief chapter to structural relations. In English we have John F. A. Sawyer, *Semantics in Biblical Research: New Methods of Defining Hebrew Words for Salvation* (SBT 2nd series, 24; London: SCM, 1972).

G. B. Caird, *The Language and Imagery of the Bible* (Philadelphia: Westminster Press, 1980), while making very limited use of linguistics, is a learned and provocative introduction to some of the characteristics of biblical language.

BIBLICAL LEXICOGRAPHY

For a valuable assessment of standard dictionaries of the biblical languages, the reader is referred to Frederick W. Danker, *Multipurpose Tools for Bible Study*, 3rd ed. (St. Louis: Concordia, 1970, pb.), chapters 6–8; cf. also Joseph A. Fitzmyer, *An Introductory Bibliography for the Study of Scripture*, revised (Subsidia biblica, 3; Rome: Biblical Institute Press, 1981, pb.), chapter 8. In spite of the valid criticisms that can be raised against the *Theological Dictionary of the New Testament*, ed. G. Kittel and G. Friedrich, 10 vols. (Grand Rapids: Eerdmans, 1964–76), this encyclopedic work remains indispensable; it should be supplemented by specialized monographs, such as David Hill, *Greek Words and Hebrew Meanings: Studies in the Semantics of Soteriological Terms* (SNTSMS, 5; Cambridge: Cambridge University Press, 1967). The *Theological Dictionary of the Old Testament*, ed. G. J. Botterweck and H. Ringgren (Grand Rapids: Eerdmans, 1974–   ), currently being produced, seeks to avoid some of the weaknesses of its New Testament counterpart.

The New International Dictionary of New Testament Theology, ed. C. Brown, 3 vols. (Grand Rapids: Zondervan, 1975–78) is more manageable than, and in some respects provides a corrective to, *TDNT* (but cf. my review in *WTJ* 43 [1980–81]: 395–99). A comparable work is *Theological Wordbook of the Old Testament*, ed. R. L. Harris et al., 2 vols. (Chicago: Moody Press, 1980), produced by conservative English-speaking scholars. The United Bible Societies are sponsoring a forthcoming Greek-English New Testament dictionary arranged on the basis of lexical fields; it is being produced by Eugene A. Nida, Johannes P. Louw, and Rondal B. Smith (cf. Louw's description, "The Greek New Testament Wordbook," *BT* 30 [1979]: 108–17).

Significant one-man contributions include Ceslas Spicq, *Notes de lexicographie néo-testamentaire*, 2 vols. (Orbis biblicus et orientalis, 22; Fribourg: Editions Universitaires, 1978), and Nigel Turner, *Christian Words* (Edinburgh: T. & T. Clark, 1980). While neither of these works incorporates modern linguistics, Turner's book is particularly disappointing. Cf. my review of Spicq in *WTJ* 42 (1979–80): 444–45, and of Turner in *Trinity Journal* 3NS (1982):103–9.

On biblical synonyms see chapter 5, notes 12 and 13. For important word-study monographs, see chapter 6, especially notes 63–66. Finally, attention should be drawn to C. J. Hemer's proposal, "Towards a New Moulton and Milligan," *NovT* 24 (1982): 97–123.

INDEX OF AUTHORS AND TITLES

Shortened titles have been used; refer to the first mention of each work for bibliographic details.

INDEX OF SUBJECTS
WITH GLOSSARY

Only linguistic terms have been glossed. Many of the definitions are deliberately not rigorous; they serve the limited purpose of helping the reader understand the use of the terms in this book.

acceptation (a dictionary definition, indicative of a generally accepted word meaning), 105, 174-76

Akkadian, 40, 41n

ambiguity (uncertainty in linguistic meaning), 136, 148-59
deliberate, 136, 149-51, 177
unintended, 136, 151-56

antonymy (a relation of oppositeness holding between the senses of two terms; *contrast* incompatibility; synonymy), 118, 130-32

Arabic, 42, 43, 110

arbitrary (*see* language, arbitrary nature of)

aspiration (an *h*-sound accompanying pronunciation), 109, 133

Authorized Version (*see* King James Version)

author's meaning (*see* intent, authorial)

Biblical Theology, 17-18

bilingualism (the use of two languages; *see* borrowing; interference; loans, semantic)

binary (consisting of two units)
contrast, 133
relations (*see* antonymy)

borrowing (the process of adopting linguistic elements from one language to another), 41
semantic (*see* loans, semantic)

calque (a French word meaning 'imitation' and used by linguists to describe various forms of borrowing), 88-89, 90n, 92, 93

case, grammatical, 150

change
in Greek language, 57
phonetic, 35, 49, 50
semantic, 50, chaps. 2-3
classification of, 75, 75-86
and etymology, 38-39, 53-54
in OT, 54-56

choice (a speaker's option in areas where the language allows for stylistic variation), 67, 100, 116-17, 136, 159-61, 177

circle, hermeneutical, 137, 146

clash, homonymic (semantic confusion created by homonyms that can occupy the same contexts), 96

cohyponym (*see* hyponymy)

coinage (a new or invented word), 75n

collocation (a distinguishable pattern in word combination), 142-43, 160

communication engineering (the application of science and mathematics to the study of the transmission of information), 136, 152, 154, 160

complementary (a set of antonyms where the negation of one member implies the assertion of the other), 131

componential analysis (a method of semantic description that focuses on the word's sense components or meaning elements), 118, 132-35

concept, 27, 107 (*see also* language and thought)

INDEX OF HEBREW AND ARAMAIC WORDS

The Words are arranged according to Hebrew alphabetization. For references to other ancient languages, see the Index of Subjects.

INDEX OF GREEK WORDS

INDEX OF BIBLICAL REFERENCES